AFRICAN ETHNOGRAPHIC STUDIES OF THE 20TH CENTURY

Volume 54

RELIGION IN A TSWANA CHIEFDOM

RELIGION IN A TSWANA CHIEFDOM

B. A. PAUW

LONDON AND NEW YORK

First published in 1960 by Oxford University Press for the International African Institute.

This edition first published in 2018
by Routledge
2 Park Square, Milton Park, Abingdon, Oxon OX14 4RN

and by Routledge
711 Third Avenue, New York, NY 10017

Routledge is an imprint of the Taylor & Francis Group, an informa business

© 1960 International African Institute

All rights reserved. No part of this book may be reprinted or reproduced or utilised in any form or by any electronic, mechanical, or other means, now known or hereafter invented, including photocopying and recording, or in any information storage or retrieval system, without permission in writing from the publishers.

Trademark notice: Product or corporate names may be trademarks or registered trademarks, and are used only for identification and explanation without intent to infringe.

British Library Cataloguing in Publication Data
A catalogue record for this book is available from the British Library

ISBN: 978-0-8153-8713-8 (Set)
ISBN: 978-0-429-48813-9 (Set) (ebk)
ISBN: 978-1-138-59731-0 (Volume 54) (hbk)
ISBN: 978-0-429-48696-8 (Volume 54) (ebk)

Publisher's Note
The publisher has gone to great lengths to ensure the quality of this reprint but points out that some imperfections in the original copies may be apparent.

Disclaimer
The publisher has made every effort to trace copyright holders and would welcome correspondence from those they have been unable to trace.

Due to modern production methods, it has not been possible to reproduce the fold-out maps within the book. Please visit www.routledge.com to view them.

RELIGION IN A
TSWANA CHIEFDOM

B. A. PAUW

Published for the
INTERNATIONAL AFRICAN INSTITUTE
by the
OXFORD UNIVERSITY PRESS
LONDON   NEW YORK   TORONTO
1960

Oxford University Press, Amen House, London E.C.4

GLASGOW NEW YORK TORONTO MELBOURNE WELLINGTON
BOMBAY CALCUTTA MADRAS KARACHI KUALA LUMPUR
CAPE TOWN IBADAN NAIROBI ACCRA

© International African Institute 1960

The publication of this volume was assisted by a grant from the National Council for Social Research of the Department of Education, Arts and Science of the Union of South Africa, which is not, however, to be understood as approving any statement made or views expressed therein

PRINTED IN GREAT BRITAIN

TO THE MEMORY OF
MY LATE FATHER
AND TO
MY MOTHER

FOREWORD

Except that it happens to be a first-fruit, a study such as this hardly calls for introduction. The importance of the subject matter, the careful collection of the material, and the academic as well as the practical equipment of the author should suffice to give *Religion in a Tswana Chiefdom* a good send-off.

The present study is a condensation of a thesis accepted by the University of Cape Town for the Ph.D. degree in 1955, under the guidance of Professor Monica Wilson. The author's experience as missionary and anthropologist amongst the Tswana-Tlhaping cluster of the Bantu family has given him special qualification for the work. The labours of his own promoter, of Language, Schapera, Willoughby, J. T. Brown, and others have provided Dr. Pauw's superstructure with the essential basic material.

It may be looked upon as mere chance that *Religion in a Tswana Chiefdom* and the Rev. John V. Taylor's *The Growth of the Church in Buganda* should be, so to speak, contemporaries. Moreover, Professor Bengt G. M. Sundkler is bringing his *Bantu Prophets in South Africa* up to date. If this be looked upon as chance, one feels like saying with the poet: *It chanced that God eternal chance did guide.*

Dr. Pauw's continual reference to Sundkler's study on Separatism has produced some very fruitful comparisons between the Tswana and the Nguni, which should prove valuable for an eventual overall study of Bantu Separatism. It is indeed gratifying that the present author has throughout endeavoured to see the Tswana-Tlhaping situation in its wider setting.

On the other hand *Religion in a Tswana Chiefdom* is indeed a 'study in depth', and is thereby related to the Uganda study. Up to now the problems of the Christian Mission in Africa have been tackled one by one, each one being examined as it appears in a number of different situations. So, for instance, the problem of marriage in Africa and the Church and politics in Africa have claimed our attention in recent years.

There is, however, the other method, which engages attention on the whole life of the Church in a given situation or a limited environment. We have the feeling that the Group Survey of the Training of the Ministry in Africa, sponsored by the International Missionary Council, may have paved the way for this latter method. In any case, Dr. Pauw may be congratulated on the completion of this study, and may

viii FOREWORD

rest assured that his labour has not been in vain. More and more the results of the impact of the Christian message on heathenism will have to be weighed and the reaction of the latter to the conquests of the Cross will have to be determined.

Approximately a quarter of a century ago Dr Edwin W. Smith, in his presidential address before the Royal Anthropological Institute, broke a lance for the proper place of social anthropology in the curriculum for the training of missionaries. Even if his plea may not have had the desired result, the reason certainly was not that this newer branch of study encroached on a realm where it has no jurisdiction. For the Christian faith and its Mission have vast sociological implications and while anthropology dare not touch the motive or the obligation of the missionary, it can and ought to criticize his methods.

After the massive labours of men like H. A. Junod and Sundkler on the 'eastern front', we are greatly heartened by this achievement on the less-known 'western front'. Once more a missionary has contributed to make anthropology 'almost a missionary science'. *Religion in a Tswana Chiefdom* deserves a place at least in all our libraries, and should be constantly at the elbow of our missionaries, administrators, and anthropologists.

G. B. A. GERDENER.

Stellenbosch, Christmas, 1958.

PREFACE

THIS book is a study of present-day religion in a rural Bantu society, viewed within the wider framework of their social structure and economy. Being a missionary it is hardly necessary to explain why I chose to investigate this particular subject, but my interest was very much stimulated by Dr. Sundkler's study of Zulu Separatist or Independent Churches, and from the outset I wish to record my indebtedness to his valuable work.[1] Dr. Sundkler's book provided numerous suggestions of lines along which a study such as this could proceed. However, although I also paid particular attention to the Separatist Churches I did try to make it more than a mere parallel of Dr. Sundkler's study among a different people. In the first place I chose a different approach by concentrating on a restricted area and investigating that as intensively as possible. On the other hand, within this restricted area I tried to conduct my investigations on a wider front by studying the social structure and economy in some detail (although only a short sketch of this has been included in this book), and by including in the study all aspects of present-day religion, i.e. not only the Separatist Churches, but also the non-Separatist Churches, and the existing remnants of traditional pagan religion.

The Tlhaping are a particularly important section of the Tswana cluster of tribes. Being the southernmost representatives of this group at the time of the European penetration of the interior, they were the first to come into contact with Europeans. Through the work of the famous Robert Moffat, who established the first permanent mission among a Tswana people, their name and the name of Kuruman, where at one time they had their headquarters, have become well known.

At present the largest and most important section of the Tlhaping inhabits the Taung Reserve which consists of two separate chiefdoms, viz. the Phuduhutswana, whose headquarters are at Taung which has given the reserve its name, and the Maidi, whose chief lives at Manthe. My investigations were mainly confined to the Phuduhutswana chiefdom which constitutes about two-thirds of the whole reserve.

I spent altogether just over a year in the chiefdom, from September 1952 to February 1953, and again from June 1953 to January 1954. I was accompanied by my wife, and at first we camped and later had a hut built adjoining some homesteads not far from the chief's court

[1] Sundkler, Bengt G. M., *Bantu Prophets in South Africa*, Lutterworth Press, London, 1948.

X   PREFACE

and meeting place (*kgotla*). When commencing fieldwork I already had a little knowledge of Tswana and it was only during the first few months that I made considerable use of an interpreter. During the first field trip I concentrated on developing my knowledge of the language and on obtaining a general impression of the culture and social structure. During the second period I concentrated on religion. My research methods included the attendance and observation of different types of activities (e.g. tribal assemblies and court sessions, weddings, funerals, and a variety of church activities), interviews with special informants on traditional matters and with church leaders, teachers, and Europeans who have regular contacts with the Tlhaping. I also collected written information from literate informants, set school children essays, and conducted a sample survey of sixty-three homesteads (for particulars of which see Appendix I).

I contacted leaders of every church known to me. In one or two cases written questionnaires were used, and occasionally I inquired, by means of correspondence, about a point which had escaped my notice, but nearly all the informants were interviewed personally. The interviews with church leaders were guided in so far as I sought information on a certain range of topics or aspects from every church, but they were conducted as freely as possible in order to discover as many details as possible. I also had interviews with ordinary church members, but my time was too restricted to conduct these systematically on a large scale. Practically all the material was collected by myself.

During a short visit to England before doing fieldwork I was able to spend a few days studying the Archives of the London Missionary Society where I collected some useful material on Taung. I am indebted to the Society for access to the Archives and for permission to use some of the material in this book.

When embarking on this study I had already worked for a short time as a missionary in Kimberley. In my field work I did not try to hide this aspect of my identity, but whenever I was questioned about my regular occupation I explained that I was not undertaking the investigation on behalf of, or to propagate, a particular denomination, but because of my interest in the Bantu people. I think the fact that I was seldom addressed as *moruti* (the form of address for ministers and missionaries), but in time became known by the name of *Rraditšô* (Father-of-*ditšô*—the word *ditšô* referring to genealogies, history, and tradition) shows that I was accepted as visiting them primarily as investigator.

In its present form the book is a condensation of a thesis accepted

PREFACE xi

by the University of Cape Town for the degree of Ph.D. in 1955. I am indebted to the University for relinquishing the publication rights which were granted to them at the time. Unfortunately circumstances outside my control delayed revision of the manuscript for publication purposes. Since I have not been in a position to make a systematic study of relevant literature and statistics that have appeared since completion of the thesis, no reference has been included to the most recent material.

This study was made possible by a bursary from the University of Stellenbosch which enabled me to spend some months at Leyden University and the Dutch Missionary College at Oegstgeest, and to undertake my first field trip. For the second field trip I received an *ad hoc* grant from the National Council for Social Research, which also made a grant partially covering the cost of publication. I wish to express my sincere appreciation to both these bodies for their assistance, as well as to the International African Institute, for undertaking the publication.

My research and writing of the thesis were supervised by Professor Monica Wilson, to whom I am greatly indebted for her very able and sympathetic guidance. Dr. John Middleton supervised part of my writing-up during Professor Wilson's absence and I very much appreciate his assistance. To Dr. Ellen Hellmann who read a draft of the manuscript and contributed valuable comments and criticisms, to Mr. Charles Johnman who revised it for style at the thesis stage, and to Dr. D. Brink of Bellville, for technical advice and assistance in drawing map B, I also owe a word of thanks.

Not only am I very grateful to Professor G. B. A. Gerdener for reading and criticizing an early draft of the manuscript, but I feel greatly honoured by his readiness to write a foreword to this book. I think of him not merely as one of my teachers, but with many others I cherish the warm friendship of which even his students have been favoured to partake.

In the Taung reserve a great number of people rendered assistance without which this study would not have been possible. I must mention Messrs. Norton and Bowen who successively filled the position of Native Commissioner while I was doing fieldwork, as well as many members of their staff, both Europeans and Africans; chief Thapama Mankurwane, councillor Morwagabuse (Samuel) Mankurwane, and the late headman Tlhapietsile (Jim) Molala, and many other headmen, as well as Mr. J. W. J. Makgothi who assisted me as interpreter and clerk. I wish to thank all the people who acted as informants, and here I include all the ministers, other church leaders and teachers, as well as

PREFACE

the European traders, the representative of the Native Recruiting Corporation, and officials of the Northern Lime Company who provided information. My wife and I wish to thank the Rev. Joseph Wing and Mrs. Wing of the London Mission very particularly, not only for their co-operation, but also for their friendship and many tokens of kindness and hospitality.

I am very grateful to my parents-in-law, who contributed in many ways to make possible the completion of this study. To my wife, who was willing to forfeit a settled home for the first few years of our married life, and to share the experiences in connection with this study, I owe particular acknowledgement. She also rendered practical assistance in many ways.

To all who contributed to my earlier training as anthropologist and as missionary, at Stellenbosch, Leyden, and Oegstgeest, I would also like to say a word of thanks.

What I owe to my own parents need not be said here. As token of my deep-felt gratitude for so much with which they have enriched my life I dedicate this book to them, who devoted the best of their years to missionary work in Northern Rhodesia.

The shortcomings in this book are, of course, numerous, but had it depended solely on my own ability, they would have been far more. Many were the times that I felt baffled and did not see the way ahead, but many prayers were also said for help and guidance. This complete dependence on God's guidance and help I also wish to acknowledge.

B. A. P.

East London,
South Africa.
January 1959.

CONTENTS

FOREWORD by Dr. G. B. A. Gerdener, Emeritus Professor of the History of Missions, in the D.R.C. Theological Seminary, Stellenbosch   vii

PREFACE   ix

I HISTORY AND SOCIAL BACKGROUND   1

History. Population. The changing society. Religious groupings.

II PAGANISM ON THE WANE   12

Examples of ritual. Present remnants of paganism. The extent of adherence to paganism.

III INTRODUCING THE CHURCHES   41

Types of churches. Historical background. Church origins. Analysis of Church statistics.

IV CHURCH ORGANIZATION   62

The church group. Leaders and other office bearers. Privileges and duties of members. The role of women in the churches. Church property and finance. Connexions with the church outside the reserve. Interdenominational relations. The churches and youth. The churches and political authorities. Attitude to Europeans. Summary.

V THE PATTERN OF CHURCH ACTIVITIES   123

The general pattern of life in the churches. The pattern of church services. Preachers and their sermons.

VI RITUAL AND REVELATION IN THE CHURCHES   146

Ritual of childhood and youth. Marriage rites. Death and its ritual. Baptism. Mass and Holy Communion. Ritual avoidance. Illness and healing. Water rites and purification. Revelation and the Spirit. Prayers for rain. Summary.

VII TRENDS AND INTERCONNEXIONS   212

Trends in paganism. General trends in the churches. Preferences for certain denominations and types. The church of the L.M.S. Some aspects of Bantu Separatism. Interconnexions.

xiv CONTENTS

APPENDIX I PARTICULARS OF SAMPLE SURVEY 243

II ST PAUL APOSTOLIC FAITH MORNING
STAR 244

III RELIGIOUS AFFILIATION OF THE BANTU
POPULATION – 1951 CENSUS 246

LIST OF REFERENCES 249

INDEX 253

LIST OF ILLUSTRATIONS

facing page

1. Site of the old capital at Taung — 16

2. Digging a grave in a cattle-byre (Note the branches closing the regular entrance) — 17

3. A Pentecostal Separatist Preacher praying and laying-on hands for his wife — 32

4. The visiting Bishop of the Holy Church of Christ officiating at a service for the laying of a corner-stone — 33

5. Minister entering baptismal pool (St. Paul Apostolic Faith Morning Star) — 80

6. Early morning prayer meeting for rain outside the chief's *kgotla* — 81

7. Laying-on of hands in the Zion Apostolic Church — 96

8. Making list of donations at funeral night watch — 97

9. The action referred to as 'tress' (running in a circle) — 160

10. St. Paul Apostolic Faith Morning Star: 'the holy place' — 161

11. Laying-on of hands causing unusual movements said to derive from the action of the Holy Spirit — 176

12. Members of the Holy Christian Apostolic Church in Zion after a service — 177

13. The Sexton ringing the 'bell'. In the background the simple church building beside some ruins (Bechuana Methodist Church) — 192

14. Interior of a Separatist Church — 193

15. The entrance to Mmoloki's Cave — 208

16. Two old people receiving baptism in Lutheran Church — 209

LIST OF TABLES

page

I DEGREE OF AFFILIATION WITH CHURCHES (SAMPLE AREAS)   10

II TOTAL MEMBERSHIP OF THE CHURCHES (Communicant and non-Communicant members)   58–9

III CHURCH ORIGINS   60

IV LOCAL GROUPS, OFFICE BEARERS, AND ETHNIC COMPOSITION OF CHURCHES   78–9

V CHURCH MEMBERSHIP—Numerical relation of the sexes   96–7

VI CHURCH AFFILIATION—Sex and age (Sample)   112

LIST OF MAPS

page

A THE NORTHERN CAPE AND ADJACENT AREAS   3

B PHUDUHUTSWANA CHIEFDOM OF THE TAUNG RESERVE: THE SOCIO-ECONOMIC BACKGROUND WITH OVERLAY SHOWING CHURCHES IN THE CHIEFDOM   *in pocket at end*

CHAPTER I

HISTORY AND SOCIAL BACKGROUND

THE people whose religion is described in this book call themselves Tlhaping, and live in a South African native reserve called Taung, in the Northern Cape, in what used to be known as British Bechuanaland. It is about eighty miles north of Kimberley, South Africa's diamond mining centre.

History[1]

According to tradition the Tlhaping, who belong to the Tswana cluster of tribes, had inhabited various parts of what is now the Northern Cape for a considerable time before their first encounters with Europeans—unsettled missionaries, travellers, and others—at the turn of the previous century. At the time they were living at a place called Dithakong and some years later moved to the well-known Kuruman, where the famous missionary, Robert Moffat, after preliminary work by others, finally established a mission of the London Missionary Society in 1821.

This was a time of continual unrest for the Tlhaping. During Moffat's early years at Kuruman they were at one stage gravely threatened by the Mantatisi, a fearful horde of fugitives of the Zulu chief Shaka. During subsequent years they were continually harassed by bands of raiding Bushmen, Griquas, and Korannas, and on at least two occasions the majority of the tribe abandoned the capital for some months to evade the marauders.

About 1829 the Tlhaping started to split up into a number of independent sections. Several groups, including one under the reigning chief Mothibi, moved away from Kuruman. Those remaining behind now regarded Mankurwane, the young son of Mothibi's deceased brother Molala, as the rightful heir, his uncle Mahura acting for him as regent. Not long afterwards the Kuruman remnant moved to Taung, again shifting to Maamusa (now Schweizer Reneke in the Transvaal) in 1846, but returning to Taung a few years later. In 1841 a L.M.S. mission was opened at Taung, and after being closed down later, was reopened in 1868. A Roman Catholic mission was started at the chief's village in 1895.

[1] For a more detailed account of the history of the Tlhaping, see Language, 1942.

R.T.C.—2

2 RELIGION IN A TSWANA CHIEFDOM

Another section of the Tlhaping, under Mothibi's son Gasebonwe, settled south of Taung, their headquarters being at Phokwane, where an Anglican mission was established in 1876. Government measures against the severe rinderpest epidemic in 1895 caused an insurrection among the Tlhaping of Phokwane, which led to the confiscation of their land and the exile of the chief Galeshewe and a large number of his followers.

None of the other groups of Tlhaping persisted as separate chiefdoms. Some Tlhaping are to-day to be found in a number of smaller reserves to the south-west of Taung, where they are administered by headmen who do not come under the jurisdiction of any chief. Many others are scattered on farms and small reserves in different districts of the Northern Cape. The eastern part of the Taung Reserve is inhabited by the Maidi Tlhaping with their headquarters at Manthe. They used to be subordinate to the main group of Tlhaping with whom they have very long been associated, but they have now for some time been recognized as an independent chiefdom by the Native Affairs Department. The main group are differentiated as the Tlhaping of Phuduhutswana, after an important chief, nine generations or more back. There is no known agnatic link between the Maidi chiefs and those of the Phuduhutswana.

The latter half of the nineteenth century saw the Tlhaping gradually engulfed by European settlement. The discovery of diamonds in the 'sixties, and the subsequent development of diggings along the Vaal River and mining in Kimberley, brought a variety of European types on to the Tlhaping doorstep and a movement of people from tribes from the interior through their territory. Mankurwanes's accession to the chieftainship in 1869 was followed by a time of dispute and strife between the South African Republic and the native tribes, as well as between these tribes themselves, the British Government, and that of the Cape Colony, eventually also becoming involved. The South African Republic had already been formed to the east of Taung and now followed the proclamation of the crown colony of Griqualand West to the south (1871), of the Protectorate of British Bechuanaland (1885), and the eventual incorporation of the latter into the Cape Colony (1895). In this process large tracts of land, to which the Tlhaping laid claim but did not always occupy, became European farms.

In view of the relatively low rainfall—an average of 17 inches p.a. was measured for the years 1936–1950[1]—and periodic droughts, the

[1] *Annual Report of the Superintendent*, Taung Irrigation Scheme, for the year July 1950 to June 1951.

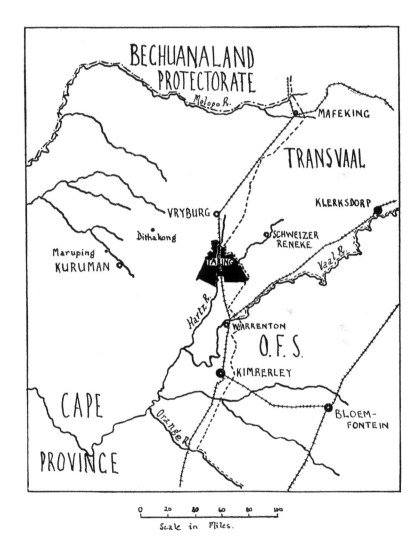

MAP A: The Northern Cape and Adjacent Areas

4 RELIGION IN A TSWANA CHIEFDOM

development of an irrigation scheme by the Native Affairs Department must be regarded as the most important change in the Reserve in recent times. The first plots for irrigation were allotted during the 1939–1940 summer. By September 1953 a total of 4,200 morgen had been developed, comprising some 1,200 fields of approximately two morgen each, and 350 smaller gardens. The scheme forms a continuation of the Vaal-Hartz Settlement to the south, where European farmers have been settled on about 1,200 holdings averaging thirty morgen each.

The topography of the reserve is dominated by a shallow valley running from north to south. The irrigation scheme stretches along the eastern slopes of the valley (Cf. Map B.)

Population

Unfortunately there are no reliable official figures for the Bantu population of the Taung Reserve or the Phuduhutswana chiefdom. In the 1951 census 22,568 were enumerated in the whole reserve, of whom approximately 18,628 were in the Phuduhutswana chiefdom.[1]

It is generally acceded that these figures are far too low. For one thing, the census was taken during the reaping season when a large but unknown number were away reaping on farms. For an estimate of the population, I used the method applied by the Native Affairs Department, viz. multiplying the number of taxpayers by $4\frac{1}{4}$.[2] In 1953 there were 7,287 taxpayers in the Phuduhutswana chiefdom, so that the native population can be estimated at $7,287 \times 4\frac{1}{4} = 30,970$ or 31,000 to the nearest hundred. This would include regular inhabitants temporarily absent at any given time during that year.

Although all members of the chiefdom pay allegiance to a Tlhaping chief and are therefore politically speaking Tlhaping, only a nucleus are Tlhaping by descent. With the exception of the Maidi, all 'true' Tlhaping putatively belong to a dispersed unilineal descent group— which might be called a dispersed clan—having the koodoo as its totem.[3] The largest proportion of the population is made up of persons

---

[1] Figures supplied by the Native Commissioner, Taung. The latter figure is an estimate, since one census sub-district includes persons from both chiefdoms (Phuduhutswana and Maidi); two-thirds of them were estimated to be Phuduhutswana.

[2] In a recent publication (Breutz, P. L., 1953b), estimates of the native population in other such areas are arrived at by multiplying the total number of taxpayers by $4\frac{1}{4}$, which the author says has been found to be reasonably reliable (p. 40). In the sample groups investigated in the Phuduhutswana chiefdom (see Appendix I), I found that the total population was 4·28 times the number of males of eighteen years and older (those required to pay tax). I therefore regard the figure of $4\frac{1}{4}$ as fairly reliable for Taung also.

[3] The Rolong, parent 'clan' of the Tlhaping, also venerate the koodoo.

HISTORY AND SOCIAL BACKGROUND 5

who are not Tlhaping by descent, but who are Tswana. There are also a number of Xhosa-speaking people (Cape Nguni) and a small number of Southern Sotho and Coloured people. The Tlhaping then form the 'royalty' or 'nobles', holding a privileged position in the political system. In other fields there is not much suggesting a cleavage between nobles and commoners, but the relation between Tswana and Nguni, who still preserve a certain degree of cultural identity, is often uneasy.

According to the 1951 census there were 586 Europeans in the reserve, of whom a large number are connected with the lime works at Buxton. Reserve natives also have a considerable amount of contact with Europeans on surrounding farms, many of whom do their regular business at Taung station.

The changing society

The same type of changes that are to-day taking place throughout southern Africa, mainly as a result of contact of indigenous populations with different 'agents' and influences of Western civilization, have been taking place among the Tlhaping, some of the influences having been at work for more than a century. Here, as elsewhere, missionaries, traders, representatives of European governments, the settlement of European farmers in the interior, and migrant labour in towns have played their part in changing the social world of the Tlhaping from one of a small-scale homogeneous society forming a small independent polity, in which kinship ties played a decisive role, to one of greater internal social diversity, of political dependence and participation in a modern state with all its international ties, one in which kinship has become much less important than it used to be. A subsistence economy based on herding and shifting cultivation has been replaced by a money economy, in which migrant wage labour is an absolute necessity, although peasant farming is still pursued. Among a considerable proportion of the population Christianity has largely supplanted the ancestor cult and other traditional beliefs and ritual.

This process of change has become familiar enough[1] to make its description superfluous, but attention must be drawn to a few features of this process in Taung to provide the necessary background for the main theme of the book.

A characteristic of Tswana social structure still encountered among many tribes at the present time is the tendency to congregate in large towns. Such towns are divided into wards and sub-wards, each con-

---

[1] Cf. amongst others Schapera (and others), 1934 and 1947; Wilson, Godfrey, and Monica, 1945, and the Keiskammahoek Rural Survey, 1952, Vol. II, Houghton, and Walton; and Vol. III, Wilson, and others.

6 RELIGION IN A TSWANA CHIEFDOM

sisting mainly of patrilineal kinsmen, each ward being administered by the senior male member of the patrilineal group around which the ward was formed. These ward headmen, whose position is hereditary, act as councillors to the chief who represents the highest indigenous authority.[1]

It is evident that this traditional pattern used to exist in the Taung Reserve, but to-day the population is scattered (see Map B), there is no large central town, and the old ward pattern, based largely on patrilineal kinship and patrilocal residence, has been superseded by a new system. The whole chiefdom is now divided into a number of areas administered by headmen appointed by the chief (or by the descendants of original appointees), who are nearly all members of royal lineages. The population of a modern headman's area is not only much more numerous than that of a traditional ward, but it is also not a predominantly patrilineal kinship group as the old wards and smaller administrative units used to be.

It is clear, then, that as a result of this scattering, kinship ties, particularly patrilineal ties, have become less important. Within the traditional wards or their component family-groups a great deal of economic, legal, and ritual co-operation used to take place between patrilineal kinsmen and their dependants, which no longer occurs. Whereas patrilocal residence was the regular custom, it is becoming much less common than it used to be.[2] Nevertheless, 'clan' and lineage distinctions, and the hierarchy of status based on descent in the male line are still recognized and play a role on different occasions.

The scattering of the population has also resulted in the delegation of power by the chief to his headmen to a greater extent than seems to have been the case under the traditional system. Headmen scattered over the reserve cannot refer matters to the chief as easily, and cannot be as strictly controlled as those living in a tribal capital. It is to be expected that they will act with a considerable degree of independence, and they do. However, the institution of chieftainship had already been undermined to a considerable extent by other factors (e.g. loss of large tracts of land to which the Tlhaping laid claim) by the time the wholesale scattering of the population started. The whole argument cannot be propounded here, but my own and comparative Tswana material suggest that, to begin with, the decline of chiefly

---

[1] Schapera, 1953, pp. 35 f., 46, and 51 ff.

[2] Quantitative material illustrating some of the trends mentioned in this section will be included in a sketch of the present-day social structure which I hope to publish elsewhere.

HISTORY AND SOCIAL BACKGROUND 7

authority contributed to the scattering of the population, but eventually was also aggravated by it.

Tribal solidarity and the authority of the chief have also been adversely affected by the diversification of a formerly homogeneous society through the introduction of missions, schools, hospitals, and voluntary associations. A money economy, making for individualism, and particularly migrant labour, have also played their part. The development of the irrigation scheme, controlled by the South African Native Trust, has meant the loss of control over arable land, a particularly hard blow to the chief's authority. These facts illustrate the complex nature of the social changes which are taking place.

Particular mention should also be made of the fact that the traditionally preferred kinship marriages, typical of the Tswana, are disappearing. Arranged marriages and preferential kinship marriages are giving way to individual taste. Another important change is that the payment of *bogadi* (marriage payment) is falling into disuse with many people, and is no longer essential to establish a man's right over the children born of a marriage. This may be because many people now get married by Christian or civil rites. It is probably also related to economic factors such as heavy losses in stock caused by droughts, combined with the readiness of the Tlhaping and other Tswana to sell their cattle, in contrast to the Nguni who are not eager to sell cattle and adhere strongly to the custom of making marriage payments (*lobola*).[1]

The school is an institution fully accepted and desired by all in Taung. Although many children do not attend school, one is not aware of any cleavage between 'school people' and those who do not send their children to school, as has been observed in other areas. On the whole there would be little difference between the way of life in the homes of those who go to school and those who do not. Most households have, or have had, connexions with the schools.

In September 1952 there were two tribal and seventeen mission schools[2] in the chiefdom, the one tribal school offering courses up to Junior Certificate. Of the 2,971 pupils in these schools, 37% were boys.

The Phuduhutswana chiefdom is very distinctly a changing society, but the marked changes that are taking place do not imply that old traditional patterns are altogether superseded by new ones. Perhaps the most remarkable aspect of the present situation is not that pro-

[1] See Houghton and Walton, *op. cit.*
[2] This was before the promulgation of the Bantu Education Act.

8 RELIGION IN A TSWANA CHIEFDOM

found changes have taken place, but that in spite of so many forces making for change, some of which have already exerted their influence for a very long time, something of the traditional background still persists. We shall pay more attention to this aspect in connexion with religion, but a few examples may be noted here from the general social background. First, the Tlhaping still have an hereditary chief assisted by headmen to whom some of his power is delegated, although they now control areas of the chiefdom and not wards of a town. The general tribal assembly is a traditional institution persisting up to the present, although it has lost much of its former pomp. The chief is still the judge of his people and litigates according to traditional procedure.

In spite of the weakening of the principle of unilineal descent in the kinship system, it still figures in the recognition of totems, names of totemic groups and lineages which are inherited in the male line. Status according to unilineal descent, though declining in importance, is still recognized and is particularly important in the initiation ceremonies which persist with remarkable tenacity and in connexion with which male and female age-grades are still being formed. Kinship generally is still reckoned much further than among Europeans, and co-operation between kinsmen still emerges on occasions like weddings and funerals. The chiefdom is perhaps ethnically more heterogeneous than it used to be, but the true Tlhaping still form the nucleus and ruling community.

Religious groupings

Groupings among and within the churches will be discussed in later chapters. Here we are concerned with the question of how far the society as a whole has been affected by Christianity, whether we can distinguish a major grouping into Christians and pagans, and how the different groups compare numerically. At the outset it must be made clear that a simple and clear-cut grouping, into Christians or church people on the one hand and pagans on the other, is not possible, because of the existence of a considerable but undefined middle 'group' consisting of people who claim to be church adherents but have no official church connexions. The existence of such a category of people is recognized by the Tlhaping in that such people designate themselves as *barati* (from *go rata*, to like or love). The term is rather vaguely used and members of this group range from people who regularly attend church services to those who hardly ever see the inside of a church but regard it as befitting present conditions to have a church which one considers as one's own, especially when it comes

HISTORY AND SOCIAL BACKGROUND

to marriages and funerals. We may henceforth refer to them as *adherents*.[1]

Some idea of the extent to which the society has accepted Christianity can be formed from official church statistics (Table II) which show the total number of communicant and non-communicant members of all the churches in the chiefdom amounts to 10,203. By non-communicant members I mean those who are members of classes which lead to full membership and who are varyingly referred to as catechumens, members on trial or members of the confirmation class. I would suggest that the total of 10,203 provides a near indication of the proportion of the population above the age of ten years observing a formal connexion with the churches.[2] According to the 1936 census 72·4% of the natives in the Union were above the age of ten. If the Phuduhutswana chiefdom were typical of the Union[3] it would mean that 22,444 out of an estimated population of 31,000 are older than ten years. The total church membership of 10,203 constitutes 45·47% of this number. This is, of course, at its best, only an approximate figure but I think the inference is justified that roughly a little less than half of the population of ten years and older have official connexions with the churches. As I shall presently show, this was actually the case in the sample areas already referred to.

As indicated above, the middle group of *barati* or church adherents is not clearly defined and this makes it all the more difficult to assess its numerical strength.[4] I did try to form some idea of this, however, by including in the sample survey information about the church connexions of the members of every homestead.

[1] The term adherent is sometimes used to include categories such as catechumens or members on trial. In the present study this is not the case, and 'adherents' always refers to people who profess adherence but have no official connexion as communicants or as members of classes.

[2] In most churches children cannot become communicant members before they are about seventeen or eighteen, but some may be attending catechumen classes from the age of about fourteen or fifteen. The Anglican and Roman Catholic Churches, which together represent about half the membership of all the churches, confirm children from the age of ten. This means that some of their catechumens may be younger than ten, but I doubt whether there are many, and at any rate their numbers would be at least equalled by those of Sunday School children older than ten, who are not included in the number given above. It seems reasonable therefore to consider the figure of 10,203 as a close indication of the number of people above the age of ten years who observe an official connexion with the churches.

[3] In the sample areas I investigated (cf. Appendix I), 73·12% of the total population were over ten years of age. This makes acceptable the supposition that the Phuduhutswana chiefdom is typical of the Union.

[4] Official census figures relating to religious affiliation in the Taung district could not be obtained.

10 RELIGION IN A TSWANA CHIEFDOM

From the particulars given by informants four categories of church affiliation could be formulated.

(1) People who were said to have *no church connexions* constitute the first category.

(2) The second consists of *adherents*. It includes all who were explicitly called *barati* or who were regarded as church people on the ground that they attended services. Children were often considered as being affiliated to churches because they were baptized (or blessed in the case of 'baptist' churches) in infancy. These have also been grouped as adherents since they may be regarded as constituting at least potential adherents. Only children under fifteen are included in the category of adherents on the grounds of infant baptism, since older people who do not claim to be adherents (if they are not catechumens or full members) can hardly be regarded as having connexions with the churches merely because they were baptized in infancy.

(3) Members of *Sunday Schools and catechumen classes*

(4) *Communicant or full members.*

The following table shows the distribution into the different categories of the 398 persons in the sample. They have also been split into two age groups, viz. those under ten years old and those above ten.

TABLE I.—DEGREE OF AFFILIATION WITH CHURCHES (Sample Areas)

Degree of affiliation	Under 10 yrs.		10 yrs. & older		Total	
	No.	*%*	*No.*	*%*	*No.*	*%*
1. Nil . . .	31	29·0	82	28·2	113	28·4
2. Adherents . .	62	57·9	68	23·4	130	32·7
3. SS. or CC. . .	14	13·1	58	19·9	72	18·1
4. Full members .	—	—	83	28·5	83	20·9
TOTAL . .	107	100·0	291	100·0	398	100·0

In the sample 48·4% of the people in the ten-years-and-over age group are officially connected with a church as full members, catechumens or members of a Sunday school. It is further significant that a considerable number of people (23·4% of the ten-years-and-over age group) claim connexion as adherents, while only about 28% of the whole population claim no connexion with the churches. Of the 82

HISTORY AND SOCIAL BACKGROUND 11

persons of ten-years-and-older, 18 (16 males and 2 females) had been baptized in infancy and therefore did have some connexion with a church as children. That leaves 64 out of 291 (22%) of the older-age group without present or past connexions.

I have no reason to believe that the sample, although small, is not typical of the society as a whole. It illustrates that the society has been affected by the churches to a considerable extent and that the majority of the people have accepted the churches as part of their life.[1] Probably even most of the people who claim no church connexions have accepted many ideas which form part of the teachings of Christianity so that these people could hardly still be called pagans or heathens. If we do distinguish between Christians and 'pagans' as constituting the major religious groupings in the society, it should be remembered that there is no clear dividing line and no deep cleavages or intense oppositions between the two groups. In this respect the existence of a considerable number of mere adherents, who have not come to a complete acceptance and profession of Christianity, is significant. Through this undefined middle group Christianity almost merges into paganism.

[1] In the whole Union 4,122,189 natives or 53% of the total native population were enumerated as professing adherence to Christian churches in 1946.

According to official census returns for the Bechuanaland Protectorate 23% of the population in the Tswana districts were enumerated as Christians in 1946, 'although the proportion varies greatly from one tribe to another (e.g. Kgatla 65%, Ngwaketse and Kwena 38%, Tawana 16%, and Ngwato only 7%)'. (Schapera, 1953, p. 47, with reference to *Census Report*, 1946, Table IV (i).)

CHAPTER II

PAGANISM ON THE WANE

ALTHOUGH the Christian churches dominate present-day religious life in the Phuduhutswana chiefdom, traditional magico-religious ritual and beliefs are by no means extinct.

It is probable that the Tswana traditionally believed in a Supreme Being whom they called *Modimo*, the word which missionaries adopted to designate God in their own teachings and in translations of the Bible. It seems as if there was hardly any cult connected with this Being. The 'dominant cult', as Professor Schapera refers to it,[1] was concerned with the dead. There was belief in a continued existence after death, and the dead were thought to have a considerable degree of control over the living, with whom they communicated particularly through dreams and divining. The living prevailed upon the dead to give them assistance and prosperity by offering prayers and sacrifices. According to Schapera, 'each family was held to be under the direct guidance of its own agnatic ancestors, who in turn were interested only in the affairs of their own descendants'.[2]

The ritual further involved the use of 'medicines' (*ditlhare*) and treatment in connexion with which there were specialist 'doctors' (*dingaka*). Illness and misfortune could be caused by deceased ancestors but sorcery (*boloi*) was also considered a major cause of misfortune, while there were still other causes more or less independent of the control of human or other personal beings, e.g. the breach of certain taboos.

Doctoring, medicine, and sorcery are usually classified as magic and the ancestor cult as religion. As the definition of magic is of particular significance to the argument developed in a later chapter, I shall discuss it there in more detail. I may just point out here that I do not think a clear-cut division can be made between the ancestor cult on the one hand and what is usually termed magic on the other. For instance, the activities of the native doctor (*ngaka*), which are often classified as magic, link up with the ancestor cult. In descriptions of the actual rites, therefore, I do not separate the ancestor cult from doctoring, medicines, and sorcery.

The fact that the traditional magico-religious system no longer functions as a complete system to which the whole society adheres

[1] 1953, p. 59.   [2] *Ibid.*

PAGANISM ON THE WANE

with relative uniformity confronts us with a problem. Science requires that we should be systematic and therefore we have to systematize, but in doing so we are in danger of over-simplifying and of describing as a complete system that which is one no longer. I shall try to avoid this by first describing examples of pagan ritual or modifications of it which are known or said to have been performed quite recently, and then analysing paganism in terms of its existing remnants and modifications.

It must be emphasized that most of the material on pagan ritual was obtained from a few reliable informants. It was not easy to gain access to the performance of pagan ritual, though I did manage to do so on two or three occasions. Further, most of the ritual described here is not often performed nowadays.

Before proceeding to a description of the ritual it is advisable to explain the most important concepts and categories implied by the vernacular terminology.

Modimo: God as single Supreme Being. Sometimes the word is used to denote an ancestor spirit or even a living person whom one honours greatly.

Badimo: the ancestor spirits. The term is not only used of one's own deceased ancestors but denotes the dead generally. I adhere to the current term ancestor (or ancestral) spirits, but in the present study it should be understood in this wider sense of spirits of the dead.[1]

Ngaka: a native doctor, using herbal and other medicines; usually he is also a diviner. ('Doctor' in this chapter always refers to such a native doctor.)

Ditaola, bola: the set of dice, consisting for the greater part of bones and pieces of bone, used by a doctor for divining.

Go alaha: to treat, doctor, or cure; used of the treatment applied by a doctor whether preventive or curative.

Boloi: the employment of medicine for evil purposes; sorcery.[2]

Moloi: a sorcerer.

Go lôwa (lôya): to employ sorcery.

Ditlhare (sing. *setlhare*): objects and substances, whether herbal or not, used as medicines by doctors or by sorcerers.

---

[1] Dr Language holds that the Tlhaping believe in two types of ancestral spirits, viz. *bamodimo*, those which are favourably disposed to the living, and *badimo*, spirits which are ill-disposed to the living (Language, 1941. Cf. also Brown, 1926, p. 103.) I came across no such distinction myself. Informants whom I questioned about the matter said they did not know of ancestral spirits being called *bamodimo*.

[2] I came across hardly any evidence of witchcraft as a true Tswana concept among the Tlhaping. The few examples of belief in witchcraft which I encountered were in terms of Nguni or S. Sotho concepts. In this chapter I shall only speak of sorcery. (Cf. Schapera, 1953, pp. 65 f.)

14 RELIGION IN A TSWANA CHIEFDOM

Molemo; More; Moriana: a medicine, whether used for socially approved purposes or for sorcery.

Moleko (from *go leka*, to try or test): a medicine used for sorcery.

Pheko: a charm provided by a doctor to safeguard against danger, to bring good fortune, or to make one invisible.

Moruti: shadow. A deceased person is thought of as being able to overshadow (*sira*) persons or things with a shadow which can be dangerous. A dangerous shadow or overshadowing may also be connected with a living person.

Sehihi: a potentially dangerous condition in which people and objects may find themselves, as a result of a death, or of a shadow of an ancestral spirit being on them. It may also result from the non-performance of ritual appropriate to a certain situation. Some informants compare it with the English term 'bad luck'. (The word has the same root as the word for darkness (*lehihi*).)

Tlhapišô (from *go tlhapa*, to wash the body): a ritual purification performed by a doctor.

Moila (from *go ila*, to avoid, dislike): an act or object which must be avoided, usually for reasons connected with ritual; taboo.

Examples of ritual

(a) Childbirth

The ritual observed nowadays in connexion with childbirth consists mostly of avoidance. A pregnant woman should not touch medicines, since by so doing she would be 'treading on'[1] them, and so aggravate the illness of the patient treated with them. According to one informant it is also taboo (*moila*) for a pregnant woman to eat excessively. When a woman is in seclusion only the women regularly attending to her may enter the house or hut in which she is confined, to avoid visitors employing sorcery against the child. During the first three weeks her husband is not allowed to visit her, but after that he may enter the house. He may resume sexual relations with her while the child is still small, provided that he is its real genitor. During his wife's pregnancy, and for some time after the birth of the child, he must abstain from intercourse with other women, however, since it would be harmful to the child.

After the birth of the child a goat provided by its maternal grandfather, is slaughtered. The mother is given a soup made of the

---

[1] The verb used (*go gatêla*) comes from the root, *go gata*, which means to tramp or tread, or lie upon. Sometimes it has the significance of making powerless. According to Schapera (1940, p. 202), persons who are ritually 'hot' (see p. 34) trample on medicines if they handle them.

PAGANISM ON THE WANE

stomach and intestines 'to cleanse the liver (*sebete*)'[1]—its ability to do so being ascribed to the vegetable substance the goat has eaten. The meat may only be eaten by the women attending to the mother.

The period of seclusion, which usually lasts several weeks, is nowadays terminated by a ceremony spoken of as 'taking the child out of the house' (*go ntsha ngwana mo tlung*), consisting of a short service, followed by a feast. During the service the child's father or his representative announces its name.[2] Only one informant connected this rite with a traditional custom. He held that the service as well as the feasting are new customs. Formerly, at the bringing out of the baby, its maternal grandmother would take it and put it in its father's arms saying: 'Here is your child,' and the father would then hold the baby for a while. This was only done in the case of a woman's first baby.

Willoughby related that in 'Bechuanaland' a rite of 'expurgation from the taboos of childhood' was performed. It consisted in treating both parents with smoke from odoriferous roots, and further treatment of their persons and the first plate of porridge they shared, and culminated in an act of sexual union signifying the resumption of marital relations.[3] The Tlhaping have no such ritual at present, but a woman who has had a miscarriage must be purified, otherwise she will be harmful to the cattle when passing through a herd or when approaching the byre. Formerly, a woman who had given birth out in the veld was fetched by some women at night, and the place where the delivery had taken place had to be purified, else the rain might be prevented from falling. This is said to have been done as recently as during the reign of chief Rabodigelo (d. 1934).

Various medicines are known and used in connexion with childbirth. Medicines for curing barrenness are known only to doctors. During pregnancy herbal medicines are taken which cause the child to be 'loose' in the womb, i.e. to ensure an easy birth. Some of these medicines, such as the plant known as *magorometšô*, are common knowledge and need not be administered by a doctor. A powder used by doctors for treating pregnant women is known as *tshitlhô*.[4] The

---

[1] Usually *sebete* means 'liver', but at least one informant seemed to use it to denote the womb.

[2] Since this is a Christian rite, it will be discussed in more detail at a later stage. (See ch. VI.)

[3] Willoughby, 1932, p. 201.

[4] *Tshitlhô* has many purposes. A layman said it is a bitter substance made from a certain kind of root and roast meat; a doctor said his *tshilthô*, which was of a light yellowish brown colour, contained 'rooistorm' and *morarane*. (According to Watt and Breyer-Brandwijk, 1932, these two plants are respectively *Rubia petiolaris DC.* and *Convulvus Hastatus Thunb.*)

16   RELIGION IN A TSWANA CHIEFDOM

child may be strengthened with medicines provided by a doctor, such as that known as *mekomišô*. If there is 'something wrong' in connexion with its birth, a child may afterwards be treated by its mother by holding it in the smoke produced by medicines smouldering on live embers. Babies often wear wristlets, anklets, and waistbands made of beads which are said to prevent the milk from 'running out'.

(b) Initiation

Various observances and avoidances connected with the initiation of boys and girls into adulthood are clearly of a ritual nature, but it is difficult to decide whether initiation as a whole essentially belongs to the domain of ritual or not. We shall therefore refer to the collective activities constituting initiation as 'ceremonial'. The initiation ceremonies provide the only remaining example of traditional ceremonial which is performed on anything approaching a tribal scale. The most important churches, however, do not allow their members to attend the ceremonies or to send their children, but after every performance of the ceremonies many church members are censured for violating this rule.

On two occasions there was a lapse of about fifteen years during which ceremonies for the tribe as a whole were not held. In his report for the year 1900, the Rev. John Brown, missionary of the London Missionary Society at Taung, wrote that there had been no circumcision ceremony at Taung for about ten years, and that he had most likely lived to see the end of these things.[1] A few years later the ceremonies were resumed, however, and were held several times during the subsequent decade. In 1940, while Dr. Language was doing fieldwork in the reserve, the general ceremonies were again held for the first time since 1925,[2] and they have been performed several times since then, the most recent having being held in 1951. The first long interval might possibly have been caused by the unsettled state of affairs in the country. This period saw the rinderpest epidemic, the rebellion of the Tlhaping under Galeshewe, and the Anglo-Boer War. The period from 1925 to 1940 saw some of the worst droughts experienced in the history of South Africa. Events such as these are known to influence the decision whether to hold the ceremonies or not. One would not be justified, therefore, in describing the resumption of the ceremonies after each long interval as the revival of customs which had become obsolete, but it seems remarkable that, in spite of

---

[1] Archives of the London Missionary Society, Livingstone House, London, *Annual Reports* (South African Field).

[2] Language, 1943b, pp. 110–134.

1. Site of the old capital at Taung

2. Digging a grave in a cattle-byre (Note the branches closing the regular entrance)

PAGANISM ON THE WANE

such long lapses in the performance, the ceremonies are adhered to with such tenacity in what is very much a changed and changing society. On the other hand the ceremonies have been abandoned by most of the Protectorate Tswana tribes,[1] among whom there is on the whole more tribal solidarity and whose chiefs have considerable authority and status.

No child should take part in the initiation ceremonies unless the rite known as *go ja dithari* (eating the animal of the cradle-skins) has been performed for the eldest child of the family. There is no fixed time when it should take place and it need only be performed for the first child a man has by his wife. A beast (bovine) or a sheep, provided by the child's father, is slaughtered at the home of its maternal relatives by the maternal grandfather or uncle. The meat is cooked and the first bit to be cut off is given to the child to eat, the second to its mother. The performer of the ritual places the fatty membrane covering the bowels of the animal (*lomipi*) around the mother's neck, the fat being allowed to drip on her body, after which it is also hung around the child's neck. The head and skin of the animal are the prerogative of the performer of the ritual. A similar rite is usually performed by the child's father at his own homestead, soon after the first, but this is not essential. Informants say that the rite is still observed by many people.

Different informants agreed that the rite was a safeguard against evil. One explained that a boy attending the initiation ceremonies without having had the ritual of the 'cradle-skin' performed, would be a danger to the other novices: he would make them senseless (*o tla tseanya bale*); his 'shadow' would fall on them (*o tla ba sira ka moruti wa gagwê*); he would 'be too heavy' for them (*o tla ba imêla*). This could, for instance, cause them to have a bad appetite. A doctor would be called to divine who was the cause, and to cleanse them all by sprinkling medicated water.

The ritual is also connected with *bogadi* and the establishment of the right of the father and his lineage over the children. The rite performed at the children's maternal relatives enables a man to say: 'These are my children,' and the animal which is sent by the former and slaughtered at the father's place, shows that 'truly, the child belongs to this man'. '*Bogadi* and *dithari* complement each other'. The ritual is also explained as the separation of the children from their mother's lineage. In view of the importance of status by patrilineal descent in the initiation ceremonies, the necessity of establishing the genealogical status of a novice beforehand is evident. The rite was also

[1] Schapera, 1938, p. 105.

R.T.C.—3

18 RELIGION IN A TSWANA CHIEFDOM

compared to Christian baptism of children, and was referred to as a 'mark' placed on them. The membrane placed around the necks of the mother and child is referred to as *sepheko* (a charm).[1]

What is known of the initiation ceremonies of the Tlhaping as they have been performed in recent years, corresponds in broad outline with older accounts of Tswana initiation.[2] The boys' ceremonies (*bogwera*) are held in temporary camps (*mephato*) out in the veld, where they live in huts, grouped in a semi-circle around an open space in which many of the activities take place. The camp is ritually 'fenced in' so that the boys should have no desire to leave it. The huts where their food is prepared at home are also 'fenced in' against sorcerers. Before the boys leave for the camp their hair is shaved and treated by a doctor before being thrown away. The camp and its precincts are prohibited ground for women and the uninitiated. Novices' parents may not eat of the same food that is prepared for them and they, as well as the boys' instructors, must abstain from sexual relations for the duration of the ceremonies.

Strict secrecy is still exercised in respect of the actual content of the ceremonies, but it is known that circumcision is still performed. Different totemic groups and lineages follow each other in order of genealogical status in undergoing the operation. The novices learn secret songs and formulas, go out hunting, perform exercises and undergo punishment. The ceremonies usually last about three months. On the day before the closing there is a procession to the *kgotla*, known as *thalalagae*, in which the new initiates wear sandals and straw skirts, and carry sticks and assegais. On approaching the homesteads, the older initiates surround the boys and form a barrier between them and the women. They return to the camp, but come in

---

[1] My Tlhaping informants' version of this rite combines two sets of information found in literature on the Tswana. The first deals with the slaughtering of an animal connected with cradle-skins (*dithari*) during or after a woman's confinement. (Schapera, 1940, p. 236; Brown, 1946, p. 417, under 'Feast'.) The second set of information deals with a ceremony in which the peritoneum or intestinal fat is hung around a woman and her child, and which is described as something apart from the *dithari* slaughtering. (Schapera, *op. cit.*, p. 72; Willoughby, 1928, pp. 187–188.) Dr. Breutz connects this ceremony with the payment of *bogadi* and legalizing the child's status. (Breutz, P. L., 1953b, pp. 110, 133. Cf. also pp. 83, 157, 170, 182, 191, 204, 217.) Cf. also Jennings, 1933, pp. 35–36, and Ellenberger, *History of the Basuto*, Ancient and Modern, London, 1913, p. 256, quoted by Willoughby, *op. cit.*, pp. 182–183.

[2] It was not possible for me to investigate the initiation ceremonies in great detail. What information I could obtain agreed with Dr. Language's account (*op. cit.*). For descriptions of the ceremonies in earlier times, see Willoughby, 1923, pp. 128–138, and Brown, 1926, pp. 73–90. Cf. also Schapera, 1938, pp. 105–107, 116; and 1939, pp. 52–59.

PAGANISM ON THE WANE

another procession (*ditime*) in the evening, the boys carrying flaming torches. After coming near to the homesteads, they return to the camp once more. The next day they finally leave the camp (which is immediately burnt), and on their arrival at the *kgotla* are welcomed by their relatives. The new initiates now wear loin skins and karosses, prepared by their parents, and anoint their bodies with ochre, and their heads with black lead. They disperse for a time and are then again summoned by the chief and ordered to wash, after which they return to normal life again. It is probably at this last gathering that they receive their name as a new age-set.

The girls' initiation is held soon after that of the boys. The ceremonies take place in separate homesteads, the girls of the same lineage gathering at one homestead. It still ends with the traditional *thojane*-night, which, according to Willoughby used to be 'famed for unflagging revelry and abundant beef and beer'.[1]

(c) Marriage

Although the prolonged ceremonial which usually accompanies a marriage in church or in the Native Commissioner's office is not held to be a part of the traditional marriage customs, it nevertheless often includes protective ritual by a native doctor. I shall describe the rites as they were actually performed for a wedding; some of them I could observe myself, the others were described to me by the officiating doctor.

The first were performed about two weeks before the wedding, when a wagon load of firewood was taken to the bride's parents' home. The firewood was to be used for the cooking in preparation for the wedding feast, and was one of the customary gifts which the bridegroom's father is expected to give the bride's parents.

The doctor, who had been summoned by the bridegroom's father, travelled by bicycle. There was nothing conspicuous about him. After the wagon had been unloaded he demanded half a crown for throwing the dice. From the saddle-bag containing his paraphernalia he produced a few dry, creeper-like twigs and an old tobacco pouch, from which he took what looked like pieces of broken crab-shell. To this he added a small ball of a substance like cow-dung. His apprentice started pounding the medicines with a stone while the doctor scratched a few scraps of a black greasy sub-

---

[1] *The Soul of the Bantu*, p. 321. A few important matters mentioned in earlier descriptions are lacking, e.g. the daily 'service of the Song of the Salt' (Brown, *op. cit.*), and a second boys' ceremony known as the 'black initiation', during which a painted pole, crowned with ostrich feathers or wildcat tails, was reverenced by the novices in the chief's cattle kraal. (Willoughby, 1928, pp. 298–299.) The female initiation ceremonies used to include daily processions with clay images, around which the novices knelt with clasped hands, their eyes fixed upon the image. (Willoughby, 1923, pp. 135–136.)

20 RELIGION IN A TSWANA CHIEFDOM

stance from a horn which had also been in the saddle-bag, and then demonstrated to the apprentice how to grind the mixture. A distinctly fishy smell came from the ground medicine.

From a small skin bag he shook his dice. In his cupped hands he took the dice with the half a crown, shook them and, while reciting the praises of the dice, threw the lot on the ground. For a short while he kept on reciting at a quick tempo, giving the pronouncement of the dice in symbolical language. The pronouncement was favourable for proceeding with the doctoring, but revealed an instance of sorcery at a former wedding of a daughter of the homestead, which was acknowledged by the inhabitants. In the meantime, the apprentice had put the ground medicine into a tin bucket with some water, and on the doctor's instructions he sprinkled the contents on the firewood by means of a brush made of horse-tail.

With his finger the doctor now applied some of the substance from his medicine horn to a stump of wood, in each corner of the hearth, and on one of the large iron pots which would be used for cooking. When the doctoring was over, all the visitors, including the doctor, were entertained to sour porridge, coffee, and beer. Later on, doctoring of a similar nature was conducted at the home of the bridegroom's 'father'. On the afternoon before the wedding, before the ox-wagon conveying the bridegroom and his following departed to the bride's home, the doctor, who was travelling with them, applied medicine from his horn to the wagon's brake and to the yoke of the leading pair of oxen. He also treated the driver and leader of the oxen by making small incisions into which he rubbed medicine from his horn.

After their arrival at the bride's home that night, the doctor performed a rite referred to as 'cooking' the bridal couple (*go apaya banyadi*). He applied medicine to the two ends of a piece of shell looking like mother of pearl, and placed it in water which was then heated. The bride and bridegroom were made to kneel, with the upper part of their bodies uncovered, and the doctor poured some of the water, said to be boiling, over their bodies.[1] He then made incisions on the outer sides of their wrists, rubbed medicine from his horn into the incisions, and made them take *tshitlhô*[2] orally. The people of the bride's home and her maternal uncle received the same treatment on the wrists and were given the same medicine. Early in the morning, before being slaughtered for cooking, the goats were also given *tshitlhô*. Later, when the fires were burning and the pots cooking, the doctor threw a pinch of *tshitlhô* into each of two large barrels filled with beer, the pots that stood cooking in the homestead enclosure, and the stock pen, and into a drum of water.

The bridal group had left very early in the morning for the Roman Catholic church where they were to be married. It was past noon before they were back at the bride's home. The wagon stopped about a hundred yards

---

[1] I could not say whether the water was actually boiling or not, because I was not invited to attend this part of the ritual.

An informant whom I asked how a doctor 'cooks' a person, explained that the person being treated is covered with blankets while stooping over a vessel of boiling, medicated water.

[2] See p. 15.

PAGANISM ON THE WANE

from the homestead and, as the couple and their following were preparing to enter the homestead on foot, the wagon proceeded to where it was outspanned. In the meantime, the doctor hastily sprinkled the ground over which the wagon was to pass, the oxen and the wagon itself, as it moved past him, as well as the path along which the wedding procession was approaching the houses.

The following day, after the feasting at the bride's home, the bridal couple travelled to the home of the bridegroom's 'father', where the festivities started anew, and doctoring similar to that at the bride's home was performed.

According to the officiating doctor the purpose of all these rites was to give protection against sorcery. Sorcerers might add harmful medicines— he sometimes used the English word 'poison', although speaking Tswana —to the food to harm the eaters, or something could be put into the fire to prevent the pots from boiling or to harm a smoker who might take a live coal from the fire to light his pipe. The doctoring of the wood, the hearth and the pots, the goats, the beer and the water, and the treatment of the bridal couple and people of the bride's home—all these were aimed at warding off this type of evil. The *tshitlhô* which was taken, and the medicine rubbed into the incisions, for example, would cause the persons thus treated to vomit whatever harmful medicine a sorcerer might have added to the food. The 'cooking' of the bridal couple was intended to strengthen them and moreover to prevent a sorcerer from harming them through their footprints. It is believed that by mixing earth from a person's footprint with medicine the sorcerer could harm the person, e.g. by causing illness or pain. Should a sorcerer try this with the bridal couple (after they had been 'cooked'), his medicine would harm not them but himself. The doctoring of the wagon, oxen, driver, and leader were aimed at preventing events such as lightning or the wagon running over somebody, both of which, it is believed, may be caused by sorcery.

The fathers of the bride and bridegroom each had to pay the doctor ten shillings for his services in connexion with the marriage, besides the two and sixpence each had to produce for his throwing the dice.

(d) Death

Since burial is nowadays generally accompanied by a Christian religious service, burial rites will be discussed in detail in connexion with the churches. A few burial customs which appear to be of pagan origin are still very common and must be mentioned here. Very often a person, whether a man or a woman, is buried in the kraal or stock pen. Only men in respect of whose mothers' marriages *bogadi* has been given, and women in respect of whose own marriages it has been given, share in this privilege. Some people feel that it is somewhat of a disgrace to have to bury a parent outside 'in the veld'. I was told that Christians do not agree to burial in the kraal, but I observed that some full church members still adhere to this custom. I asked many

22 RELIGION IN A TSWANA CHIEFDOM

people about its significance: to most of them it was merely a traditional custom to which they attached no special significance, but a few connected it with the belief that the dead wished to be near their cattle and if buried elsewhere would call the cattle to them, i.e. they would die. In olden times manure was not taken from the kraal because this would mean taking away the 'blanket' of the deceased.

When burial takes place in the kraal, the regular entrance is closed with a pole or with branches, and a temporary opening is made at the back of the kraal before digging the grave. From then onward only the temporary entrance is used. When the funeral service is over and the grave being closed up, the temporary opening is closed and the regular entrance opened, and the people who entered the kraal for the burial service, now leave by the regular entrance. No explanation could be given for this. One informant called it taboo (*moila*) to return from the grave by the same way one came, but could not say what would be the result of the breach of this taboo. He connected it with the custom, formerly observed, of removing a corpse through a hole in the back wall of the hut.[1]

At funerals I attended, even funerals held with full Christian burial rites, I was usually struck by the careful manner in which all the earth that had been excavated in the digging of the grave, was scraped back on to it. At least one informant intimated that 'people say' this care is taken to prevent sorcerers from taking some of the earth. (A grave outside the kraal is usually covered with stones.)

From the grave all the people return to the homestead, where the men wash their hands in a dish or a bath of water. No soap is used, neither is the water medicated. When all have finished washing, the vessel is immediately overturned where it was standing. Some explain this act as just washing the earth from their hands. (All the men usually take turns in helping to carry the coffin to the grave and to fill up the grave.) One said 'they wash off death, because they come from burying'. Another explained it by saying that they 'have conveyed dust; dust is the deceased; dust is earth' (*mbu*). This washing seems to be connected with the actual burial and not with touching the corpse, since the corpse of a woman would be laid out by women, yet they do not wash their hands on returning from the grave.

The men now gather apart, usually at the *kgotla* or kraal, and one or more men closely connected with the deceased say a few words. These speeches are called 'announcing the death' (*go latolêla*) and usually include references to the deceased and expressions of thanks to those who attended. At one funeral the eldest son of the deceased,

[1] Cf. Willoughby, 1932, pp. 135, 136.

PAGANISM ON THE WANE

a youth of about sixteen was called and told that his father now being dead, he should 'listen to the law of his father, this one'—the speaker pointing to the boy's junior paternal uncle. He was reminded that he still had fathers and was not an orphan. On another occasion one of the speakers ended by saying: 'He [the deceased] refuses to leave us rain.' When questioned afterwards, he explained: 'We prayed to him, that he should pray to God, that God should let it rain for us.' After these speeches, food is usually served. Sometimes an animal might have been slaughtered the previous day, merely for food, it is said, but some people nevertheless apply the name *mogôga*[1] to it, although the best informants on traditional matters hold that *mogôga* is something slaughtered some time after the funeral.[2] It may be that the speeches 'announcing the death' were formerly also connected with the slaughtering of *mogôga*.

Sometimes the implements used for digging the grave, even if they were borrowed from other people, are kept in the house from which the corpse was taken to the grave; they must 'spend the night' there, but on the following day they may be used for other purposes or returned to the owners.

If relatives and friends of the deceased and the people of his homestead were not able to attend the funeral, they are expected to pay the homestead a visit soon after the funeral. Such a visit is spoken of as *matshedišô* (from *go tshedisa*, to cause to live; to sympathize with the bereaved).

After the funeral, usually early on the following day, the floor of the hut or room where the corpse lay and the veranda or stoep are smeared with fresh dung, and the clothes and bedding of the deceased are washed. Often a doctor is summoned to perform a ritual of purification, either on the same day or the following one. It usually includes washing of the upper part of the bodies of close relatives of the deceased with medicines, and sprinkling medicines on his personal belongings, on the house, on the doorpost and in the entrance to the enclosure, or in the enclosure generally. Some doctors demand a goat which has to be slaughtered, and then the half-digested contents of the stomach (*mošwang*) are added to the medicines, or the persons undergoing the rite are smeared with it. On some occasions the hair of a deceased man's unmarried children is shaved. The rite has to be performed either in the morning or in the afternoon, when a person casts

[1] See pp. 24-5.
[2] A man of Southern Sotho stock told me that the Tswana say of a beast slaughtered at someone's death: 'It is the beast which he causes to go before (*eteletsapele*) him; he drives it; it is his last gift.'

24 RELIGION IN A TSWANA CHIEFDOM

a shadow, and not in the middle of the day. It is explained that the death of a person brings *sehihi* over the homestead and its inhabitants, and over the personal belongings of the deceased. The rite is performed to remove this *sehihi*, otherwise the 'shadow' of the deceased will remain and weigh them down,[1] or the deceased will be troublesome. The wife of the deceased should not go about in public before she has been purified.

It is taboo to take the possessions of a dead man from one place to another[2] during summer, because it 'spoils' the rain. 'They say it is *sehihi*.' If the chief hears of a person breaking this taboo, he is fined and has to get a doctor to perform another purification ceremony. Observance of this taboo is still considered to be of great importance.

When a mother of unmarried children has died, the children are taken to their maternal relatives by their father a week or two after the mother's death. On their arrival they do not enter the homestead at the usual front entrance, but through an opening specially made for them at the back of the enclosure. A sheep, brought by the father, is slaughtered by the children's maternal uncle, and eaten by all present. Their hair is also shaved. In former times the sheep was slaughtered before the children entered the enclosure, and portions of the contents of the stomach (*mošwang*) were placed at intervals, from the special opening at the back of the enclosure, to the front, where the animal was slaughtered. When the children entered, they stepped on the *mošwang* as they walked to the front of the house. Before the performance of this rite the children should not visit their maternal relatives, but after this rite they may freely do so. If this rite is neglected, *sehihi* will be attached to them; 'they will be stupid' (*ba tla tseanya*). One informant also spoke of it as a purification (*tlhapišo*). Various informants said that this rite is still performed by some people to-day. It is spoken of as 'shaving the hair' (*peolô*), or 'letting the children break through' (*go thobisa bana*), with reference to the breaking of the wall or hedge.

Some time after a man's death—about a month, some say—a head of cattle is slaughtered. This animal is known as *mogôga* (from *go gôga*, to draw), and its purpose is generally described as announcing the death of the deceased, especially to his children (*go latolêla bana*). Some informants, however, also described it as a gift to the ancestor spirits (*go ha badimo*). One informant said the bones were collected and thrown on the father's grave with these words: 'These are your cattle. Now the remaining ones are ours. Leave them to us.' If the rite

---

[1] The verb used comes from the root *go gata*. Cf. above, p. 14, note 1.

[2] E.g. some must be sent to a man's maternal uncle.

PAGANISM ON THE WANE

was neglected, the cattle might die and follow their owner.[1] By no means all informants connected the rite in such a clear manner with the ancestor spirits. When I asked a group of men in a headman's *kgotla* why the animal is called *mogôga*: what it draws (or whom), and where to, I received the answer: 'It draws the deceased to where he has gone. We do not know where it is. He has gone to heaven, to God who made him.' A few denied any connexion with the ancestor spirits, even when I suggested the possibility, and added that the Tswana do not have the custom of 'giving to the ancestor spirits'— it is a custom of the Southern Sotho and Nguni people. The rite is probably very seldom performed nowadays. Many people speak of the animal which is slaughtered for food at the funeral as *mogôga*. The formal 'announcing of the death' at funerals nowadays, might also be an innovation, and might formerly have been connected with the eating of the *mogôga*. Mention is sometimes made of an animal called *tatolô* or *molatolô* (the announcing of the death), but this might be the same as the traditional *mogôga*.[2]

Someone who has lost a spouse may not remarry or begin cohabiting with another partner during summer. Moreover, both the widow or widower and the new spouse or partner must be ritually purified and 'joined' by a doctor before they have sexual relations. The breach of these rules 'spoils' the rain and the culprits are said to 'eat' the rain, or to have 'stolen' by their act. Such an act is punishable by the chief or headman and culprits are submitted to a most unpleasant punishment, besides their having to be purified at the *kgotla* of the chief or headman concerned.

(e) Illness and other forms of misfortune

Traditional views relating to illness are still recognized by many people, and a number of native doctors remain active in the Phuduhutswana chiefdom. In serious cases, when causes connected with traditional beliefs are suspected, a native doctor is summoned and he divines the cause by his dice. Usually he also performs the appropriate ritual.

Dikgaba. It is believed that an individual who has offended one of his living seniors, may meet with misfortune known as *dikgaba*. This is held to 'come from' the displeased person, although he does not wilfully cause it and is ignorant of his being the cause. It may bring

---

[1] Willoughby writes that the Tswana 'believe that the spirit lingers about the grave till sacrifice is offered, a month after burial, for the repose of the departed, or, as they express it, for sending the spirit home to the abode of the gods. (1928, p. 36.)

[2] The Ngwaketse, however, have *mogôga* as well as *tatolô*. Schapera, 1939, p. 95.

26   RELIGION IN A TSWANA CHIEFDOM

illness, stupidity, wastefulness, diminution of one's stock, and it may cause one's work and efforts to be fruitless. A year or two before I was doing fieldwork, doctors who were summoned to divine the cause of a minor drought ascribed it to *dikgaba* coming from the chief. The appropriate ritual purification was performed. The seniors from whom *dikgaba* emanates are usually relatives of a senior generation, or of the sufferer's own generation, but senior in genealogical status.

After a doctor has divined the cause and indicated the offended person, a purification rite is performed in which the names of the offended and other seniors are called out. The sufferer is washed with medicated water; sometimes the offended person spits into this water before the sufferer is washed. Some doctors order the slaughtering of a goat of which the stomach contents (*moswang*) are placed in the water.

Sorcery[1], it is held, may be the cause of illness, pain, death, drought, lightning, and wind. Snakes as well as other small animals, otherwise harmless, may be 'sent' by means of sorcery to bite an enemy, with unexpected death as the result. As far as my information goes these animals are not kept as familars by the people sending them.

Sorcery is believed to be disclosed by doctors through divination, and in former times this would result in the sorcerers being put to death by the chief. It is believed that when a doctor divines that some misfortune is caused by sorcery, he can take measures to 'send it back' to harm the sorcerer who 'sent' it.

Ancestor spirits. When a child talks or groans in its sleep, or dreams of a deceased father or mother, this is held to be a sign that the 'shadow' of the deceased is above the child (*ngwana o ôkangwe ke moruti wa ga mmagwê kapa rragwê*). This may result in illness, of which it is said: 'It is the mother's *sehihi*.' Such symptoms may also be interpreted as signs that the deceased is trying to 'take' the child. Therefore it must be purified 'to drive away' the deceased. Some earth from the grave of the deceased is usually used in this purification ceremony.

'*Hot blood.*' Some people are believed to have 'hot blood' (*madi a a mogote*) or 'bad blood' (*madimabe*). The same condition is also referred to as having 'bad' or 'hot' hands. Some men and women, are born in this condition and then it cannot be healed, but all women have 'hot blood' while menstruating. A man who was not born with 'hot blood' may come into this condition by having sexual intercourse with a woman whose blood is 'hot'; but in this case a doctor can give treatment to free him from it.

[1] For methods of working sorcery, see p. 33.

PAGANISM ON THE WANE

A person with 'hot blood' should not come into a house where someone is ill, because he will aggravate the illness. Therefore people are warned of the presence of a sick person or a confined woman with the expression: 'The branches have been placed' (*matlhaku a beilwe*).[1] If a person with 'hot blood' slaughters an animal the meat becomes tasteless and stock castrated by him will die. People who permanently have 'hot blood' are incapable of conceiving or begetting children. Various precautions and taboos are still observed in connexion with menstruation. Some of these also apply to childbirth.

Preventive ritual. Perhaps it is in the field of preventive ritual that doctoring and medicines are still most commonly applied nowadays. The preventive ritual in connexion with marriage ceremonies has been described in detail.[2] Doctors are employed to treat a new homestead, amongst others, by placing medicated pegs in the ground before it is built, and by making cross-marks on doors with medicines. Such treatment offers protection, especially against sorcery and theft. The head of the homestead also receives a horn filled with medicine, itself a protection against sorcery, but the greasy contents may also be used as a cure for various ailments. Homesteads are ritually protected against lightning. It is said that small stock are still sometimes treated against jackals with a mixture of jackal's excrement and medicines. Another preventive measure is that which a husband and wife should take before resuming sexual relations after a long time of separation. One method of treatment involves the use of two bits of dry twig, provided by the doctor. Each partner soaks one of these in his or her own urine and then the other burns it and takes the ashes as snuff.

(f) Drought

In former times it was a special responsibility of the chief to ensure that enough rain fell in the chiefdom, either by performing the appropriate ritual himself, or by summoning rain-makers to perform it. This idea is still held, although it is not as strong as in former times. Much of the rain-making ritual has become obsolete, but purification rituals for removing the causes of drought are still performed. If the rains are delayed, the chief summons doctors to divine the cause, which may be *dikgaba*, breach of the taboo and the rule of purification applicable to widows and widowers, or the presence of objects

---

[1] In former times signs were actually placed at the house. Such a sign was a stick across the doorway or a twig in the thatch above the door. (Willoughby, 1932, p. 193.)

[2] See pp. 19–21.

28 RELIGION IN A TSWANA CHIEFDOM

known as *dibêla*. A stillborn child, an aborted human foetus, and the foetus of certain animals (horses, donkeys, goats, and dogs), lying unburied in the veld, prevent the rain from falling. Sorcerers can also place harmful medicines in the veld with the express purpose of driving the rain away. If the doctors should divine the presence of *dibêla*, the chief or headman organizes a hunt to locate the object which is finally identified by the doctors. A ritual of purification must then be performed on the spot where it has been found.

Such a case occurred in the area of a sub-headman not far from the chief's place in August or September 1950. The ritual performed was described to me by a reliable informant, an eye-witness, in the presence of other eye-witnesses.

The doctors required a billy-goat which they slaughtered at the place where they found the *dibêla*. The contents of the goat's stomach (*mošwang*) were mixed with water and medicines from the doctors' medicine horns, and the mixture was sprinkled on the *dibêla*. While doing this, the doctors spoke in the following vein: 'We are praying; we are asking God; we are asking for rain.' Eventually they threw the *dibêla* into the river to be carried far away by the water. In this case the *dibêla* consisted of medicines only, including a piece of crocodile skin, and a small piece of elephant tusk. This type of medicine was considered as not being 'of this country.'

Another method of purification is that of burning the *dibêla* along with medicines, and then sprinkling medicated water on the fire. Cases of purification for *dibêla* have been reported in another headman's area as having been performed in 1951 and 1952.

If a widower has 'eaten' the rain, or if *dikgaba* is the cause of the drought, the appropriate purification ritual must also be performed.

It is customary to begin or close speeches with expressions such as: 'May the rain fall!' (*A pula e nne!*) or 'Rain!' (*Pula!*) or 'I cause rain to fall' (*Ke nesa pula*), and people are more particular about doing this during the rainy season. During the summer months I sometimes observed that speakers who failed to use these expressions in public speeches were scolded for not 'causing it to rain' as if these expressions were regarded as magical formulas having the power to cause rain.

Present remnants of paganism

Pagan ritual and belief have now been subjected to various disintegrating forces for a long time. Partly changes in other aspects of the social structure have influenced and undermined ritual and belief, but a very direct attack has been made not only by Christian missions, through religious teaching, schools, and medical work, but also by administrative measures, especially those punishing the imputation

PAGANISM ON THE WANE

of 'witchcraft'. We have observed that in spite of these disintegrating forces paganism has not become obsolete, but it is difficult to form an idea of what is still left in quantitative terms. The most that can be done is to summarize the existing belief and ritual and to try to assess tentatively the extent to which these are still adhered to.

(a) The ancestors (*badimo*) and God (*Modimo*)

Several of the rites which still persist are connected with the belief that the living and the dead may mutually communicate with and influence each other. Undoubtedly this is the case with *mogôga*, and it probably also applies to the rite of eating the animal of the cradle-skins, the custom of burial in the kraal, and the entrance of the corpse at the back of the kraal.

The purification rites to drive away the 'shadow' of the deceased after the funeral or when a child has dreamt of a deceased ancestor, further illustrate the belief in ancestor spirits. There is also the belief that if a person dies in discontent, or if his children misbehave after his death, he 'troubles' them by appearing in dreams or otherwise. When the wrong has been righted he will go and 'lie down' or 'sleep' (*rôbala*) again. One or two informants mentioned the possibility of having to slaughter something for an ancestor spirit coming to one in a dream.

It is known that the custom exists of praying in the name of one's ancestors, even when praying to God himself. Some people hold that a doctor's ability to divine is a gift of God, while others hold that it comes from the ancestor spirits. When throwing the dice the doctor pronounced a praise in which he said: 'I ask my ancestor spirits (*badimo baka*) . . . who have given me these things.' At least two of the names figuring in the praises were included in his direct male line of descent.

My own informants did not connect belief in *dikgaba* with the ancestors in any way and seemed rather to regard *dikgaba* as something which results almost automatically from the anger or displeasure of a senior relative, but according to Professor Schapera it is closely connected with the ancestor cult among the Kgatla.[1] Of these few remnants of the ancestor cult at least one (*mogôga*) seems to be very seldom performed nowadays, while many people who still adhere to the burial customs mentioned above, and to the eating of the

---

[1] Schapera, 1934, pp. 298 ff. Cf. also 1940, p. 254 and 1953, p. 61. Willoughby, 1928, p. 194 n. does not mention any connexion between *dikgaba* and the spirits of the dead.

30 RELIGION IN A TSWANA CHIEFDOM

animal of the 'cradle-skins', are no longer aware of any connexion these customs have with the belief in ancestor spirits.

In former times there were people who were believed to converse with the ancestor spirits. They are referred to as 'prophets'.[1] One by the name of Tolonyane, who was active during chief Mankurwane's reign, is especially remembered by some older people. I devote some space to present-day memories of him, since these throw interesting light on the activities of some modern religious leaders with whom we shall deal at a later stage. Tolonyane is spoken of as a 'man of the ancestor spirits' (motho wa badimo) who conversed with or prayed to them, and there are certain caves which people say he used to visit for this purpose. His ability to foretell coming events, especially diseases and drought, resulted from his contact with the ancestor spirits, who revealed these matters to him. When people came to consult him, he expected them to bring a small gift for the ancestor spirits, such as a bracelet, a little corn, or the skin of a civet cat (tshipa).[2] Such trifles he would place in the cave where he consulted them, and some, it is said, were then taken during the night; those remaining were the spirits' gifts to him. Some informants held that it was God to whom he spoke, and who revealed matters to him.

One manner of treatment which was revealed to him, was to pray that the disease should be 'cool', i.e. moderate, and to make the people drink water 'for which he had prayed.'[3] He is said to have predicted a smallpox epidemic, for which he prescribed inoculation of pus from the pox of a patient who had the disease in a moderate degree. On another occasion he prescribed the wearing of necklaces plaited from rushes (mokhasi). Although he was considered different from other doctors, and did not 'dig for medicines' as they did, he is held to have acted in accordance with Tswana custom. 'He was a real Tswana prophet, not one of European type.' He is also referred to as a rain-maker (morôka), and is reported to have performed a rain-making rite in which little girls walked along the paths, making a wide tour through the chiefdom, sprinkling water from small pots they were carrying, and saying: 'We ask rain, we ask rain.'[4] On another occasion he required a head of cattle to be slaughtered as a gift to the ancestor

[1] The barôka (sing. morôka), the doctors who knew the special rain-making rites and rain-medicines, are also nowadays often referred to as baperofeta.

[2] An old informant who provided most of the information about Tolonyane spoke of the skins of the tshipa and thwane (lynx) as 'the tax (lekgetho) of the ancestor spirits'.

[3] The term go rapêlêla metsi, lit., to pray for the water, is a technical term often used in connexion with ritual.

[4] Cf. Schapera, 1930, pp. 211 ff.

PAGANISM ON THE WANE

spirits. Its bones were thrown into a fire from which a thick cloud of smoke ascended.[1]

The high esteem in which he was held, is illustrated by an event which is related of a native minister who is said to have had such awe-inspiring experiences in Tolonyane's cave that he called out, 'Are you a god, Tolonyane?' (*A o modimo, Tolonyane?*)[2] This incident gave rise to a song in which the people sang: 'Are you a god, Tolonyane? Are you a god, Tolonyane?' A doctor who despised him is said to have met with such calamity, that he hastened to the prophet, calling out: 'Truly, you are a god, Tolonyane.'

Besides communicating with particular individuals known as 'prophets', the spirits of the dead are also still believed to influence the lives of their living relatives by scolding or giving advice, e.g. in dreams, or, in the case of diviners, by revealing the unknown through their dice. It has also been hinted that the ancestor spirits pray to God for rain on behalf of the living.

Whereas in former times each Tswana family 'was held to be under the supernatural guidance and protection of its deceased ancestors in the male line',[3] there no longer seems to be such a clear distinction of one's own lineage ancestors. I still found it in prayers said to have been pronounced in connexion with certain rain rites, but the last such rites were performed about 1925. In the eating of the animal of the cradle-skins the idea of the lineage ancestors' particular importance seems to be present, but here we should again remember that not all people are aware of this significance of the rite but perform it primarily on account of its connexion with initiation, and to avoid misfortune which may result from non-performance. Informants who were questioned as to the identity of the deceased persons who might communicate with them, or for whom animals would be slaughtered, mentioned paternal as well as maternal relatives, both male and female.

The idea that the ancestor spirits stand in an intercessory position between the living and God, the Supreme Being, does not seem to be a modern innovation.[4] However, it is probably much more prominent than before, even among non-Christians. Whereas it was taboo in former times to use the name *Modimo* when referring to the Supreme

---

[1] (i) In several aspects the description agrees very closely with that given by Willoughby (1928, pp. 120–121) of a prophet by the name of Marethe, who arose among the Rolong at Morokweng in what is now the Vryburg district.

(ii) For Tswana rain-making rites, see Willoughby, *op. cit.*, pp. 204–205.

[2] According to Willoughby, 'a "prophet" was known as a *modimo* (god) in Bechuanaland before Europeans came'. (*Op. cit.*, pp. 113.)

[3] Schapera, 1951. Cf. *The Tswana*, p. 45.

[4] Cf. Schapera, 1951, p. xxi, 1953, p. 59; and Willoughby, 1923, pp. 76–78.

32 RELIGION IN A TSWANA CHIEFDOM

Being,[1] it is now much more commonly heard in everyday conversation than references to the ancestor spirits. This is very markedly so in connexion with rain: 'We look to God to give us rain,' or 'God has helped us with rain,' are expressions often heard during the summer months. 'Remain with God' (i.e. may God be with you who remain behind), and similar expressions are used as greetings. The use of such expressions is by no means restricted to pious Christians. Some people also ascribe to God attributes which used to be connected with the spirits of the dead. They believe, e.g. that the fall of the diviner's dice is controlled by God, not by the spirits, and some believe that the traditional 'prophet', Tolonyane, received revelations from God and not from the dead.

(b) Doctors, medicines, and sorcery

Many native medicines are known and in use among the population at large. Others are known only to the native doctors (*dingaka*). What I got to know about the ingredients of such medicines, and the manner in which they are used, is in keeping with the nature of the morphology of 'magic' as described by Schapera[2] in respect of the Tswana generally.

Native doctors are still common, but one often hears the opinion that to-day's doctors are very much inferior to those of long ago. Nevertheless, considerable use is made of their services. The *ngaka* is often also a diviner, but doctors who perform healing but do not divine are also called *dingaka*. Such a doctor is called 'hornless' (*ngaka e tšhotšha*), because a doctor without dice is like an ox without horns. There are no doctors who only divine and do not give treatment. A special kind of doctor is known as *ngaka ya sedupe* (or *sedupi*, from *go dupa*, to suck an object from the body of a person) because of his special method of treatment, viz. placing his mouth to the body of a patient, and producing an object through which, it is believed, a sorcerer has harmed the person. One informant said he makes strange sounds, and people have to sing during his performance. Nobody is allowed to smoke or use snuff during the performance. If someone should do so furtively the doctor would faint and the people would have to sing, pray, and clap hands to revive him. This informant ascribed the abilities of the *ngaka ya sedupe* to the fact that '*badimo* are in him'. Such doctors are scarce nowadays; I heard of only one in the chiefdom, and he came from another district.

The commonly known type of doctor who divines with bones is trained by completing a period of apprenticeship with a practising

---

[1] Brown, J. Tom, 1926, pp. 114–115. [2] 1953, pp. 63 f.

3. A Pentecostal Separatist Preacher praying
and laying-on hands for his wife

4. The visiting Bishop of the Holy Church of Christ, officiating at a service for the laying of a corner-stone

PAGANISM ON THE WANE

doctor, which includes their living in the veld for a while. The apprentice is prepared for handling the dice by a regularly repeated rite in which medicated fluid and beer are poured into a dish into which the doctor throws the dice. The apprentice must now recite the formulas describing the fall of the dice, after which he has to consume the mixture so that their actual positions become visible. Mention was also made of spending a night in a pool so as to be charmed by the fabulous water snake. Women can also become doctors but seldom do. I heard of no woman practising when I was doing fieldwork.

Doctors do not regularly wear special regalia by which they can be recognized, and there is usually nothing about a doctor's person which distinguishes him from other people.[1]

Doctors are employed to divine the cause of misfortunes such as illness and drought and, where necessary, to apply the appropriate treatment, to perform the protective ritual referred to above and to perform purification ceremonies for the various purposes which will be discussed below. One man acknowledged to an African demonstrator that he had had his field on the irrigation scheme treated by a doctor when it was allotted to him.

It is maintained that the same substances used as medicines for socially approved purposes may also form the basis of 'medicines' used for sorcery, but in different combinations. Methods often mentioned are the adding of medicine of sorcery to the victim's food or drink, the 'sending' of the animals already referred to, or dangerous elements such as lightning or wind. A person can also be harmed by mixing some of his excrement or earth from his footprints with medicines. Earth from a grave is supposed to be useful to sorcerers. Sorcerers are believed to cause drought by placing the appropriate medicine out in the veld. Sometimes these medicines are combined with a foetus (or part of it), which in itself may withhold the rain from falling if it lies unburied.

(c) Various causes of misfortune

Several notions have been referred to involving causes of illness or other misfortune which are not believed to be purposely caused by

---

[1] For a description of a Tswana doctor's regalia, see Brown, 1926, p. 127. One doctor with whom I had close connexions posed for me to take his photograph in a garment of jackal-skins which he draped around his body; he wore a cap made of the skins of a porcupine (*noko*) and hyena (*kgwereme*) adorned with a few feathers. In his hand he held the effigy of a black snake cut out of wood. When I inquired about the significance of this apparel he intimated that he wore it when he was 'fighting' another doctor with medicines. He claimed that the snake, which could change its appearance, helped him in such a contest.

R.T.C.—4

34 RELIGION IN A TSWANA CHIEFDOM

other human beings, as in the case of sorcery, and which are mostly not thought of as being wilfully and directly caused by the ancestors or God. These are notions about hot blood, *sehihi*, or shadow, *dibêla*, and the breach of some taboos, which require further elucidation here.

Besides saying that a person could be born with *hot blood*, my own informants connected the condition with menstruation. According to Professor Schapera, the Kgatla also connect it with sexual intercourse, pregnancy, childbirth, and menstruation, and with the first year of bereavement of a widow or widower. People returning from a long journey, from a funeral, or from visiting a woman in confinement, are 'hot'; a woman is 'hot' when she has been mixing earth or smearing walls or floors of the homestead, and a doctor is 'hot' for two or three days after the death of a patient.[1] Furthermore, an aborted foetus is considered as being 'hot' and as preventing the rain from falling, for which reason it must be buried in damp ground.[2] These examples, particularly the last mentioned, suggest that it is not only hot blood which is dangerous, but that there are other things which can possess dangerous 'heat', and that such heat can also affect the rain adversely. This resembles the concept of 'heat' as described for the Lovedu by the Kriges, who explain it against the background of the importance of rain to the people. 'To them [the Lovedu] the ultimate good is rain. Rain is regarded as not merely the material source of life and happiness and the physical basis of man's security; it is also a symbol of spiritual well-being and a manifestation that the social order is operating smoothly. Hence coolness denotes a state of euphoria: man and matter to be in order and to function properly have to be kept cool; angry ancestors must be kept cool by means of medicine; even witches can be cooled and so made to forget their evil purposes. On the other hand, heat as the antithesis of the main basis of man's security, the cooling, life-giving rain, is conceived as a destructive force leading to a state of disphoria.'[3] Our evidence is not sufficient to state definitely that the same ideas are implied in the Tswana concept of 'heat', but it seems very probable that the ideas of heat and coolness, drought and rain, euphoria and disphoria are connected by the Tswana in a similar manner.

As further evidence may be added here the fact that the prophet Tolonyane prayed that an imminent disease should be cold or cool (*tsididi*). He also made the people drink water over which he had prayed and which people called *letsididi* (coldness). One informant spoke of the purpose of a rain-making rite which the prophetess

[1] 1940, pp. 194, ff.   [2] *Ibid.*, ch. VIII.
[3] Krige, D. and E. J., 1954, p. 68.

PAGANISM ON THE WANE 35

Botlhale (see pp. 48 ff.) performed as being to let the earth be cooled (*tsidihalêlwa*).[1] A Christian woman, the wife of an evangelist, in saying grace prayed that God would give the food, 'with cool hands'.

Another notion is implied in the term *sehihi*. It is difficult to define its content but this can be said: the presence of *sehihi* in any situation is regarded as unfavourable, if not dangerous, and a purification rite must usually be performed to remove it. Some informants said it had a similar meaning to the English term 'bad luck'.[2] The homestead and close relatives of a deceased person are endangered by *sehihi*, and must undergo a rite of purification to be freed from it. The 'spoiling' of the rain by sending away the deceased's belongings during summer is also ascribed to *sehihi* and requires a rite of purification, while the rite of letting the children 'break through' after the death of their mother is also said to be a safeguard against *sehihi* and is spoken of as a form of purification. A child's dreams of a deceased parent denote the presence of the parent's *sehihi* which may cause illness. As to the results that may follow if *sehihi* is not removed, I only came across the idea that it could cause illness and stupidity or senselessness and that it could 'spoil' the rain.

Sehihi is sometimes used interchangeably with 'shadow' (*moruti*).[3] The *sehihi* attached to the lately bereaved or that connected with a child's dreams of a deceased parent was also spoken of as the shadow of the deceased weighing down the living. A boy attending the initiation ceremonies without the rite of eating the animal of the cradle-skins having been performed is also spoken of as casting his shadow on the others. Although I did not come across an instance of the latter, also being referred to as *sehihi*, it is significant that it calls for a purification rite involving the sprinkling of medicated water, as in other cases of *sehihi*.

The nature of objects to which the term *dibêla* is applied has already been explained above. Here I would draw attention to the fact

---

[1] This verb is also used of the abating of sickness. (Brown, 1946.)

[2] According to the Rev. J. Tom Brown (*Secwana Dictionary*) *sehihi* is a noun denoting 'a person who is forbidden to journey because of the death of a relative; a grave'. In his *Among the Bantu Nomads* (pp. 137, 138) he uses it in connexion with a person whose 'whole nature is changed' so that 'there is an overshadowing of the true relationships of life, and a deterioration of character, as when a child neglects or repudiates his duty to his parents, or a parent fails in his duty as such; or when a subject treats as of little account his allegiance to his chief'.

[3] (i) If *sehihi* and *moruti* are not the same thing, they seem to be at least related in meaning, since *sehihi* comes from the same stem as the word which means darkness (*lehihi*), which has a lot in common with a shadow.

(ii) Cf. here the Lovedu concept of *muridi* (shadow), which is also a 'malignant force'. (Krige, *op. cit.*, pp. 69 f.)

36   RELIGION IN A TSWANA CHIEFDOM

that there seems to be some connexion between *dibêla* and the idea of heat. Foetuses, which prevent the rain from falling, are included in the category of *dibêla,* and according to information quoted above (from the Kgatla) their adverse influence on rainfall derives from the fact that they are hot. Moreover, it appears as if there is an etymological connexion with the concept of heat. A menstruating woman whose condition is one of 'heat' is denoted by the term *medibêla.*[1]

The Tlhaping also connect some instances of misfortune with the breaking of *taboos* (*meila,* sing. *moila*), although this does not always result in misfortune. Many traditional taboos are remembered and even school children could list quite a number of them. Many of these are no longer adhered to, but there are still a number which many people observe. The taboos in connexion with menstruation (hot blood), pregnancy, and childbirth, initiation, and death are still important. To these may be added certain taboos connected with natural phenomena. A hut of the old type may not be pulled down in summer as it might cause hail or lightning. Certain trees and bushes, particularly *motlhaje* (Blue bush, *Royena pallens Thunb.*), *mohatlha* ('vaalbos' or wild cotton, *Tarchonanthus Camphoratus* L.) and *mokgalo* ('blinkblaar', *Zizyphus mucronata*) may not be cut in summer. Breach of the taboo may also cause hail. In late spring or early summer, a public announcement is made in a general assembly prohibiting the cutting of these bushes and trees from a certain date onward. This also marks the beginning of the period during which it is taboo for widows or widowers to remarry. It is important to note that breach of the last two taboos mentioned is held to be punishable by the chief, probably since these breaches may cause calamities which endanger the well-being of the whole society.

Heat, *sehihi,* shadow, *dibêla,* and misfortune resulting from breach of taboos must not be seen as mutually exclusive categories. It has already become clear that they are in some instances connected with similar conditions and that the different concepts tend to overlap. It is possible that this overlapping is the result of a certain degree of confusion in the ideas that are at present held about these concepts, which one could understand in view of the general disintegration of

---

[1] I must point out here, however, that there is some information suggesting that the word for rain-preventing objects is not *dibêla* but *dibêêla* (from the verb *go bêêla* which is the 'applied' form of the verb *go baya,* to place). If this is so, *dibêêla,* then, primarily denotes objects which are 'placed' with the purpose of preventing rain. Brown (*Secwana Dictionary*) gives only a verb *go dibêla* which means to 'guard or keep from harm', but neither *dibêla* nor *dibêêla* are given as nouns. He connects *medibêla* with *go dibêla.*

PAGANISM ON THE WANE

the traditional magico-religious system. However, it is not impossible that they did overlap traditionally.

There is one point to which attention must still be drawn and that is that purification rites (*ditlhapišô*) take place in connexion with each of these concepts, although this not does necessarily happen in every particular instance.[1] All these concepts therefore seem to imply the notion of 'impurity'. I know of no Tswana term for this common 'impurity' which the rites have to remove and probably no such explicit idea is commonly held but it is nevertheless implied.[2] It must not be thought of as an idea involving an ethical valuation but rather as something dangerous connected with certain substances, conditions and happenings. The fact that all these different notions (heat, *sehihi*, etc.) are connected with purification rites which usually consist of sprinkling or lustrating with medicated water, suggests the hypothesis that 'heat' is the basic form of impurity in all these cases. The essential significance of purification rites would then be that they have a 'cooling' effect which neutralizes the dangerous 'heat'.[3] My material is insufficient to prove this hypothesis, however.

(d) Dreams

The belief that future events may be revealed through dreams is still wide-spread. All dreams do not necessarily have significance as revelations, but if a dream is remembered it is sure to have significance. People discuss their dreams with one another and try to ascertain their meaning if this is not immediately clear. Dreams are variously interpreted. We have already observed the significance of dreams about the dead. Sometimes it is believed that events taking place in a dream foreshadow similar events in actual life. To some people certain dreams signify just the opposite of what is taking place in the dream. Thus, one man said that if he dreamt of someone who was ill as being dead, it was a sign that the patient would recover.

Some people maintain that they have formulated certain standard clues for themselves which they use to interpret dreams. One man

[1] None of my own informants mentioned purification rites in connexion with 'hot blood' (heat), but they did mention it in connexion with foetuses which, according to Schapera, derive their dangerous effect from being 'hot'. (See above, p. 34.)

[2] According to Willoughby '*leshwe* is used [in Tswana] of the contamination of taboo-contact'. It is 'the common word for "dirt", and its ritual significance is evidently "defilement".' (1932, p. 197.)

[3] I may also point out that purification rites sometimes include the use of *mošwang* (the contents of a slaughtered animal's stomach). Cf. with this fact that among the Lovedu 'the green undigested chyme from a sheep or goat's alimentary canal' figures prominently in ritual as one of the substances having 'cooling' properties. *Krige, op. cit.*, p. 69.)

38   RELIGION IN A TSWANA CHIEFDOM

said that if he dreamt of *phikakgolo* (the fabulous water snake) when a woman in his family was expecting a baby, it would be a boy. For another man the same dream would signify the birth of a female child, but if he dreamt of a hare, the child would be a boy. They hold that they arrive at such clues by dreaming about the same thing on different occasions.

(*e*) The water snake

Finally the belief in the existence of a species of large water snake (*nôga ya metsi, phikakgolo*) is still held by many people. It is said to be found in rivers, pools, and dams, and is credited with 'taking' people when they are in the water, or fascinating them by changing its colours when they come near the water, so that they eventually go to it. A male snake sometimes takes a woman to stay with him as his wife in his home under the water, while a female snake may take a man. If a snake does not 'marry' its victim, it sucks his blood and then lets him go. A person who has been fascinated but not yet taken, must be treated by a doctor to break the spell, and made to vomit, otherwise he will return to the water. Some doctors are believed to have medicines with which they are able to make the water snake powerless, while it is said that the hardened urine of the snake is a potent medicine. These snakes are also believed to be the cause of whirlwinds.

*   *   *   *   *

We may say then that much of pagan ritual has become obsolete while the ideas held about traditional rites and beliefs are frequently confused. Many rites performed in former times, have been dropped. In this respect special mention must be made of rites which were of extreme importance to the whole chiefdom, such as some of the rain rites[1] and the ceremony of the first fruits.[2] The initiation ceremonies, which still concern a considerable proportion of the people, have probably lost much of their ritual character. Many taboos are no longer observed. Ritual which has become obsolete in more recent times, such as certain rain rites, is still remembered by older people, and with the memory some of them still preserve and adhere to the beliefs attached to the rites. The general impression is that in the totality of traditional belief and ritual the ancestor cult has disintegrated more than the rest. Only a few rites are left which are concerned with the ancestors. Some of these, though still common, have either lost their traditional meaning for the people (as in the case of burial in the cattle byre), or are a matter for treatment by medicines or puri-

[1] Willoughby, 1928, pp. 204–212.   [2] *Ibid.*, pp. 226–234.

PAGANISM ON THE WANE

fications to ward off danger rather than direct personal dealings with the ancestors, as in the case of the belief in *dikgaba* and the ritual connected with it. On the other hand doctoring, medicines, and sorcery and the beliefs and ritual connected with 'heat', *sehihi*, shadow, *dibêla*, and taboos are still relatively important. We shall return to this point later, but I wish to point out here that in terms of the definition of magic which will be used in this study, the traditional beliefs which are predominantly magical tend to persist with greater vitality than the ancestor cult. Another aspect of the changes taking place is that the belief in God has become much more prominent than it used to be, and is tending at least partly to take the place of the ancestor cult, even among non-Christians.

The extent of adherence to paganism

Now that we have formed an idea of the volume of extant pagan belief and ritual, the question arises how widely these occur. Partly this has already been answered by our pointing out what is still quite often encountered and what is almost extinct. Further, it is important that a very substantial proportion of the population, probably about half, have official connexions with churches and must be considered as Christians and not pagans (p. 9). Nevertheless remnants of paganism are still found among these people. In later chapters we shall pay special attention to the influence the pagan background has had on the public life of the churches, but mention must here be made of the fact that many church members in their private life still adhere to pagan customs and beliefs which their churches do not officially accept. This is especially the case with consulting a native doctor, to which at least the most important churches are opposed. Ministers of several churches said of their own accord that many church members nevertheless still have pagan ritual performed by these doctors. However, there are those—and I think they form a substantial core of the church people—who have no such private connexions with paganism.

Then there is the middle group of church adherents or *barati*, many of whom probably combine some pagan beliefs and customs with their leanings toward Christianity. This leaves a minority who might be called 'pagans', but even some of these do not seem to adhere to the extant traditional magico-religious beliefs and customs very strongly. Moreover, I have the impression that Christian belief and practice have penetrated even to all pagans, to such an extent that it seems doubtful whether one is justified in referring to them as pagans. This is especially the case with beliefs concerning God and directing prayers to him. An apt example of this is the native doctor who

40 RELIGION IN A TSWANA CHIEFDOM

claimed that he went to church to be 'prayed for' by the priest so that his doctoring should be successful. He was referring to the Roman Catholic Church where a priest would certainly not pray specially for the practice of a native doctor, but I take it that he considered that the usual prayers said in church would benefit his practice.

CHAPTER III

INTRODUCING THE CHURCHES

THE preceding chapter has illustrated the fact that pagan religion is no longer predominant, and has, in fact, to be searched for. On the other hand the Christian religion, which finds organized expression in the churches, is very evident and one is continually kept aware of its prevalence. Moreover, a considerable proportion of the population has formal connexions with one of the churches, while many of the rest profess adherence as *barati*.[1] It is natural, therefore, that in a discussion of present-day religion, our main interest will be with the churches.

Types of churches

I was able to trace thirty churches which are active in the Phuduhu-tswana chiefdom at present. (For their names see Table I.) In grouping them according to different types we must first of all bear in mind the division between Roman Catholicism and Protestantism. The *Roman Catholic Church* is clearly set off from the other churches by its large following (see below), the imposing and ambitious set-up of its mission enterprise, and the predominance of European mission workers. I have the impression that Bantu Christians do not consider the cleavage between Roman Catholicism and Protestantism as being deeper and different from the cleavages between different Protestant churches. Certainly it is not as profound to them as it tends to be in European communities.

Roman Catholicism is present in Taung with its typical hierarchical organization, elaborate ritual, and comprehensive approach. The latter is not only evident from the fact that besides its strictly religious work it also has educational, industrial, and medical enterprises, but also from its large range of associations and a co-ordinating Catholic African Union.[2]

Among the *Protestant churches* I treat as a group those which have Europeans in the ranks of their members (not necessarily in the reserves, however), or which are under the supervision of European missionaries, or at least in some way or other connected with European leaders. To these I refer as 'churches connected with Europeans'. Over against this group there are the churches usually referred to as Native Separatist churches. They have no Europeans in their ranks,

[1] See pp. 8–11.   [2] See p. 124.

42 RELIGION IN A TSWANA CHIEFDOM

and do not observe a formal connexion with any particular European church or church leaders.

The terminology used to denote these two categories of churches presents some difficulty. Dr. Sundkler has pointed out the undesirability of the name Native Separatist churches and adopted the name 'Bantu Independent churches' for the latter group. This may, however, give rise to confusion, not only because the term '"Independent" in English usage often stands as synonym for "Congregational"',[1] but also since another type of church to which the term 'Independent' applies, is developing from missionary activities purposively aimed at building self-governing Bantu churches which may in time become completely Bantu or African in membership and leadership, independent of any control of missionaries. Such churches could, in fact, be completely independent and, nevertheless, voluntarily observe a certain connexion with a European church or missionary body, from the missionizing activities of which it has developed. I see no other alternative, therefore, but to refer to these 'all-Bantu' churches as Bantu Separatist churches. There are, of course, also European churches which are separatist in nature, but to avoid confusion with them I shall confine the use of the term 'Separatist' to the churches which have no connexions with Europeans. Where I speak of 'non-Separatist churches' it must be understood as meaning the same as 'churches connected with Europeans'.

Because of its American connexions there might be some objection to classifying the African Methodist Episcopal Church (A.M.E.) as a Bantu Separatist church. The Church in South Africa forms an Episcopal District of the Negro Church of the same name in the United States and is presided over by an American Negro Bishop.[2] I may point out, however, that the Church originated in South Africa as a result of the so-called Ethiopian Movement which marks the beginning of the growth of Bantu Separatist churches in this country. The 'Ethiopian Church' was first formed by Bantu Christians who separated from missions and churches under European leadership, and only subsequently did their leader, Dwane, contact the A.M.E. Church of America and was the Ethiopian Church incorporated in the American Church.[3] In spite of its American connexions the A.M.E. Church is therefore very closely associated with the Bantu Separatist movement in South Africa.[4]

[1] Sundkler, 1948, p. 18.
[2] *The Doctrine and Discipline of the A.M.E. Church*, published by Order of the General Conference held in New York City, N.Y., May 1936.
[3] See Sundkler, *op. cit.*, pp. 39–40.   [4] Cf. also *Ibid.*, pp. 65 f., 69.

INTRODUCING THE CHURCHES

Cutting across the division between churches connected with Europeans and Bantu Separatist churches are other differences dividing the Protestant churches into three groups or types. This typology is based on the stress laid on certain aspects of ritual and teaching, such as observing Saturday as Sabbath, recognizing only adult baptism by immersion, the avoidance of tobacco, alcoholic drinks, and certain forms of food, and giving particular prominence to healing activities and the receiving of direct revelation through the Holy Spirit.[1] I distinguish three types to which I refer as 'A', 'B', and 'C'.

Type 'A'. Those churches which do not lay particular stress on a combination of some of these aspects, have been grouped together as group 'A'. Two 'Baptist' churches which do stress adult baptism by immersion, but not the other aspects mentioned above, have also been included. In this group the predominating pattern of sermons is that in which there is a single text and theme. The six churches in this group which are connected with Europeans are all branches of well-known denominations, and need not be further qualified. Of the Separatist churches in group 'A' several follow the Anglican pattern of terminology and ritual (the African United Church, Ethiopian Catholic Church in Zion, African Catholic Church and perhaps the Ethiopian Church of Christ by Religion).[1] The Ethiopian Church follows many Anglican liturgical usages, but the terminology used in respect of church organization shows greater similarity with that used in the Methodist Church (e.g. Church Steward, Exhorter, Local Preacher, Deacon, Minister (though Priest is also used), Presiding Minister, President, Annual Conference). It also follows the Methodist 'class' system.[2] The patterns followed by the other Separatist churches of type 'A' are reflected in their names (Native Independent *Congregational* Church (an offshoot from the L.M.S.), African *Methodist*

---

[1] I am not quite sure about this church, since I could not obtain its constitution, while the only service I attended was very simple and without any ritual, being conducted by the minister's daughter in his absence.

[2] According to Dr, Sundkler (*op. cit.*, pp. 39 ff.) the *Ethiopian Church* was founded by a '*Wesleyan*' minister, Mokone, and other 'malcontents' from the Wesleyan Church in 1892. A few years later the Ethiopian Church was incorporated in the African Methodist Episcopal Church (A.M.E.) of America. From Dr. Sundkler's information one is led to think that the Ethiopian Church ceased to exist. According to a Constitution which contains references to Annual Conferences of 1930 and 1951, the Ethiopian Church which is represented in Taung was established in 1892. In connexion with the initial organization of the Church the names of ten ministers are listed, four of whom were ordained by Bishop H. M. Turner, four by Bishop L. J. Coppin, and two by Bishop W. B. Derrick. Turner and Coppin were American (Negro) officials of the A.M.E. Church. (See Sundkler.) Perhaps the Ethiopian Church, after being incorporated into the A.M.E., was later again revived as a separate church by the ten ministers mentioned above.

44 RELIGION IN A TSWANA CHIEFDOM

Episcopal Church, S.A. Native *Baptist* Church Mission, and Bechuana *Methodist* Church (an offshoot from the A.M.E.).

Although the two Baptist churches included here, lay stress on adult baptism in common with the Pentecostals, they have not been grouped with the latter, since they do not tend to such extreme forms of religious expressions as the Pentecostals do.

Type 'B'. The observance of Saturday as Sabbath has been taken as the basis for a separate group of churches (group 'B'), and I therefore also refer to them as *Sabbatarian churches.* In common with the churches of group 'C' they recognize only adult baptism by immersion, observe specific ritual avoidances, and perform a rite of foot washing before Holy Communion. Their services are quieter and more orderly, with less display of emotion than most of the Pentecostal services. A particular type of sermon, consisting of a series of related texts with comments on each text separately, is common with them.

The three Separatist churches in this group are very similar, which is to be explained by the fact that all three in some way or other have developed out of the same larger Separatist church, the Church of Christ (*Ibandla lika Kreste*, see p. 55). In Taung their membership is almost exclusively confined to Nguni people, which is consistent with the fact that the parent church is under Nguni leadership and is centred in Port Elizabeth. All three churches sing only unrhymed portions from Scripture to original melodies. Two of the churches pay particular attention to healing and include rites of healing in their regular services.

Type 'C'. The common characteristics of the churches of this group (to which I shall also refer as *Pentecostal churches*) are insistence on adult baptism by immersion, the observance of ritual avoidances, and particular stress on healing activities. These they share with churches of type 'B', from which they are, however, differentiated by observing Sunday, and not Saturday, as a day of rest. Some also perform rites of purification and claim that they receive direct revelations from the Holy Spirit and that certain bodily movements which they perform and sounds which they utter ('speaking with tongues') are a sign of the Holy Spirit working in them. It is often believed by such churches that these were the essential characteristics of the Primitive Church after the pouring forth of the Holy Spirit. Sometimes the avowed affinity with the early church after Pentecost is expressed in designations such as 'Pentecostal' or 'Apostolic' which form part of the name of the church.[1]

---

[1] (i) As I use the term 'Pentecostal' it does not therefore refer only to such churches as are officially called Pentecostal.

(ii) Bantu Christians belonging to these churches particularly to those which are Bantu Separatist churches, may not always be aware of this appeal to the Primitive

INTRODUCING THE CHURCHES

These churches' services often last several hours and usually fall into two parts, the main feature of the first part being a series of sermons, while the second consists of the ritual of healing. In varying degrees these churches tend to a more extreme type of religion than the others. In this respect they form a continuing series with the non-Separatists at the one end and some of the Separatists at the other. However, it is not merely a contrast between Separatists and non-Separatists. The extreme ends of the series contrast sharply, but a Separatist church such as the Zion Apostolic Church of South Africa is not so profoundly different from the non-Separatist Pentecostal Holiness Church; in fact, it is more similar to the latter than it is to some of the Separatist churches which have an extremely violent and elaborate ritual.

Three of the churches which have the most elaborate ritual also share more or less the same set of rites. (They are the New Apostolic Church in Zion, the Holy Christian Apostolic Church, and the Foundation Apostolic Church in Jerusalem.) They share a few techniques of healing with the other Pentecostals, but only these three use *ashes* and wear special *clothes* for healing, carry *staffs* and *flags* to give strength, and perform rites of *purification* in a *river* or *pool*. I attended services of two of these churches, and in both cases they were of an extremely violent nature (see ch. V).

Another church which also has very elaborate ritual is the St. Paul Apostolic Faith Morning Star, but a great deal of the ritual is different from that of any of the other churches. There are also differences in other aspects and although it conforms to the basis which we have chosen for grouping together the churches of type 'C', it is amongst these almost a type on its own.[1]

It does not seem possible to classify the Watch Tower Bible and Tract Society with any of the above-mentioned groups, and since it is thus far of little importance in the set-up of the churches in the chiefdom, it is ignored in the classification.

The typology used here differs somewhat from that applied by Dr. Sundkler in his account of Zulu Separatist churches. He distinguishes between two types of churches, viz. Ethiopians and Zionists. As *Ethiopians* he classifies 'such independent Bantu churches as have (a) seceded from White Mission churches chiefly on racial grounds, or (b) other Bantu churches seceding from the Bantu leaders classified

---

Church and Pentecost to account for the practices referred to above, but in the 'European' or 'Western' churches, from which this ritual has spread to the Bantu, this is usually the trend of the argument.

[1] For more details of this church, see Appendix II.

46 RELIGION IN A TSWANA CHIEFDOM

under (*a*)'. With this type of church he associates the 'chief-type' of leader. Of *Zionists* he says that they are 'a syncretistic Bantu movement with healing, speaking with tongues, purification rites, and taboos as the main expressions of their faith'. With this type of church he associates the 'prophet-type' of leader.[1] I have not used this typology in the present treatise since Dr. Sundkler formulated it particularly with a view to Bantu Separatist churches, whereas my own investigation included churches connected with Europeans, so that a typology had to be formulated which was applicable to Separatist and non-Separatist churches. But Dr. Sundkler's typology would not have been adequate, even if we had been concerned only with the Separatist churches in Taung. To a certain extent my type 'A' churches probably fall into Dr. Sundkler's Ethiopian type, and the type 'C' churches into the Zionist type, but I do feel that the Sabbatarians, although they have much in common with the Pentecostals, stand apart as a type by themselves. Moreover, it is not possible to distinguish between distinct types of leaders in the Taung churches.[2] Finally, neither racial antagonism nor syncretism are obvious enough in Taung Bantu Separatist churches to make these the bases of a typology as Dr. Sundkler has partly done.[3]

Historical background

We have already observed that the origins of sustained missionary activity among the Tlhaping take us as far back as the beginning of Moffat's work as representative of the London Missionary Society at Kuruman (1821).[4] Although they subsequently left Kuruman, they remained under mission influence, and since 1868 Taung has been a permanent station of the L.M.S.

The Anglicans were the first to follow the L.M.S. A mission was established at Phokwane by Messrs. Crisp and Bevan in 1876. Canon Bevan remained at Phokwane for nearly fifty years. The Tlhaping of Phokwane, we should remember, did not belong to the Phuduhutswana chiefdom of Taung, although both groups split off from the same tribe at Kuruman. However, a remnant of the Phokwane group now lives at Modutung in the southern part of the Phuduhutswana chiefdom. I do not know exactly when the work of the Anglicans was extended into the Phuduhutswana chiefdom, but it must have been at an early stage, because in 1904 St. Mary's Church at Matolong already existed.

---

[1] *Op. cit.*, pp. 54–55, 106 ff.   [2] See pp. 71 ff.   [3] See pp. 231 ff.
[4] See p. 1.

INTRODUCING THE CHURCHES   47

One of the earliest secessions in the history of 'Separatism' in South African missions and churches, even before the rise of the actual Ethiopian movement, took place in the Taung reserve, and was a split from the L.M.S.[1] In 1885 discontented members of the Manthe congregation in the Maidi chiefdom seceded from the L.M.S. as a result of which the Native Independent Congregational Church was founded. I do not know whether people of the Phuduhutswana chiefdom joined the secessionists immediately, but to-day the Native Independent Congregational Church has a considerable following in the latter chiefdom, the largest of all the Bantu Separatist churches in the area.

The first denomination to start work beside the L.M.S. at the headquarters of the tribe at Taung was the Roman Catholic Church. St. Paul's Mission was founded in 1895 by Father Porte, a French priest, who had previously been working in Basutoland.

During the years between the Anglo-Boer War and World War I, Separatist church leaders were particularly active in Taung.[2] This was for instance reported by the L.M.S. missionary at Taung during 1904 and 1905.[3] The report for 1909 mentions the presence of 'numerous "minor prophets" in our midst' during the preceding two years. Special reference is made to the appearance of two 'youths' during June 1909, 'one of whom claimed to be the Lord Jesus and the other John the Baptist. By this time most of the church members were accustomed to those vagaries, but among the unbelieving there was great excitement. Multitudes went to hear them preach and to be baptized by the so-called visitors from the Lord. . . .' They taught that 'God was going to destroy all the white people and the blacks were to have everything, and far more, that they could desire.'[4] Regular teaching such as that given by the mission churches, was to be despised, and if the people only believed and followed the prophets 'they

[1] Cf. Sundkler, *op. cit.*, pp. 38–39.

[2] This was a time of rapid growth for the Ethiopian Movement as a whole. In Natal, Ethiopians were actively connected with the Zulu Rebellion of 1906. (See Sundkler, *Ibid.*, pp. 66, 68 f.)

[3] All references to L.M.S. reports in this section are to Annual Station Reports for Taung. (Annual Reports, South African Field, L.M.S. Archives, Livingstone House.)

[4] The destruction or expulsion of the white people is a recurring theme in the teachings of indigenous prophets both of pagan and Christian extraction, in South Africa as well as in other parts of Africa. Well known is the case of Mhlakaza and the girl Nongqawuse whose 'prophecies' led to the tragic 'cattle-killing episode' among the Xhosa in 1856–1857. For anti-European tendencies with African prophets see, besides Sundkler, *op. cit.*, Willoughby, *The Soul of the Bantu*, pp. 115 ff., Hunter, Monica, *Reaction to Conquest*, O.U.P., London, 1936, pp. 561 ff.; and Schlosser, Katesa, *Propheten in Afrika*, Albert Limbach Verlag, Braunschweig, 1949. The latter work describes a number of prophet-inspired anti-European movements from different parts of Africa.

48   RELIGION IN A TSWANA CHIEFDOM

would be enshrined in glory both during this life and the next'. The
prophets were eventually arrested on a charge of seditious teaching,
and were finally sentenced to four and a half and five years hard
labour respectively.[1]

These two were apparently the same men as Johane and Sehapano,[2]
of whom I was told by one of my older informants, Molala Baisitse,
who was a personal acquaintance of theirs. According to Molala they
were not local men but came to Taung from the north. They called
themselves messengers of the ancestor spirits and said that they had
been sent by God. My informant gave a vivid description of their
arrest, telling how they sang their songs, blew a trumpet made of the
horn of an ox, and uttered queer sounds. They were wearing ordinary
clothes, but at the magistrate's office they suddenly appeared dressed
in robes.[3] They did not perform healing, but my informant held that
they could foretell events and could speak many different languages.
They preached that white and black should be one, that the Europeans
should give the Bantu good treatment, and that the Bantu should be
friendly to the Europeans. The black man had been punished because
he had laughed at his father, but the white man had prospered because
he had honoured his father.[4] They said that they had come to end
this condition. 'You (pl.) should make peace with each other', they
said, 'and you (sing.) are liberated from the bond with which you have
been bound because you laughed at your father'.

About the same time as these two men, a local woman, known as
Botlhale, also emerged as a prophetess. My informant Molala, who is
recognized as having been a confidant of hers also, views her in
the same light as Tolonyane, and ascribes some of the same activities
to her as to the earlier prophet. He holds that the ancestor spirits
(badimo) gave her extraordinary powers. Her own son, however,
ascribes these powers to the Spirit of God. As a girl Botlhale belonged
to the L.M.S., but became an Anglican through marriage. In 1909,
when she must have been at least near the age of forty, the Spirit of
God 'entered' her, making her exceedingly ill, so that her own spirit
left her temporarily. The Spirit 'took her out of the Church' and
directed her to go out among the people and preach to them to
refrain from doing evil. She was enabled by the Spirit to predict
events, and to prescribe treatment for the sick, making special use of

[1] The prophet mentioned by Willoughby, 1928, p. 121, is probably one of these
two men.

[2] Sehapano: a cross.

[3] *Dipurapura. Purapura* (sing.) means purple (fr. Afrikaans, purper), and is used
by some of the Separatist Pentecostal churches of the robes they wear.

[4] Cf. Genesis 9: 21 ff.   [5] See p. 30 f.

INTRODUCING THE CHURCHES

prayer and water that had been 'prayed for'. She is remembered as having been especially gifted in connexion with rain. The chief and his headmen and councillors used to go to her to ask her to pray for rain. In 1910, after successive years of severe drought, the people reaped an exceptionally good crop as a result of abundant rains. That year is still spoken of as *mabele a ga Botlhale* (Botlhale's crop). She was recognized as a prophetess for many years, and died at Taung in October 1952. She never organized a church or congregation of her own, and was buried by the African United Church.

Kgokong is another prophet of local origin belonging to the period under consideration, who is remembered by many people. He told his followers to kill their goats and to throw away their household utensils,[1] and prophesied that they would be enabled to fly. He is said to have promised immortality to his followers who had to forsake homes and families. He posed as 'saviour of the people' (*mmoloki wa batho*), and is still often referred to by the name of Mmoloki. He performed adult baptism by immersion, and the candidates for baptism had to go 'naked'. Eventually, after a boy was drowned while being baptized in a deep pool where the Kgathumane stream joins the Hartz River, Kgokong was sought by the police and fled into a near-by cave, but he was arrested after being driven out by hunger. Cross-signs, said to have been made by him, are still to be seen on the rocks around the entrance of this cave, which is known as Mmoloki's cave.[2]

Suping, a prophet who appeared after Kgokong, was of Kgatla stock and came from Kanye in the Protectorate, but his mother was a Tlhaping. Some of the activities of the former prophets are also ascribed to him. He is said to have repudiated the teachings of Kgokong, however, preaching submission and advising the people to pay their taxes. Nevertheless, the police were suspicious, but before they took any steps against him, he was arrested by the chief, who bound him to a post (*mokgôrô*)[3] with outstretched arms. He was afterwards set free, however. It is related that Johane and Sehapano, on the day of their arrest, had prophesied that another would come who would be tied to a post.

[1] Perhaps he was concerned particularly with utensils of European origin. Cf. Willoughby, *op. cit.*, p. 115 n.: 'A prophet who caused some trouble in Bechuanaland not many years ago demanded that his followers should cease wearing trousers and using things made by the white man'.

[2] The L.M.S. report for 1911, after mentioning the activity of prophets, adds that 'even now the police are hunting for some who, during the performance of their rites of baptism, have compassed the death of a boy by drowning'. (December 31, 1911.)

[3] *Mokgôrô* in the Tswana translation of the Bible denotes the cross used for crucifixion.

R.T.C.—5

50 RELIGION IN A TSWANA CHIEFDOM

In February 1914, the Rev. J. Tom Brown of the L.M.S. referred to the spread of 'Ethiopianism' and reported that the chief was now at the head of the movement, which was from his point of view a political rather than a religious one. 'It has not affected in any way the Church,' he wrote, 'but the low standard of conduct required for Church membership required [*sic*] by that sect will not tend to help the work of raising the ideals of the tribe.'

Unfortunately, the L.M.S. reports to which we have referred do not mention the names of specific churches which were involved in the Ethiopian activities in Taung. Of the Separatist churches at present existing in the Phuduhutswana chiefdom, however, the A.M.E. and the Bechuana Methodist Church were introduced during the period we have been discussing. None of the prophet movements have left any persisting corporate groups, although there is evidence that at least some of the prophets collected groups of followers around them which broke up after the disappearance of the leaders.

During the two decades following 1914, several churches, Separatist and others, started working in the chiefdom. It should be remembered that some of them had already existed in neighbouring areas (such as the 'Barkly West Reserves') for some time prior to their introduction into the Phuduhutswana chiefdom.

The dates of origin of the churches (Table II), show that of the thirty in the chiefdom at present, thirteen existed by 1933: six Protestant churches connected with Europeans, six Protestant Separatist churches, and the Roman Catholic Church. Of the Protestant churches connected with Europeans, four belonged to Group A, one was Sabbatarian (Group B), and one Pentecostal (Group C), while five Separatist churches were of Group A, and one of Group C. All of the other seventeen churches entered the field after 1938. Four of these are connected with Europeans (two belong to Group A, one to Group C, while the fourth is the Watch Tower), and thirteen are Separatist churches. Of these Separatist churches five belong to Group A, three to Group B (Sabbatarian), and five to Group C (Pentecostal). Two points are shown up clearly by this chronological grouping of the churches: first, the marked increase in the number of Separatist churches in the chiefdom from 1939–1951, and secondly, the fact that with one exception all the Separatist churches of Sabbatarian and Pentecostal type originated during the latter period.

Church origins

None of the churches in the chiefdom originated locally (i.e. within the chiefdom) as altogether new churches. All spread to Taung from

INTRODUCING THE CHURCHES 51

neighbouring areas or from other parts of the country. Since our study is concentrated on a restricted area, viz. the Phuduhutswana chiefdom, our first concern is with the manner in which the different churches started in the chiefdom, i.e. how they spread to the chiefdom from other areas.

A number of the churches started as the result of a definite and organized attempt to make converts or win members for the church. Such attempts involved one or more office-bearers of the Church in question, coming from another part of the country, to visit the chiefdom or settle there with the express purpose of expanding the church. These may be considered as missionary enterprises. A second factor involved in the origin of some churches, is the existence of a Church or mission in a neighbouring area, such as the Maidi chiefdom, the Barkly West Reserves, or the Vaal Hartz Irrigation Scheme, from which it spread into the Phuduhutswana chiefdom, perhaps by gradual infiltration or by organized attempts, or both.

Sometimes, members of a church came from another area to settle in the chiefdom for economic or other reasons, but not in the first place with the purpose of expanding their church. When such new inhabitants found that their own church was not represented locally, they attached themselves to another church already existing, but occasionally they started their own church activities, or were visited by the leaders from the nearest centre where their church existed, who organized a local congregation. The same type of thing happened when a local native joined a church while he was abroad, working or visiting, and started his own church activities on his return home, if there was no local branch of the church. A last factor is the occurrence of a secession of a local congregation or part of it from the church to which they belonged. We have observed how this happened in the Maidi chiefdom, where it led to the founding of a completely new church, but in the other instances in which splits took place, the seceding group made contact with another church, not represented in the chiefdom, and usually of the same type as the one from which they seceded. They were then incorporated into such a church, and this meant the origin of a new church in the chiefdom.

In Table III a summary is given of the manner in which the different churches originated, and it shows that in Separatist as well as non-Separatist churches missionary enterprise has been the most important factor in their origin. The joining of a new church by local natives while abroad, new inhabitants of the chiefdom, and secessions each played a part in the origin of several churches. An important fact which this illustrates is that beside missionary enterprise, the

52 RELIGION IN A TSWANA CHIEFDOM

present mobility of the native population of South Africa plays an important part in the multiplication of denominations in a given area.

More must be said about the role of secessions in connexion with the origins of Bantu Separatist churches. It was not possible to investigate the circumstances under which each particular Separatist church originated (in the sense of its initial origin or founding, not its introduction into the chiefdom), as this would have taken me too far afield from the more immediate concern of the present investigation, but where such information was easily accessible I did pay attention to it.

The Ethiopian Church, the A.M.E., and the Ethiopian Catholic Church in Zion (E.C.C. in Z.) grew out of the early Ethiopian movement of the eighties and nineties of the previous century.[1] The founder of the E.C.C. in Z., the Rev. James Brander, was educated as a Methodist, but later joined the Church of the Province. As a 'missionary' of this Church he is said to have been involved in a dispute with his superior church officials about certain expenditures he had made after which he 'lost fidelity in the English Church' and resigned from the Church in 1890. He now joined the Ethiopian movement, and with other Ethiopian leaders entered the A.M.E. Church. The latter, however, because of its subordination to the American body of which it was a branch, did not fully satisfy some of the Ethiopian leaders, so that Brander eventually again seceded in 1904 and founded the Ethiopian Catholic Church in Zion.[2] In 1905 another group seceded from the A.M.E. Church in Bloemfontein to form the Bechuana Methodist Church.[3] According to the present 'Head' of this Church, the cause of this secession was dissatisfaction with the use of the English Bible in church services, and the fact that sermons were delivered in English and had to be interpreted into Tswana. In the historical sketch prefaced to the Constitution we read that 'during the run of the Church there arose disputes between its ministers of a superiority claim'. Fortunately the Rev. Marks Molotsi, who succeeded his father as head of the Church, later 'managed together the whole of the . . . Church under one superiority'.

The main cause for the founding of the Native Independent Congregational Church was inter-'tribal' feeling between the two chiefdoms in the Taung reserve. The Phuduhutswana hold that the Maidi are subordinate to them, while the Maidi claim that they are independent

[1] Cf. Sundkler, *op. cit.*, pp. 39–43.
[2] *Constitutions and Canons of the Ethiopian Catholic Church in Zion*, pp. 3–6, cf. Sundkler, *Ibid.*
[3] *Constitution*, Bechuana Methodist Church, Bantu Printing Press, Johannesburg.

INTRODUCING THE CHURCHES   53

of the former. To-day, the Native Affairs Department recognizes their independence, but they apparently had to struggle for this recognition for a considerable time. Any hint of their being subordinate to the Taung chief was, and is still, much resented. In L.M.S. Church organization, Manthe, the Maidi chief's place, was merely an outstation of the Taung Mission, and this caused resentment, since it seemed to sanction the claim of the Phuduhutswana to political superiority. The actual split followed the request made by the Maidi to the L.M.S. that an ordained minister be stationed at Manthe.[1] Part of the L.M.S. Church at Manthe then seceded (1885), and requested the Maidi chief to find them a minister. For some years the secessionists were pastored by an African Congregationalist minister from Kimberley, who visited them periodically. On his death chief Kgantlapane of Manthe personally visited another Congregationalist minister at Kimberley, Rev. Solomon M. Matolo, and eventually induced him to settle at Manthe in 1893. According to documents in the possession of the late Rev. Matolo's son, he took the view that the Native Independent Congregational Church was founded by himself in 1893, after his going to Manthe. There are at present two factions in this Church (see below) of which one (which we may call the Schmidtsdrift faction because its most prominent congregation is at Schmidtsdrift) upholds the above-mentioned view. The other faction (which we may call the Manthe faction) claims that the Church was founded in 1885, i.e. the year when the secession from the L.M.S. originally took place.

The L.M.S. retained some of their followers in the Maidi chiefdom and later also stationed an ordained African minister at Manthe. The 'Independent' Church, however, has very distinctly become the 'tribal' Church of the Maidi, and is at present more of a tribal church than the L.M.S. is in the Phuduhutswana chiefdom. There is little doubt that it is numerically the strongest church among the Maidi.[2]

It did not confine its activities to the Maidi chiefdom, but has spread far afield into other parts of the Northern Cape, the Transvaal, and the Orange Free State. This tendency toward geographical ex-

[1] In accounts given by members of this Church, the inter-chiefdom feeling was not explicitly mentioned as the cause of the split, but it is clearly reflected by the facts, particularly the subsequent development of the Church.

[2] The Native Churches Commission reported in 1925 that: 'One of the most experienced missionaries of the London Missionary Society writes, "History will assure you that it (the Native Independent Church) was not so much a schism from the London Missionary Society (though some men disciplined by the London Missionary Society did join) as a desire to have a tribal church distinct from that at Taungs [sic], as the chief at Manthe sought for and ultimately received his independence from the chief at Taung".' Union of South Africa, Report of the Native Churches Commission, U.G. 39–25, Cape Times Ltd., Cape Town, 1925.

54 RELIGION IN A TSWANA CHIEFDOM

tension of the Church eventually proved to be incompatible with its origin and character as a 'tribal' church. In time sections of the Church outside the Maidi chiefdom came into conflict with those who wished to centralize the activities at Manthe. The former are those whom I have called the Schmidtsdrift faction, the latter are the Manthe faction. Both factions, of course, have their own version of how the trouble arose, and it is difficult to make out exactly how the schism started and developed. What is clear, however, is that it started in connexion with the succession of a certain Rev. Monyakoane to the post of Rev. Matolo at Manthe. No doubt personal factors also played their part, but it seems that the position of the Manthe congregation in the Church as a whole lies at the root of the trouble. The Manthe faction holds that Manthe is the official centre of the Church, and that the minister of Manthe (elected by the local congregation) is *ipso facto* the Moderator of the Church. The Schmidtsdrift section refuses to recognize Manthe's pre-eminence and holds that the Moderator should be elected by the Conference of the whole Church. In practice the Schmidtsdrift congregation appears to enjoy a certain degree of pre-eminence.[1] This dispute has now been going on since 1922, and successive attempts to come to an agreement have up till now been unsuccessful.

Strangely enough, the members of the church in the Phuduhu-tswana chiefdom are not openly split into two separate factions. Some of the leaders who regularly conduct services, belong to the Schmidts-drift-faction, but the church is also visited by the Manthe minister and most of the members receive the sacraments from him. This gives one the impression that the dispute is largely one between leaders and that the rank and file of church members are not particu-larly interested.

The African United Church is a happy exception to the rule, being the result of a church union between the Native Congress Catholic Church and the African Catholic Bantu Church which took place in 1912–1913.[2] The Zion Apostolic Church of South Africa is mentioned by Dr. Sundkler as one of the main secessions of the period 1917–1920 from the Zion Apostolic Church, the latter being the result of foreign missionary activity.[3] Further particulars as to the circumstances of its origin are not known.

[1] In an agreement reached in 1950 and signed by ministers of both factions the one faction is also referred to as 'some [members] of the N.I.C.C. at Schmidtsdrift who are under Rev. R. F. Mohapanela'. (The co-operation to which they agreed broke down in 1952.)

[2] *Constitutions and Canons of the African United Church,* Johannesburg, 1917.

[3] Sundkler, *op. cit.,* pp. 48–49.

INTRODUCING THE CHURCHES 55

The Holy Church of Christ originated as a separate church by a secession from the Church of Christ. The cause of the split, which took place in 1945, was described to me as follows by a visiting minister of this church:

> We left X because he did not want to have a Constitution. The Church made lots of money; the Church is rich, but now it all belongs to him. He had all of it written in his name by an agent [i.e. an attorney]. In the beginning we did not take notice of these things because we trusted him. When we saw these things we said these things should be in the name of the Church. X refused and said that if we were not satisfied we could leave. Then we went out there and made this Church. With us the buildings are written in the name of the Church.[1]

As I have shown above, a few secessions took place within the Phuduhutswana chiefdom, but none of these resulted in an altogether new church since the seceding groups attached themselves to other churches already existing outside the chiefdom. For instance, the leader of the Ethiopian Church of Christ by Religion used to belong to what was presumably a Pentecostal Separatist church. Because of a dispute with his superior church officials about the portion of the contributions of members which should fall to him he deserted the church, taking his congregation with him. After some time he went to Kimberley where he contacted the head of the Church to which he now belongs, into which he was accepted with his flock. Another group again were deserted by their leader and then contacted the Head of the Holy Gospel Church in Zion, which they ultimately joined.

The nucleus of what is now the Holy Church of Christ (in the chiefdom[2]) used to belong to the Church of the First Born. They hold that they could not get on with that church and that the Church could not get on with the chief either, so that the latter, with the Native Commissioner's sanction, ordered the leader out of the chiefdom. One section of the Church, which centres in another part of the chiefdom, remained in the Church, but those living in the vicinity where the trouble arose dissociated themselves from it and contacted the Holy Church of Christ, to which they now belong.

These examples illustrate that dislike of European control as well as of American Negro control in missions and churches was a major cause of secessions in the earlier stages of Separatism. Inter-tribal politics played a part in the origin of the Native Independent Congre-

---

[1] A clause in the Constitution of the Holy Church of Christ requires that church buildings be registered in the name of the Church.

[2] Above I referred to the origin of this church as a whole; here we are dealing with the local branch of it in Taung.

56 RELIGION IN A TSWANA CHIEFDOM

gational Church. It is well known that many further secessions and re-groupings take place within Separatism. Our examples show how tribal affiliation, dislike of the predominance of the English language in church, financial disputes, and the departure of leaders play a role in this process.

Analysis of church statistics

The present state of the churches is reflected by the statistics presented in Table II. With the exception of the St. Paul Apostolic Faith Morning Star Church, these figures were provided by Church leaders themselves.[1] From the church mentioned above no statistics whatsoever could be obtained.[2] In that case I made an estimate based on my observation of numbers actively taking part in important church festivals, making allowance for a number who would be absent. I tried to get a total of all adults observing a formal connexion with the churches, by adding members of confirmation classes or members on trial, and catechumens—collectively called non-communicant members—to the number of communicants.

These figures immediately reveal the numerical strength of the Roman Catholics. Their members form 47% of the total membership of all churches in the chiefdom. To a large extent their predominance is probably the result of the fact that their missionary effort is far more imposing than that of any other denomination: on their staff they have three priests, two European, and one Coloured, besides a number of European lay Brothers and Sisters, whereas the L.M.S. missionary is the only European Protestant missionary in the chiefdom; the R.C. buildings and equipment are not only more numerous, but much more imposing than those of any of the other churches; the scope of their work is much wider: they have an industrial department and a boarding school, which none of the others have, and, probably most important of all, they are the only Church doing medical work, and they do it on a large scale. The possibility that

[1] I often struggled through their registers with them to make sure of getting the correct numbers. Most of the figures were collected during the latter half of 1953, and a few during January and February of 1954.

[2] The local leader, referred to as 'Field Gospel Servant' in official correspondence of the church, was quite co-operative in the beginning, but after he had mentioned my investigation in a letter to his superior church officials, they wrote and told him to notify me that 'any informations and particulars of services in which this servant is serving are the privileged informations [*sic*], and are only obtainable from Quarters of the Divine Government Offices through the above office only. The servant . . . is himself not entitled to say anything about same . . .' My attempts to obtain further information through correspondence were fruitless. I remained friends with the local leader, visited him occasionally, and was allowed to attend church services, but he was not willing to divulge any further information or explanations.

INTRODUCING THE CHURCHES 57

something inherent in Roman Catholicism appeals particularly to the Bantu, will be discussed later.

Another striking fact is that the Methodists are the strongest of all Protestant churches, even stronger than the L.M.S. which entered the field long before them. We note, however, that the latter still have more communicants than the Methodist Church (Table I), but the fact that a very large proportion (46%) of the Methodist members are members on trial, suggests that Methodism is pushing forward rapidly. The reasons for the success of Methodism will be discussed in our final chapter.

A comparison of the membership of churches connected with Europeans with that of Separatist churches, shows that the Separatists have about 20% (2,070) of the total for all Protestant churches. The only available norm beside which these figures can be placed so as to judge their significance, is the 1936 and 1946 population census figures for the Union. A comparison of the statistics collected by myself in the Phuduhutswana chiefdom, with returns from the two Union Censuses, gives us the following:

	Phud. Chiefd.	Union 1936	Union 1946
Bantu Separatists as % of all churches	20·3	33·9	18·6
Bantu Separatists as % of all Protestants	37·9	36·6	20·5

If the 1946 figures for the Union are to be accepted, the numerical relation of Separatists to other churches is about the same for the Phuduhutswana chiefdom as for the Union, but if the Roman Catholics, who are relatively far more numerous in Taung than in the Union, are not taken into account, the Separatists can be said to be a good deal stronger in Taung than in the Union as a whole. Unfortunately not much value can be attached to this comparison, since the great disparity between the figures for the two Union censuses makes their reliability rather doubtful.[1]

[1] Cf. the following figures for Bantu membership of a few churches in the census returns:

		1936	1946
Seventh Day Adventists	..	3,682	105,241
Apost. Faith Mission ..	..	13,003	177,298
Diverse Christian Sects	..	1,076	48,051
Bantu Separatist Churches	..	1,089,479	758,810

I suggest that many who were enumerated as Bantu Separatists in 1936 were enumerated as S.D.A., Apost. F.M., or Diverse Christian Sects in 1946.

58 RELIGION IN A TSWANA CHIEFDOM

TABLE II.—TOTAL MEMBERSHIP

	Churches connected with Europeans	Date of origin	Present membership		
			Non-Communic. members	Communicant members	Total membership
GROUP A	Methodist . . .	pre 1923	574	671	1,245
	L.M.S. . . .	1830–40	343	854	1,197
	Anglican . . .	1880–90?	128	265	393
	Lutheran . . .	± 1910	29	69	98
	Bantu Baptist .	1939	25	22	47
	Dutch Reformed	1951	6	25	31
	TOTAL FOR GROUP A .		1,105	1,906	*3,011*
GROUP B (Sabbatarians	Seventh Day Adventist	pre 1920	24	169	193
	TOTAL FOR GROUP B .		24	169	*193*
GROUP C (Pentecostal)	Full Gospel . .	1947	23	66	89
	Pentecostal Holiness .	1918	—	83	83
	TOTAL FOR GROUP C .		23	149	*172*
UNCLASSIFIED	Watch Tower . .	1951	9	3	*12*
	TOTAL FOR PROTESTANTS		1,161	2,227	*3,388*
R.C.	Roman Catholic . .	1895	708	4,037	*4,745*
TOTAL FOR ALL CHURCHES . .			1,869	6,264	*8,133*

INTRODUCING THE CHURCHES 59

OF THE CHURCHES

Separatist churches	Date of origin	Present membership			Total for all churches
		Non-Communic. members	Communicant members	Total membership	
Native Independent Congregational . . .	1885 or 1893	?	?	304	
African Methodist Episcopal	1904–06	61	144	205	
African Lutheran . .	1925?	67	133	200	
S.A. Native Baptist Church Mission . . .	pre 1947	54	129	183	
Bechuana Methodist . .	pre 1914	35	87	122	
African United . .	1919	35	65	100	
Ethiopian Church of Africa.	1943	38	58	96	
Ethiopian Catholic Church in Zion	1944	6	33	39	
African Catholic . .	1947	18	20	38	
Ethiopian Church of Christ by Religion . . .	1951	12	6	18	
		326+?	675+?	*1,305*	4,316
Witness of Christ (Sabbath).	1941	—	116	116	
Church of the First Born .	1941	—	97	97	
Holy Church of Christ .	1950	4	14	18	
		4	227	*231*	424
Zion Apostolic Church of S.A.	1932	60	88	148	
New Apostolic Church in Zion	1950	21	101	122	
St. Paul Apostolic Faith Morning Star . .	1944	?	?	120	
Holy Christian Apostolic .	1947	24	47	71	
Found Apostolic Church in Jerusalem .	± 1949	—	40	40	
Holy Gospel Church in Zion	1945	—	33	33	
		105+?	309+?	*534*	706
		—	—	—	12
		435+?	1,211+?	*2,070*	5,458
		—	—	—	4,745
		435+?	1,211+?	*2,070*	10,203

RELIGION IN A TSWANA CHIEFDOM

TABLE III CHURCH ORIGINS

Type of church[1]	Name of church	Missionary enterprise	Expansion from neighbouring area	Local native joined abroad	New inhabitants	Secession	Unknown
R.C.	Roman Catholic	×					
	Methodist[2]						×
	L.M.S.	×					
Prot. C.E. A	Anglican		×				
	Lutheran		×				
	Bantu Baptist				×		
	D.R.C.		×		×		
Prot. C.E. B	S.D.A.	×					
Prot. C.E. C	Full Gospel	×					
	Pentecostal Holiness	×		×			
Unclassified	Watch Tower	×					
Prot. Sep. A	Nat. Ind. Cong.		×				
	A.M.E.	×	(or ×)				
	Afr. Lutheran						×
	S.A. Nat. Bap. C. Mis.	×					
	Bech. Methodist	×					
	Afr. United						×
	Eth. C. of Afr.	×					
	Eth. Cath. C. in Z.			×			
	Afr. Catholic		×				
	Eth. C. of X. by Rel.					×	
Prot. Sep. B	Witness of X. (Sab.)	×					
	C. of the First Born	×					
	Holy C. of X.					×	
Prot. Sep. C	Z. Ap. C. of S.A.				×		
	New Ap. C. in Z.			×	×		
	St. P. Ap. F.M.S.	×		×			
	Holy Zion Ap. C.			×			
	Foundation Ap. C. in J.	×		×			
	Holy Gospel C. in Z.					×	

[1] Prot. : Protestant;
C.E. : Connected with Europeans;
A, B, or C: Belonging to Group A, B, C;
Sep. : Separatist.
[2] The churches in each group are listed in order of their relative numerical strength. (Cf. Table II.)

INTRODUCING THE CHURCHES   61

No single Separatist church in the chiefdom has a distinct numerical lead on the others. Moreover, none of these churches really has a large following, certainly nothing approaching that of the leading churches connected with Europeans. However, in the neighbouring Maidi chiefdom, the Native Independent Congregational Church claims to have 1,500 members in that chiefdom alone.

A comparison of the different types of Protestant churches shows that in respect of churches connected with Europeans, the churches of Group A have the great majority of the members (89%). Among the Separatist churches, however, those of Group A have only 63% (1,305) of all the members, while the Sabbatarians have 11% (231), and the Pentecostals 26% (534). Closely connected with this phenomenon, that Sabbatarians and Pentecostals are proportionately stronger among Separatists than among non-Separatists, is the fact that of the non-Separatist Protestants only a very small proportion belong to churches of more recent origin, while more than half of the Separatists belong to churches which originated after 1938. With one exception, all the Separatist Sabbatarian and Pentecostal churches belong to the latter group. This means that there is a greater tendency within Separatism toward Sabbatarianism and Pentecostalism, than within non-Separatism, and that this tendency is relatively recent.

CHAPTER IV

CHURCH ORGANIZATION

THIS is not the place to enter into a theological discussion of the nature of the Church, but I do want to make it quite clear that although I subject the churches to a sociological investigation this does not mean that I view the Church merely as a voluntary association like any other. To me the Church is the Body of Christ and I cannot treat it as anything else. Nevertheless, in its visible form, the Church is an association, in fact many different associations, of human beings existing not apart from, but within, society. It therefore involves, and is involved in, social relations and it is with these relations as they factually exist that we are here concerned. I shall try to describe the pattern of relations within the small, regularly co-operating church groups, and the relations of these groups with the rest of their own church, with other churches, and with society at large.

The church group

The important unit in church organization is the local church group by which is meant the group of people regularly meeting for weekly devotions and other church activities. Church members usually attend devotions at the church centre most accessible to them, and there do not seem to be clearly defined territorial boundaries between the different local groups of a certain church.

One of the most striking characteristics of such local church groups is their small size. Table IV, which shows the number of local groups for each church beside its membership, gives an impression of the average size of local groups. Only the Roman Catholic Church has local groups of considerable size. Their mission work is centralized at Taung, where they have a local group of over two thousand members.[1] Even two of the other local groups consist of over five hundred members each. Formerly the following of the L.M.S. also used to be strongly centralized at Taung, but with the scattering of the population, the Taung church has shrunk considerably. It still has the largest membership of all the L.M.S. local groups in the chiefdom, but nevertheless it comprises only about 220 members. Only two of the other L.M.S. local groups have more than a hundred members. The mem-

[1] 'Members' in this chapter will refer to the total of communicant and non-communicant members, unless otherwise specified.

CHURCH ORGANIZATION

bers of the Methodist Church are grouped into a number of societies, of which the largest is the Taung Society, with a membership of 350, which is considerably larger than that of any of the other societies. However, in practice the Taung Society consists of two local groups, so that none of the Methodist local groups can be considered as a large central group.

Two of the Separatist churches show some centralization. The 200 members of the African Lutheran Church form a single local group; they are mostly from Buxton and Mocweding in the south-western part of the chiefdom. The members of the St. Paul Apostolic Faith Morning Star are scattered over a wide area and actually there are several places where church members meet fairly regularly, but the church activities are strongly centralized at the church and the leader's homestead: nearly every Sunday, and even during the week, one finds members from the more distant places taking part in the activities at the church centre. This church resembles what Dr. Sundkler has typified as the Bethesda type of church among the Zulu,[1] and I consider the members as forming a single group which is not clearly sub-divided into local groups. Table IV shows clearly that none of the other churches can have local groups of considerable size.

Various distinctions divide the local group into sub-groups; communicant members and non-communicant members usually form two distinct groups, while there is also a distinction between office bearers and the other communicant members. Members of the women's associations usually constitute a separate group. Many of the children of members usually form an integral part of the local group, and are sometimes organized into a Sunday School. Moreover a number of adult adherents (*barati*) often maintain a close connexion with the local church group. In the Methodist Church the 'class' system for church members[2] cuts across the line dividing full members from members on trial. Three Separatist churches which have a Methodist Episcopal type of church government also have the class system incorporated in their constitution, but it is seldom put into practice in these churches, probably because the local groups are often too small to be further sub-divided.

The amount of contact between the different local groups of a single church varies. In the case of the L.M.S. the first week-end of every month is the occasion for the *phuthêgô* (gathering, or congregation;

---

[1] 1948, pp. 151 ff.

[2] The reference is not to 'classes' in the sociological sense of different strata of society, but to the division of church members into a number of small groups or classes which regularly meet for religious instruction or discussions.

64 RELIGION IN A TSWANA CHIEFDOM

church) for the whole sub-district, which consists of all the local churches (including one outside the chiefdom). This monthly *phuthêgô* is held at Taung, and Leaders and Deacons from the local churches have to attend the business meetings, while other members who are able to do so also make the journey to Taung to attend the numerous services held over the week-end, and the Communion service on Sunday afternoon. I do not know of other churches which have such regular contacts between their local groups, but such contact usually takes place on the occasion of the administering of the sacraments and on special occasions such as the dedication of a new building.

One church consists of three sections, existing relatively independently of each other, each section consisting of one or more local groups. This is the result of ministers of the same church each gathering a flock of his own. One, who claims to be the 'General Overseer' for a large area, had already been working in the chiefdom for about two years when a local man who had joined the Church and had been made a minister while working abroad, returned home and started doing church work without any reference to the 'General Overseer'. The second minister had already been propagating his church for nearly a year when I left the field, and the two leaders had never yet been in touch with each other. There is even a third minister who also has a separate following. The work of these ministers does not seem to overlap in any single locality, but there is no clear division of the chiefdom as a whole between them. Each one communicates with the head of the church independently of the others. This illustrates the loose character of church organization in some of the Separatist churches.

The geographical distribution of the different local church groups (see Map 'B') does not show any regular pattern. Some of the churches with a smaller membership are more or less concentrated in one area. On the other hand, even small churches may have several local groups in different parts of the chiefdom, while the members of the St. Paul Apostolic Faith Morning Star, though forming only one local group, live in many different parts of the chiefdom. The population of any given area may be quite heterogeneous in respect of their church affiliations. In 21 sample homesteads at Mokgareng, which had a total population of 143, ten different denominations were represented. The whole area in which these homesteads are situated could not have been much larger than half a square mile. However, a particular denomination does sometimes predominate in a particular area.

The proportionate strength of the different ethnic elements which are found in the chiefdom[1] varies considerably between different

[1] See pp. 4 f.

CHURCH ORGANIZATION 65

churches (Table IV). The Roman Catholic Church and the L.M.S. are virtually exclusively Tswana. The Methodists, on the other hand, are very distinctly an ethnical mixture, and although the majority are Tswana, many of the leaders who are of Tswana stock are not people of the chiefdom by birth but came from other areas. Group feeling between Tswana members on the one hand, and Nguni on the other, is not missing in this church, and a tendency toward the formation of three different factions has been evident in some local groups, viz. a Tswana faction, a Nguni faction and a middle group, which strives at co-operation between the ethnically differing sections. The Anglican Church also has a strong Nguni element beside the more indigenous Tswana, while in the A.M.E. Church Tswana, Nguni, and Southern Sotho elements intermingle. In some of the churches the non-Tswana element is very conspicuous. The Dutch Reformed Church members, e.g., are almost exclusively Southern Sotho, which goes to illustrate that it originated locally largely as a result of its members coming from elsewhere to settle in the chiefdom. The (Separatist) Zion Apostolic Church of S.A. has a strong Southern Sotho nucleus, although the Tswana members seem to form the majority of its total membership in the chiefdom. Members of a certain Southern Sotho lineage were instrumental in bringing the church into the chiefdom, and the most important leaders still come from this lineage. The three Separatist Sabbatarian churches, and the (Separatist) Holy Christian Apostolic Church are very distinctly predominantly Nguni churches. Less is known about the ethnic composition of churches that have not been mentioned, but they are all predominantly Tswana.

To some extent the ethnic composition of the membership of a church can be explained with reference to its geographical distribution. On the whole it would probably be true that the non-Tswana element in the ranks of the churches is not to be accounted for so much by local conversions but rather by immigration of people who already belonged to churches and who joined the local branches of the churches to which they belonged, or introduced their own churches if these were not yet represented. This would explain, for instance, why Methodists and Anglicans have many non-Tswana members and why the L.M.S. is only Tswana. Except for their work in the Rhodesias, the L.M.S. is very largely confined to the Tswana language-areas, so that the only accretions to their membership that could result from immigration would consist of Tswana people. The ranks of the Anglicans and Methodists, on the other hand, have certainly been increased by immigration of Nguni members of their churches. This does not explain, however, why the large Roman Catholic membership

R.T.C.—6

66   RELIGION IN A TSWANA CHIEFDOM

includes virtually no non-Tswana people, since Roman Catholic work is certainly not confined to Tswana areas.

As far as my information goes, each of the three Sabbatarian Separatist churches is predominantly Nguni, not only in Taung, but throughout the whole Church. The reason for this is that the mother church out of which these three have developed through secessions, i.e. the Church of Christ (*Iɓandla lika-Krestu*), is centralized in Port Elizabeth and is oriented to the Xhosa language.[1]

The small size of the local church group makes for intimate in-group relations. The intimacy of the relations is often increased by the fact that the church services are held at the homestead of a church leader or one of the other members.[2] Moreover, some of the most important opportunities for joint activities and social contacts are provided by the church.[3] Where the local group is formed by people belonging to a single ethnic group forming a minority of the population, this circumstance also binds the members more closely together. The local church group is undoubtedly one of the most important social groups in the society to-day, and this applies to Separatist as well as non-Separatist churches. This group solidarity, however, is not expressed in extreme isolationism such as that found among some Zulu Zionist churches, which keep together as a group even in activities in which the whole community takes part. Neither are there any of the unstable roving Zionist groups which follow their leader about the country,[4] although it seems that such groups were formed by some prophets who were active in Taung in the years preceding World War I.[5]

The kinship element is not altogether excluded as a factor influencing church membership since in some cases children join the same church as their parents, more or less as a matter of course. Quite often, however, the children of parents who are church members or adherents, do not have any connexion with a church, not even as adherents, while the reverse is also the case. Moreover, it is not uncommon for parents and children to belong to different churches, the reason often being that the children attended the school of a different denomination from that to which their parents belong, and were drawn into that church through the influence of its educational work. It seems probable that in some cases the element of ethnic origin also plays a role in deciding which church a person joins. A

---

[1] Cf. Mqotsi and Mkele, *op. cit.*

[2] It is not uncommon for a cup of tea or coffee to be served after the Sunday morning service.

[3] See pp. 124 f.   [4] Cf. Sundkler, *op. cit.*, pp. 95–97.   [5] See pp. 47 ff.

CHURCH ORGANIZATION 67

Nguni would rather join a church with a strong Nguni element among its members, I should think, than an exclusively Tswana church, while a Tswana would not be so easily attracted to a church which is very predominantly Nguni.

When trying to understand the social significance of the local church group, the nature of traditional Tswana social structure should be remembered. The most important social units were the family group, consisting of several households, and the ward, consisting usually of a few family groups. The members of the same family group or ward were mostly connected by agnatic kinship ties. Within the family group there was constant co-operation in economic, cere-monial, and legal affairs, and there was also a great deal of co-operation between the family groups composing the ward. The set-up of the homesteads of the ward around a common byre and meeting-place, resulted in their members sharing much of each others' lives.[1]

This old ward system has disappeared from Tlhaping society, and with it most of the opportunities for social contacts and group activity which the traditional society had to offer. In the changed and changing society the church is the only institution which has so far emerged as a possible successor to these important functions. The inhabitants of the new type of headman's area hardly form a corporate group, and within it there are no clear sub-divisions with any degree of solidarity. It is therefore clear why, in these circumstances, the church group has become so important socially. Its small size and intimate in-group relations, which make it comparable to the traditional family groups and wards, may have contributed to its acceptability as successor to some of the functions of these groupings.

With the decay of the old social structure many of the excitements and amusements of tribal life in the past have disappeared. There are no more inter-tribal wars and cattle raids, no important tribal cere-monies apart from initiation, and enthusiasm is lacking for tribal assemblies. Moreover, beer drinks are less and many Christians may not attend them, and there are few work-parties nowadays. Undoubt-edly the social activities of the churches have been stimulated by the dearth of opportunities for recreational and other activities which provide some excitement and diversion in a condition under which life can be dull and uninteresting.

Leaders and other office bearers

In the Roman Catholic Church indigenous leadership is much less prominent than in Protestant churches. There is no R.C. African priest

[1] Cf. Schapera, 1953, pp. 40, 46–47; 1943, p. 29.

68 RELIGION IN A TSWANA CHIEFDOM

in the chiefdom, but one of the three fathers in the Mission is a coloured man who was born at Phokwane, while one of the five brothers attached to the mission is a Tswana from Kimberley. A number of local men and a few women assist in church work as Catechists and Elders by teaching the catechism, visiting the sick, and burying the dead. African leaders play an important role in all Protestant churches.

In the L.M.S. most of the work is done by the African church leaders, and the missionary gives only part of his time to the churches in Taung, the chiefdom being only one of four sub-districts under his supervision. None of the other churches connected with Europeans has a missionary stationed in the chiefdom, and visits from European ministers who supervise the work are few and far between. The strong Methodist Church, e.g., is altogether supervised by an African minister stationed at Kimberley. In several instances the missionaries who supervise the Taung Church are as far away as the Witwatersrand, and the degree of supervision exercised by European church leaders is usually small. On the whole one is not aware of any resentment of their control. The Evangelist of the S.D.A., for instance, said that he preferred belonging to a church with European leadership, and explained his preference by referring to the tendency of Separatist churches to split. 'There is no agreement amongst them because of the desire for superior positions.'

The trend of the official policy of the L.M.S. toward greater independence of the mission church is most conspicuous in the organization of the Regional Council which includes a number of districts, and in the still wider Church Council, which has only recently been formed. In the Regional Council Europeans and Africans are equally eligible as officials and in 1953 the Chairman of the Southern Regional Council, which includes the Taung district, was an African. In the Taung sub-district five schools have recently been placed under the management of the African minister, to give some expression locally to the new tendency in mission policy. The idea of the gradual withdrawal of the Missionary Society from the indigenous church has so far not infrequently been interpreted by members of the church as 'the Fathers are throwing us away', although the more educated members realize the necessity for this development. It must be remarked, however, that in the Taung churches the leadership is largely in the hands of older people (many of them women) who have had little formal education, so that younger and more highly educated members have little opportunity for taking responsibility.[1] It must be

---

[1] For a possible explanation why the older generation monopolizes the church, see p. 229.

CHURCH ORGANIZATION 69

said that some of the younger 'intellectuals', although formally members, show little interest in the church.

It was difficult to assess the relation between the European missionary on the one hand, and the African leaders and the church on the other. I went to the field only a few months after the missionary and his wife had settled at Taung as their first station, so that it was necessarily still a time of adaptation on both sides, the more so since there had been no missionary for two years. Nevertheless, it is clear that the missionary's numerous administrative activities restrict the opportunity for direct and personal contacts with the church members. He is not highly integrated into the life of the local church groups, but his presence in the district and his connexion with the church is still regarded as necessary. He attends the business meetings of the sub-district if he happens to be at Taung, but does so merely in an advisory capacity. Interference on his part in the ordinary affairs of the church would be resented, and suggestions on his part, which entail some deviation from a course or a custom that is traditional in the local church, are not easily accepted. On the other hand, in special circumstances which require a little organization falling outside the ordinary course of events, the responsibility is readily placed on his shoulders.

Every local church of the L.M.S. has its 'Leader' and a number of Deacons who together form a local church council which is responsible for the organization of the local church. They conduct their own meetings, but have to report monthly to a meeting of the whole local church. Every month all the local church councils in the sub-district meet at Taung under the chairmanship of the African minister in charge of the sub-district, who is stationed at Taung. This council again either has to report to a more representative gathering of all the churches in the sub-district, or its decisions are referred back to the local churches. The minister visits the different local churches in turn to take the Sunday services, but the Leader and Deacons form the corps of regular preachers in each church. Other members of the church who have the ability, may, however, also be asked to preach. The Leader and Deacons for each local church are to be elected from its members for a period of three years, but it is the tendency in the churches to let them carry on for longer. As a rule only men are eligible as Leaders in the L.M.S., but in some local churches where no suitable men are available, women—who are in any case eligible as Deacons—act as Leaders.

On the whole the patterns of organization in the other churches are less formal and clear-cut, but they follow much the same lines.

70   RELIGION IN A TSWANA CHIEFDOM

The office bearers form the church council for the local group under leadership of the one who holds the most senior office. Since local groups are small, such business as may arise—even the disciplining of members, which usually forms the largest proportion of business ransacted—is often discussed in gatherings of the whole church group. The distinction between members and office bearers varies, but is on the whole not very conspicuous, although the holding of an office in church always carries a certain amount of prestige. Even in the non-Episcopal churches the different types of office bearers are considered as a hierarchy, and it is here that one more often finds consciousness of rank, i.e. between different office bearers. This idea of rank is by no means confined to the Separatist churches. In the Separatist churches the range of offices is usually a long one, starting with the Bishop, who is head of the church, followed by the Overseers; then come Ministers, Priests or Pastors, and Evangelists. Below Evangelists there are often as many as three or four minor types of offices to which various names are applied, such as Leaders, Stewards, Preachers, Deacons,[1] and Prayers. Usually there is not a very clear distinction between the activities of the different junior office bearers. Preaching, praying for the sick, and conducting funeral services are their most common duties.

In both Separatist and non-Separatist churches office bearers seldom hold office for a defined period, even although the church law or constitution may state this to be the case. The natives seem to feel that once a member becomes an office bearer, he remains one, unless he has to be censured for some misdemeanour. Moreover, when once his foot is on the first rung of the ladder, he rises, although perhaps only very slowly. Each promotion usually follows some form of examination, by the Bishop or a council of examiners, which takes place at the Synod or Conference of the whole church. In the churches connected with Europeans, and in the A.M.E., however, a period of special training is required for the holding of senior offices. In the churches with an episcopal form of church government, difference in rank is reflected in the ecclesiastical robes worn by different office bearers. In the Separatist churches within the chiefdom these differences are not very conspicuous, however, since none of them have office bearers of high rank. In Pentecostal churches in which the members wear robes and uniforms, these uniforms are worn by all members, and individual differences usually do not reflect differences in status, although in one such church the use of a metal staff, as

---

[1] In one or two churches the men called deacons more or less rank as ministers.

CHURCH ORGANIZATION 71

opposed to a bundle of sticks or palm branches, is the prerogative of Preachers and their seniors.[1]

Against this general background of church organization we may now consider leadership in the churches. When speaking of leaders here, I use the term in the general sense of people who hold a responsible position in the churches, whether they are called Leaders, Ministers, Evangelists or another name. Most of the people to whom the information in the following paragraphs refers are the most senior office bearers in the chiefdom, i.e. each the most senior within his own church.

Dr. Sundkler has shown[2] that in Zulu Separatist churches the leaders—by which he means men, each of whom is the head of a whole church—can be divided into two classes, viz. the chief-type of leader and the prophet-type. Since the present study is limited to churches in one chiefdom, and does not deal with the churches, each as a whole, there has been little opportunity to study the position of leaders who are the heads of whole churches. Nevertheless, provided that this fact is kept in mind, it is not inappropriate to discuss the rural church leaders with whom this section is concerned, in terms of Sundkler's typology. We find, then, that it is not possible to formulate distinct types to which church leaders conform, and that it cannot be said that many of these leaders reveal characteristics which are part of the Tswana ideal of chieftainship. There are, however, aspects of church organization, which remind one of aspects of the political organization. One such aspect is the hierarchical ordering of church officers in Separatist and non-Separatist churches, which is comparable to the hierarchy of tribal authorities. In the St. Paul Apostolic Faith Morning Star great stress is laid on respect and submissiveness to one's seniors: members to the local leader, and the leader to his superiors. This is not confined to relations within the church, and the whole church is known for its respectful attitude to the government and tribal authorities. Occasionally, also, the idea of offices being hereditary is attached to leadership in the Separatist churches. Rev. D—— M—— of the S.A. Native Baptist Church Mission told me, for instance, that his father had left the 'Free Baptist Church' and founded the present church. M—— had joined a 'Zionist' church of which he became a minister, but after his father's death the members of the S.A. Native Baptist Church Mission asked him to come back and take his father's place as Bishop of the church. Other examples of sons taking up

[1] Uniforms and rank in connexion with the women's associations will be discussed in a later section. For a more detailed description of robes and uniforms, see ch. V.

[2] *Op. cit.*, pp. 106–109.

72   RELIGION IN A TSWANA CHIEFDOM

important positions held by their fathers are very few, however, and nowhere is the idea of inheritance as clearly expressed as in the instance quoted above. In the tribal gatherings speakers occasionally complain that the *baruti*[1] do not attend these gatherings, and that each one only wants to be a *kgosi* (chief or headman). The assistance that church members sometimes lend in household activities at the church leader's homestead, such as smearing the floors and walls, might be regarded as reflecting a chiefly status awarded to the leader. On the other hand, this usage, which is found not only in Separatist churches, is usually said to be quite voluntary, or is connected with the responsibility of the church to provide the minister's home and keep it in good repair. The custom of the L.M.S. congregation to rise for a moment when the preacher enters is comparable to the rising of the men in the tribal assembly when the chief enters.

The parallel between church organization and political organization seems to be implied in the following statement of a member of the Pentecostal Holiness Church, who was attending a service of another Pentecostal-type church where he said: 'I belong to a different "ward" (*lekgotla*), I am a "Pentecostal" (*Mopentekoste*), but even so we are all "Apostles" (*Baapostola*).'

A certain leader of a Separatist Pentecostal Church displays very clearly the characteristics of the prophet-type of leader as described by Dr. Sundkler: he is thin and highly strung, with large eyes. He joined this church as a result of a very serious illness. Many doctors and long hospital treatment could not cure him, but he was eventually cured by a minister of this church. Before his recovery, however, his spirit 'was taken'; it 'left him' from eleven o'clock in the morning till after seven that night, and while in this condition, he 'saw' that this minister would come to him. He cured him with water: he 'prayed for' the water and the patient had to drink it. After this experience he joined the minister's church, of which he is now himself a leader. He is now known as a healer, divines with the use of the Bible and claims that he receives visions and auditory revelations, but it is rumoured that he also throws the dice like a Tswana doctor. He is the only church leader who is seen going about with clothes adorned with crosses and other signs, and carrying a staff or flag, in the everyday course of events. Others are seen with these only when engaged in church activities. One or two other leaders of churches of the same type also possess some of these characteristics, but most church leaders do not strike one as unusual personalities. It may be that

---

[1] Officially the word for ministers, but in practice used for a wide range of church officers, from Bishops down to Evangelists.

CHURCH ORGANIZATION

some of the earlier prophets described in the previous chapter were unusual types. It is significant that the prophetess Botlhale received her call in connexion with a similar crisis.

Crises such as the one experienced by the leader described above are not confined to leaders of one particular type of church, but also figure in the life histories of leaders belonging to churches of group 'A' and 'B' which are connected with Europeans. The Evangelist of the S.D.A., a serious and honest man, gave the following account of how he joined this church. (He was a member of the Anglican Church before.) During a serious illness he had a vision which he believed was shown to him by God. He was shown the buildings of the different churches in the town where he was living one after another, as if illuminated by the light of a torch. Each time, he asked whether that was the one to which he was to go, to which he heard a voice say: 'No,' but when he saw the S.D.A. church, the voice said: 'Hasten! Go, that they may pray for you in that Sabbatarian church.' An untrained evangelist of another non-Separatist church which believes in adult baptism by immersion, left the L.M.S. and joined this church as the result of dreaming, during a period of illness, of being baptized in Jordan. In the dream he was told that this would bring him recovery from his illness.

On the whole, then, characteristics which belong to the prophet-type of leader in the Zulu Zionist churches, are also occasionally encountered in the churches of the Phuduhutswana chiefdom, but some of these characteristics are found even in leaders of churches which are not Separatist and not Pentecostal. One or two individuals conform to the prophet-type of leader, but it cannot be said that the Separatist Pentecostal leaders as a group represent a distinct type. We should remember, however, that the Zulu Zionist prophet follows a pattern well known in Zulu society, viz. that revealed in the character and activities of the diviner and his or her pupils. The Zulu diviner, however, is quite different from the commonly known Tswana diviner.[1]

The life histories of church leaders show that several Separatist leaders did not belong to another church before they joined their present church, and some of them have been in these churches since childhood. The majority, however, have drifted from other churches to the one to which they now belong. Some of them have drifted from non-Separatist churches to Separatists, while others have come from one Separatist church to another, usually from churches of group 'A' to Sabbatarian and Pentecostal churches. Several have already changed

[1] This point is discussed in detail in Ch. VI.

74 RELIGION IN A TSWANA CHIEFDOM

their church connexions twice in their lives. We should note, however, that among the churches connected with Europeans, some of the
leaders have also drifted from churches of group 'A' to those of group
'B' or 'C'. The general direction of the drift between the churches as
illustrated by the histories of leaders is therefore not merely from
churches connected with Europeans to Separatist churches, but also
from churches of group 'A' to the Sabbatarian and Pentecostal
churches.[1] I have no indication of what proportion of the membership of Separatist churches is formed by those who have gone over
from churches connected with Europeans. One occasionally hears
allegations that people who are disciplined in the latter churches cross
over to Separatists and are accepted by them but I do not have the
impression that this is so very common. The local leader of the St. Paul
Apostolic Faith Morning Star, for instance, has the reputation—even
among members of mission churches—of not accepting people from
other churches as members of his church unless they have already
been estranged from their church for a considerable time. What does
perhaps happen more commonly is that people who regard themselves
as adherents of one church are eventually gathered into the fold of
another church, but this can hardly be regarded as 'sheep-stealing'.
It is said that Separatist churches as well as those connected with
Europeans accept such people.

While I was doing fieldwork there were only three African church
leaders in the chiefdom who had received special training for church
work. They were the L.M.S. Minister (Std. VI, plus seven years'
training), the Anglican Priest (Std. VI, plus four years' training), and
the A.M.E. Minister (Std. VI, plus three years). A few men have
voluntarily followed Bible courses by correspondence—one with
Wilberforce Institute and a few with the Voice of the Prophecy Bible
School.[2] Although the latter is an undertaking of the S.D.A., the
course is also followed by non-Sabbatarian Separatists. Besides the
minister of the A.M.E., a few other Separatist church leaders have had
a good school education. A minister of the Native Independent Congregational Church is an agricultural assistant who has had two years' agricultural training after Junior Certificate, while a school teacher has been
made Evangelist of this church. Among the Pentecostals we find another
agricultural assistant who is an Evangelist, and a former school teacher
who is an Overseer. Several other Separatist leaders have had schooling,

---

[1] Cf. p. 61, where other information has also illustrated the tendency toward
Sabbatarianism and Pentecostalism. This will be further discussed in Ch. VII.

[2] Mention must here also be made of an L.M.S. preachers' class once a month for
the Leaders and Deacons who form the regular corps of preachers.

CHURCH ORGANIZATION 75

the standards passed by them varying from three to six. Yet several others have picked up the ability to read and write without attending school —a few by attending lessons in the mine compounds. Three of the men who have had no school education have the status of 'minister' or 'priest' in their churches, but the others are mostly Preachers. I must point out here that three of the churches connected with Europeans have as their most senior office bearers in the chiefdom Evangelists who have had no school training. None of the men who hold the most senior office in their church in the chiefdom are completely illiterate. Quite often church members or junior office bearers may boast a higher educational qualification than their leader. In one Separatist church a highly educated Evangelist is the secretary to the minister who has had no school education. In the split in the Native Independent Congregation Church the educational qualifications of leading church officers undoubtedly play a role, the leaders of the one faction having conspicuously higher qualifications than those of the other.

The three trained church workers as well as the Pastor of the Full Gospel Church (non-Separatist), and the Bishop of the S.A. Native Baptist Church Mission (Separatist), are supposed to devote all their time to church work and to be completely dependent on the income accruing from this work. A number of other office bearers of different churches (Table IV) have some income from church work, but also have other work from which they make a living. On the whole we may say that the leaders of the Separatist churches and some of the non-Separatist churches are mostly peasant farmers or wage labourers who devote some of their time to church work.

A few of the men who devote all their time to church work receive regular salaries or stipends. Of these the L.M.S. minister is probably the best paid with a fixed salary of £80 a year, complemented by an allowance of £1 a year for every child, and contributions in kind given by church members from their crops on the Irrigation Scheme and from returns from reaping on farms. Members of the church must further collect firewood for the minister's household and do the smearing of mud floors and walls in his house, which is provided by the church. In most of the other churches the income that church leaders receive from church work is not a fixed sum but is supposed to be a proportion of the church fees collected from their flock. On the whole these rural leaders are only the collectors of the fees, which they have to pass on, all or in part, to their superior church authorities. None of them seem to be particularly wealthy, even by native standards, and they are usually not men of high genealogical rank.

76   RELIGION IN A TSWANA CHIEFDOM

The figures in Table IV illustrate that a considerable number of church members have authority to preach—about one in every nineteen in Protestant churches. It should be kept in mind, further, that in some churches ordinary members of the church are also allowed to preach at times, and in others members may also speak during the service after the text has been introduced by one or two office bearers. On the one hand this means that church members have considerable opportunity for self-assertion in church work. On the other hand a great deal of church work, both in Separatist churches, and churches connected with Europeans, is done by untrained people who are not in full-time church work. The important role of the lay element in church work is a common characteristic of the work of Protestant missions and native churches in South Africa.[1]

In part, the presence of a large number of leaders is a concomitant of the fact that local church groups are small and therefore numerous, but even in the small local church groups there are often several people who may officiate as preachers.

This trend in connexion with leadership may be related to some aspects of the traditional social structure and the social changes taking place. In traditional society the most important leaders were the chief and his advisers, the ward headmen and their advisers (and perhaps to some extent also the more successful doctors). These offices offered opportunities for leadership to a considerable number of men and were not exclusively held by members of the 'royal' lineages, since there were also 'commoner' wards which had their hereditary leaders with their own advisers. Moreover, all male members had (and have) the right to speak in tribal assemblies. However, the offices of chief and headmen were hereditary and to a considerable extent their choice of advisers was decided by the descent of the men, so that opportunities for non-hereditary leadership were restricted in traditional society. Moreover, none of the opportunities mentioned were open to women.

The scattering of the population and the decay of the old ward system have given rise to the new type of headmen's areas of which there are only eighteen at present. Judging by the number of remnants of old wards still observable at Taung there must have been a considerably larger number of wards of the old type than there are of the new type at present. This means that the opportunities for leadership have become less. Moreover, headmen nowadays all come from the ranks of the royal lineages, so that the commoners particularly have very little opportunity for exercising leadership in the sphere

[1] Sundkler, *op. cit.*, p. 135.

CHURCH ORGANIZATION 77

where almost all the available opportunities offered by traditional society were found.

The opportunities for leadership in the churches[1] now make up for the loss of such opportunities in the political and administrative sphere. Church leadership also makes up for a lack of opportunity for non-hereditary leadership which always used to exist even in traditional society, while women, who had hardly any such opportunities may now also become leaders in the churches. Opportunities for leadership in the churches are complementary to the opportunities for leadership which still exist in the sphere of tribal politics and administration. This is consistent with the fact that on the one hand none of the men holding important political positions take a keen interest in a particular church, and on the other hand church leaders do not show a very keen interest in tribal politics.

Dr. Sundkler connects the desire for leadership as expressed in Zulu Separatist churches with the colour bar in South African society.[2] No doubt the fact that the Bantu are excluded from most opportunities for political and economic leadership open to Europeans is significant in respect of leadership higher up in the hierarchy of church organization, but in the rural churches which I have investigated leadership does not seem to be strongly conditioned by this factor.

What is perhaps significant is the example of the pattern of leadership in European society. As we have seen, the predominant pattern of leadership in traditional Tswana society was that in which leadership was connected with offices which were inherited in the male line. In a patrilineal society this pattern is consistent with the whole social structure so that the absence of non-hereditary leadership did not worry anybody. However, the contact of the Bantu with non-hereditary leadership in European society, and to the important role it plays there, may have created and stimulated the ambition or desire for such leadership. Further the weakening of the principle of unilineal descent adds to the significance of this new type of leadership which exists independently of the lineage structure.

Privileges and duties of members

I do not doubt that the majority of people who join the churches, do so because they have sincerely accepted the Gospel which the Church proclaims, but this does not exclude the possibility that in joining a church, many people are also influenced by certain privileges connected with church membership. On my inquiry a woman who

[1] Here I think of all who hold office in churches as leaders or potential leaders.
[2] *Op. cit.*, p. 100.

78 RELIGION IN A TSWANA CHIEFDOM

TABLE IV.—LOCAL GROUPS, OFFICE BEARERS,

		Total member-ship	Local groups		
			Build-ings[1]	Home-steads[2]	Total
Churches connected with Europeans	Methodist	1,245	6	5	11
	L.M.S.	1,197	12	4	16
	Anglican	393	2	4	6
	Lutheran	98	1	2	3
	Bantu Baptist . . .	47	—	2	2
	D.R.C.	31	—	1	1
	S.D.A.	193	2	2	4
	Full Gospel . . .	89	—	3	3
	Pentecostal Holiness .	83	—	3	3
	Watch Tower . . .	12	—	1	1[3]
Separatist churches	Nat. Ind. Cong. . .	304	1	7	8
	A.M.E. . . .	205	—	7	7
	Afr. Lutheran . .	200	1	—	1
	S.A. Nat. Bap. C. Mis. .	183	1	2	3
	Bechuana Methodist .	122	1	3	4
	African United . .	100	2	—	2
	Eth. C. of Afr. . .	96	—	1	1
	Eth. Cath. C. in Z. .	39	1	3	4
	Afr. Catholic . .	38	—	4	4
	Eth. C. of X. by Rel. .	18	—	1	1
	Witness of X. (Sab.) .	116	—	2	2
	C. of the First Born .	97	—	2	2
	Holy C. of X. . .	18	—	2	2
	New Ap. C. in Z. .	122	—	5	5
	St. Paul Ap. F.M.S. .	120	1	—	1
	Z. Ap. C. of S.A. .	148	—	2	2
	Holy Xian Ap. C. .	71	—	1	1
	Foundation Ap. C. in J. .	40	—	1	1
	Holy Gos. C. in Z. .	33	—	1	1
	TOTAL FOR PROTESTANTS .	5,458	31	71	102
R.C.	R.C. Church . . .	4,745	6	4	10

[1] Local groups meeting in church and school buildings.

[2] Local groups meeting in homesteads, hired buildings, etc.

[3] The Watch Tower services are actually house-to-house visits, but they do meet occasionally for Bible study.

[4] Office bearers authorized to preach (i.e. excluding trained workers). The figures in this and the following two columns refer to *Bantu* office bearers and workers only.

AND ETHNIC COMPOSITION OF CHURCHES

Bantu trained workers	Office bearers authorized to preach[4]	Fully paid workers	Partly paid workers	Ethnic composition
—	33[5]	—	?	Mixed
1	app. 90	1	?[6]	Tswana
1	5	1	5	Mixed
—	6	—	—	Predominantly Tswana
—	3	—	—	Predominantly Tswana
—	2	—	—	Southern Sotho
—	9	—	1	Predominantly Tswana
—	6	1	1	Predominantly Tswana
—	7	—	1	Predominantly Tswana
—	1	—	—	Predominantly Tswana[7]
—	18	—	—	Predominantly Tswana
1	?	1	?	Mixed
—	4	—	—	Predominantly Tswana
—	3	1	—	Predominantly Tswana
—	4	—	1	Predominantly Tswana
—	2	—	—	Predominantly Tswana
—	7	—	1	Predominantly Tswana
—	3	—	1	Predominantly Tswana
—	2	—	—	Predominantly Tswana
—	1	—	1	Predominantly Tswana
—	3	—	—	Predominantly Nguni
—	14	—	—	Predominantly Nguni
—	5	—	1	Predominantly Nguni
—	7	—	2	Predominantly Tswana
—	10+?	?	?	Predominantly Tswana
—	6	—	—	S. Sotho nucleus
—	24	—	—	Predominantly Nguni
—	2	—	—	Predominantly Tswana
—	3	—	—	Predominantly Tswana
3	280+?	5+?	15+?	
—	—	—	5	Tswana

[5] This is only the number of Full Preachers. There are also a number of Preachers on Trial.

[6] A few 'Leaders' of local churches receive only a small payment.

[7] The 'Witness' who introduced the movement to Taung is a Lozi who was working at Mafeking before he was sent farther south.

80   RELIGION IN A TSWANA CHIEFDOM

joined a church when she had already been married and had had children, said that the fact that all her friends were church people had induced her to join it. She further explained that when one goes visiting, and one is not a church member, one feels lost. This not only illustrates again the importance of the church group but it also shows how church connexions tend to take the place of kinship ties. In former times, if a tribesman was away from home and found himself among another tribe, he would have sought and found hospitality with some kinsman. The kinship relation would have decided the mutual behaviour of these people and would have prevented excessive uneasiness on the part of the foreigner. To-day church membership is seen as providing one with connexions in a foreign community.

A privilege commonly associated with church membership is a decent burial. An old woman, prominent in the L.M.S., was speaking one day to a young man who came from a Christian family, and asked him why he had not yet made any move to become a full church member. In encouraging him to do so, she pointed out that a church member was sure of being properly buried, and even if he were to die in hospital away from home, if he had his church 'papers' with him, he would be buried by the church. One who had nothing with him to show his church connexions, would simply be buried by convicts. Observation also indicates that funerals of church members tend to be conducted with more ceremony than those of people who have no formal link with the church, even though the latter type of funeral is also usually conducted by a church official. Some churches have a special graveyard in which its members are buried.

Within the churches there are varying degrees of membership. In *Protestant churches of group 'A'* the initial step toward church membership is not marked by much ceremony: a person wishing to become a church member informs the minister or another church leader of his desire, and after perhaps being informally questioned, he or she is entered as a member of the class in which regular instruction is given to would-be communicants. In the L.M.S. the ability to read is a condition for admission to church membership, but persons with a disability, such as blindness or old age, are exempted from this rule. In the R.C. Church acceptance into the catechumen class is marked by a small ceremony at which the new catechumen receives a medallion which he or she wears in future. In the churches connected with Europeans (type 'A') preparatory instruction usually lasts from two to three years, but Separatist churches tend to make it shorter. Catechumens who have not been baptized in infancy, mostly receive baptism after the expiry of part of this period. After having given evidence of a

5. Minister entering baptismal pool (St. Paul Apostolic Faith Morning Star)

6. Early morning prayer meeting for rain outside the chief's *kgotla*

CHURCH ORGANIZATION

satisfactory knowledge, they are confirmed, and thereby become communicant members.

In the Sabbatarian and Pentecostal churches, baptism is the all-important step in becoming a church member. In a few of these which are Separatist churches hardly any instruction is given to new members, but in most cases at least a little is given, either before or after baptism.

Admission to full membership invariably carries with it the privilege of admission to Mass or Holy Communion, which is sometimes guarded from outsiders and non-communicants as a kind of mystery (see ch. VI). Full membership of women's associations and the wearing of the uniform connected with it (see pp. 86 ff.) is also reserved for communicant church members only. In the Pentecostal Separatist churches it is only after full admission into the church that members start carrying the sticks and wearing the robes and cords peculiar to them.

Besides the general Christian conduct which is expected of church members, there are few formal duties, the most important being the regular attendance of services and the giving of church contributions. These contributions are fixed at a certain sum per month, quarter, or year, and tickets or receipts are issued for their payment. These are kept very carefully, and sometimes placed in a member's coffin at his funeral, together with other church certificates (see ch. VI). Undoubtedly there is a tendency, not only among Roman Catholics, but also among Separatist and non-Separatist Protestants, to consider the giving of these church contributions as an important part and condition of one's salvation, and the receipts and other papers placed in the coffin before burial, have at a funeral of a female church member been spoken of as the certificates (ditšupô) of the works the deceased had done, with which she would arrive in heaven.

This attitude to church contributions is part of a general tendency to stress proper behaviour and the doing of good works, in other words, part of a general moralistic trend, which will be discussed in more detail in the last chapter.

In some churches members are expected to part with certain traditional customs. The traditional institution on which views conflict most strongly amongst the natives themselves is initiation. From the early stages of its work the L.M.S. followed a policy of strong opposition to the initiation ceremonies, and members who went to be initiated, or who sent their children to the ceremonies, or consented to their attending, have invariably been expelled from the church. If such expelled members repent and wish to be re-accepted into church

R.T.C.—7

82 RELIGION IN A TSWANA CHIEFDOM

membership, they have to remain in the catechumen class for at least
a year. The fact that to this day a considerable number of members
have to be disciplined after every performance of the tribal initiation
ceremonies, shows that the policy of opposition, after all these years,
has not been completely accepted yet. Several other churches, both
Separatist and non-Separatist, discipline members who openly have
connexions with the initiation ceremonies, while most of the churches
at least express opposition.

In several instances, however, it is evident that adherence to the
custom is condoned. A few church leaders take the view that if people
take part in the ceremonies quietly, and more or less try to keep it as
secret as possible, they may be left alone. Others hold that young
people should avoid trouble by first going to be initiated, and then
coming to join the church. I was also told by some church leaders that
although their church is opposed to the ceremonies, the members
'steal', i.e. go and attend the ceremonies but keep the church officials
in the dark about the matter.

According to the Anglican priest, who is a Xhosa-speaking Nguni, his
church allows the attendance of initiation ceremonies if they are performed 'in a Christian way', by which he meant that a priest or
preacher should be allowed to visit the boys in the camp. It must be
remembered, however, that the same secrecy is not attached to initiation among Nguni tribes which have such ceremonies, as among the
Tswana. It is doubtful whether a priest or minister would be allowed
to enter a Tswana initiation camp, most certainly not if he had not been
initiated himself. This difference between the Tswana and Nguni
ceremonies has also given rise to difference of opinion among Methodists. The Tswana church members on the whole are opposed to
initiation, but some Nguni members feel that church members should
be allowed to undergo initiation. The official attitude seems to remain
one of opposition, but attendance of the ceremonies is condoned, provided that those who attend do not give too much publicity to the
matter.

The Evangelist who is leader of the Bantu Baptist Church said
that he allowed his own children to go, and added that 'it is the law of
Christ'. Of all the Separatists only the three Sabbatarian churches
openly allow initiation, but we should remember that they are all
predominantly Nguni churches. (The S.D.A., also Sabbatarian, which
has mostly Tswana members does not allow it.)

A certain Separatist Bishop holds the view that 'Christian' usage
used to be the same as Tswana custom in respect of circumcision, but
when Christ came, 'then the Lord only discovered: the Lord cannot

CHURCH ORGANIZATION 83

be served with the flesh: He must be served with the Spirit'. That is why baptism then took the place of circumcision. References to 'the law of Moses' are commonly made in defence of the ceremonies, and in a tribal gathering a headman who suggested that the ceremonies should again be performed, clinched his argument with the words: 'Christ was circumcised.'

An interesting example of reference to Scripture is found in the Church of the First-born. Not only do they refer to Old Testament evidence as others do, but they also quote New Testament passages dealing with the issue of circumcision and other prescripts of the Mosaic law in the Primitive Church. They take the view that as in the early Church it was left to the discretion of the individual non-Jewish convert whether to be circumcised or not, so to-day also Christians may make their own choice whether to attend initiation ceremonies or not. They do not realize that the issue in the Primitive Church was of a different nature from the issue of circumcision among Bantu Christians. This clearly results from a literal application of a fragment of Scripture—the free choice to be circumcised or not—without taking into account the context in which it occurs. There are other examples of the same kind of application of Scripture. They base their opposition to native doctors on Deut. 18: 10–12, but there is no objection to going to European doctors, for, so they argue, with reference to Rom. 13: 1, one should honour those placed in authority. Opposition to the use of tobacco is based on Ezek. 8: 17, where 'put[ting] the branch to their nose' is listed as one of the abominations committed by the house of Judah. This kind of literal application of fragments of the Bible is very common among Separatists, but is not limited to them.[1]

Some churches, not only Separatists, are positively in favour of the giving of *bogadi*, but all insist that members should be married by church or civil rites as well. The L.M.S. is the only church opposing this institution, but according to the L.M.S. minister, many church members adhere to it nevertheless, although some call it merely a 'gift'. Others, again, give it secretly. According to church leaders, the opposition is based on the connexion of *bogadi* with the initiation ceremonies: if *bogadi* has not been given in respect of the marriage from which a child is born, that child has to be ritually treated, or, according to another church informant, one of the animals constituting *bogadi* is slaughtered in a ceremony which has as its purpose the preparation of the children born from the marriage for undergoing the initiation ceremonies.[2] From this explanation one may deduce that

[1] See further pp. 195 f.
[2] Cf. the rite of eating the animal of the cradle-skins, ch. II, pp. 17 f.

84 RELIGION IN A TSWANA CHIEFDOM

native Christians do not consider *bogadi* itself as undesirable, but oppose it on the grounds of its connexion with the undesirable initiation ceremonies.[1]

Since polygyny seems to be fast disappearing, it is no longer a very important issue in the churches. None of the churches allows their members to contract polygynous marriages, and all discipline them if they do so. It is rumoured, however, that one Separatist minister has allowed such cases to go undisciplined. In respect of people who are already partners in a polygynous marriage at the time of their conversion, the Separatists are more lenient than some of the other churches, and accept them as members. The practice varies in churches connected with Europeans; in one church such people may be baptized but cannot become full members, while others accept women already married to polygynists, but do not accept the men, or they require that one wife be married by church or civil rites and the others be sent away.

On the whole the churches are opposed to native doctors, and Roman Catholics and Methodists may even be censured for consulting a native doctor.[2]

In most church courts seduction and adultery are the most commonly recurring offences which have to be dealt with. In view of the frequency of pre-marital sexual relations, one Separatist church does not accept young people into full membership before they are married, 'so that they do not go wrong again after having been confirmed'. Drunkenness and beer drinking, attendance of initiation ceremonies, and the settlement of domestic disputes are also among the cases frequently heard by these courts. The following typical description of the procedure in a case of seduction of a girl, was given by an Anglican Church Steward.

The father of the girl reports the matter to the priest who summons a meeting of the congregation, at which the father of the girl and the man whom he accuses—or his father, if he is an unmarried youth—must be present. At this meeting the priest presides, assisted by the church wardens, and the father of the girl, as complainant, has to put his case before the congregation. In the ensuing discussion, the congregation has to form an opinion about the case, by questioning both parties, and individual speakers indicate their personal opinion as to who is guilty. Finally the priest gives his verdict, without a vote being taken. The matter is then referred to the European minister who supervises the district, and he decides what the punishment should be.

[1] A much more radical type of opposition is expressed in a brochure published by the L.M.S. (Jennings, 1933).

[2] On the attitude of churches to traditional techniques of healing, see further, pp. 174 ff.

CHURCH ORGANIZATION

Whether this description is accurate or not, it shows how such procedure is seen through the eyes of a church member, who evidently views it in much the same light as the hearing of a case in a chief's or headman's court.

The rules of the L.M.S. state that 'if a child is at fault and it is proved that this has been due to the negligence of the parents, the parents themselves will be considered to have been at fault'. This attitude is also taken in other churches, especially in cases of illicit sexual relations of young people, and of boys and girls attending the initiation ceremonies.

The punishment inflicted by a church court is often spoken of as 'putting (a member) backward' (go busetsa kwa morago), and in some churches, Separatist and non-Separatist, it literally implies that those disciplined may not sit in the front seats with the full members, but must sit farther back with non-communicant members or children. It further implies that the sacraments are withheld from the disciplined member for a certain period, which is either fixed beforehand, or is terminated when the leader or members feel that the period has been long enough, and the erring member is 'put on his chair' again. The periods of discipline tend to be shorter in the Separatist churches than in those connected with Europeans.

The role of women in the churches

In the churches differentiation is made between the sexes in various manners. Men and women usually sit apart in church services, and when these are held in homesteads, all available chairs and benches are occupied by the men, while the women and children sit on mats on the floor. When Holy Communion is administered in one of the Separatist Pentecostal churches, both bread and wine are first served to the men, and then to the women. In at least two Pentecostal Separatist churches a clear difference is observable between the manner of participation in church services of men and women. In one church one sees women contorting their bodies and one hears them making hissing and buzzing sounds when 'the Spirit enters them', whereas the sounds and movements made by the men are less observable. In the other church the position is just the reverse: the men shout and jump about while the women act less violently. In the latter church the men also wear a greater profusion of cords tied around their body, and carry more sticks than the women. Through the women's associations, the churches nowadays provide more opportunity for women to take part in church activities than for men. Women are also given considerable opportunity for exercising

86   RELIGION IN A TSWANA CHIEFDOM

leadership, although the more senior church offices are only open to men.

The numerical predominance of women in the membership of Bantu churches has been reported from various areas[1] in South Africa. In the Phuduhutswana chiefdom women form 72% of the total membership of all the churches (see Table V). There is hardly any difference in this respect between the Roman Catholic Church and the Protestant churches taken as a group, but there is considerable variation among the different Protestant churches. In only three churches (one Separatist Sabbatarian and two Separatist Pentecostal) men are in the majority, and in the case of the Holy Christian Apostolic Church this majority is largely, if not altogether, the result of the fact that many of the male members are men from the mine compound at Buxton. I can give no explanation for the deviation in the other two cases. A very small Separatist church of group 'A' has an equal number of male and female members. In all the other churches women are in the majority. The highest proportion of women in a single church is found in the L.M.S. where women constitute no less than 92% of the total membership.

The numerical predominance of women is more marked in churches connected with Europeans than in Separatist churches. In the Pentecostal churches (Separatist and non-Separatist) this predominance is distinctly less than in the churches of groups 'A' and 'B'. On the whole the churches of longer standing have a larger percentage of women in their ranks than the churches which have been introduced into the chiefdom more recently. If the churches are grouped in chronological order of their origin, it appears that 73% of the total membership of churches originating prior to 1933 consists of females, while they constitute only about 57% of the total membership of the churches of more recent origin.

Women's associations play an important role in church life, and through these, women are given most of their opportunities for leadership in the churches, but some such opportunities exist apart from these associations. Women may become Deacons in the L.M.S. and Class Leaders in the Methodist Church, and in several churches women often conduct services in the absence of male leaders. In churches which have Sunday Schools, women can also become Sunday School teachers. In one Separatist church of group 'A', female mem-

[1] Pondoland (Hunter, 1933); the Ciskei (Wilson, and others, Keiskammahoek Rural Survey, Vol. III, 1952); Zululand and Natal (Sundkler, *op. cit.*, p. 140); Swaziland (Kuper, 1946, p. 183); and the Bechuanaland Protectorate (Schapera, 1953, p. 38).

CHURCH ORGANIZATION 87

bers who have erred are disciplined, not by the minister and church council, but by the minister's wife and a committee of women.[1] The very fact that men form a minority among church members has also opened up opportunities for leadership to women. In the R.C. Church and the L.M.S. women have been appointed as Catechists and local Leaders respectively, in places where no suitable men were available. However, women are only admitted to the lesser offices, and are not allowed to become Evangelists or Ministers in any church. There are no female 'prophet'-leaders in any of the Penetcostal churches, although the prophetess Botlhale (see pp. 48 f.) might have been an example of this type of female leader, but it should be remembered that she did not have a regular following or church of her own.

On the whole, then, it does not appear as if the difference Dr. Sundkler found between 'Ethiopian' and 'Zionist' churches in this respect,[2] is evident in the Separatist churches in the chiefdom. The opportunities for leadership offered to women in churches of Pentecostal type do not differ essentially from those in the other churches. In Pentecostal churches which allow opportunity for public testimonies or relating of dreams on the part of the congregation, women make use of these opportunities as readily as the men do, but they do not hold more prominent positions than women do in other churches. The prophetess in Zulu Zionist churches, however, has a precedent in traditional Zulu society, namely the female diviner, who becomes a diviner by spirit possession.[3] There is no such precedent in Tswana society, and this is probably the reason why such prophetess-leaders are not found in Tswana Pentecostal churches.[4]

Attention must also be drawn to the fact that churches connected with Europeans offer women just as many opportunities for leadership as Separatist churches.

Only a few of the churches do not have women's associations, and one or two of these were planning to form local branches of such associations at the time I left the field. In the L.M.S. there is no association including a large number of women members, but there is a small group of women forming what may be termed an order or guild of 'Leading Women'. In view of the very prominent position of these women in the L.M.S., and in view of the fact that this order or guild

[1] It is not unusual for a member of the women's association who has been disciplined by the church council to be taken to task by the association also.

[2] *Op. cit.*, pp. 141–144.

[3] *Op. cit.*, pp. 313–316. Cf. further pp. 203 ff.

[4] Among the prophets described and referred to by Katesa Schlosser in her survey of prophets and prophet-movements in Africa there are not many women. (Schlosser, *op. cit.*)

88 RELIGION IN A TSWANA CHIEFDOM

differs somewhat from the women's associations in most of the other churches, we may pay special attention to it first.

Seen within the wider framework of the L.M.S., the Leading Women form an unofficial order for which no provision has been made in church laws. It is largely a local development and is found in only a few of the L.M.S. churches outside the Taung mission district. Probably the order originated in 1915, when it was reported in the annual station report that at the head station (Taung) eight women 'who took a leading part in church activities' had been formed into 'a sort of guild of deaconesses' during the year. Some of them had gone out, two by two, into neighbouring villages to preach and teach among the women. They had agreed to abstain from the use of alcoholic drinks. Such Deaconesses were later appointed at other places as well.

At present the official position in the L.M.S. is that each local church has a number of elected Deacons, some of whom may be women. All Deacons are supposed to be elected for three years at a time. In practice we find that some of the female Deacons have at some time or other been elected as 'Leading Women'. These Leading Women remain part of the body of Deacons, but nevertheless form an order of their own, and are regarded as superior in status to other female Deacons. They hold the position of Leading Women—and consequently also of Deacons—for life, unless they are deposed for a breach of conduct.

On the local church level the Leading Women are perhaps more important as individuals, and not so much as a group, but on the sub-district and district level they figure very distinctly as a group. During the monthly meeting of the sub-district at Taung they sit together in church, and usually eat together at the minister's homestead. At the beginning and middle of the year, when the district meetings of the church are held, the Leading Women from the whole district meet separately at times and place their own resolutions before the district meeting of the whole church. The order moreover has certain funds of its own.

The distinction between Leading Women and other Deacons is further stressed by the fact that the ordination in office is accompanied by the putting on of the cape which completes their uniform. Although the ordinary formula for the ordination of Deacons is read—which includes instruction about their duties—all the Leading Women of the district meet separately after the service and in this closed circle the novices are instructed about their duties and conduct. When a new Leading Woman has to be elected, the Leading Women in the

CHURCH ORGANIZATION 89

local church nominate two candidates of whom the local congregation elects one.

There are no formal laws or written constitution to which the order is bound and it is difficult to know how the order is organized and exactly what their relation is to the rest of the church. It seems as if these Leading Women more or less rule the church, regulating church affairs according to their own ideas, and they show dislike of attempts on the part of senior church officials to examine their activities and to probe their internal and external relations.

The minister's wife *ipso facto* presides over the Leading Women of the sub-district, and the wife of the leader of the local church holds the leading position among the members of the order in that church. Besides the special position held by the wives of church officials, the Leading Women also have a system of rank based partly on the length of time each member has served in the order, and partly on age. It decides the order in which they take turns to preach at the various services for which they are held responsible. Outsiders do not pay particular attention to it, but amongst themselves the women are particular about the recognition of their individual status.

The order is prominent in all church activities. Formally the status of Leading Women is lower than that of the local church leader or the minister but these men would have little co-operation if they were not to act in accordance with the views of the Leading Women. This is the more so in the case of the minister, since they especially are the people who keep an eye on the minister's household to see that he is not lacking in anything which it is the church's responsibility to provide. Members of the order are prominent in the services held every Monday and Friday afternoon, at which the women Deacons act as preachers. They take turns, a few at a time, in assisting the minister, together with a few male Deacons, in administering communion, and at baptism two members of the order line up with the parents or with the adults who receive baptism, as representatives of the congregation. At the funeral of a female church member these women conduct the first part of the service inside the house or hut where the corpse has been kept, nobody else being inside with them. They bring out the coffin and deposit it outside the hut, where a male Leader or Deacon conducts the rest of the service before the coffin is carried to the grave, men now acting as bearers. Such evangelistic campaigns as are held by the church are the responsibility of the order. I was told that the men hold that they lack the gift for this kind of work.

Unlike the other Deacons, the Leading Women have a particular uniform. Special significance is attached to the cape which completes

90   RELIGION IN A TSWANA CHIEFDOM

it. A Leading Woman may only wear her cape if she is accompanied by another member of the order, or by a member of the church, and it is said that when two walk together and then part, the capes are promptly removed. When a Leading Woman is deposed, someone is sent 'to take her blanket' (*go tsaya kobô*), i.e. to take back her cape, but if she dies in office, the cape is placed in her coffin along with other articles relating to her church membership. (See further ch. VI.) The cape may not be worn during a meal.

Particular significance is attached to these uniforms, and in Tswana the Leading Women are called Women of the Uniform (*Basadi ba Seaparô*). When asked about the purpose of the uniform, one woman explained that it was to remind them of their duties. There is no doubt that social prestige is attached to wearing it, and that the members of the order are proud of it. Some of the rules and customs connected with the wearing of the uniform suggest some magical association connected with it, but I was not able to obtain further evidence to verify this impression. However, the danger of an exaggerated value being attached to the uniform was recognized by the African minister in his address to new members of the order, when he aptly compared the uniform to a matchbox which does not serve its real purpose if there are no matches inside.[1]

Women's associations are found in all types of churches. In the other churches these associations are less exclusive than the order of Leading Women of the L.M.S., and also less closely connected with the ordinary church offices. In some churches all the women who are communicant members of the church, are taken to be members of the association, while others confine membership of the association to married women only. If all female communicants are not automatically considered members of the association, they may at least join it if they wish to, but then they are usually first subjected to a period of trial and to an examination of their conduct and their Scripture knowledge before being admitted to full membership. Members of the association then have a somewhat higher status than women who are ordinary communicants. Mostly the members are older women, and in some churches younger women are definitely not admitted to membership, even if they are married. The R.C. Church has a separate association for the younger married women (even apart from a third one for

[1] The wearing of special regalia as a sign of office does not seem to have been very important in the traditional culture of the Tlhaping. At his investiture the chief wore certain insignia—Dr. Language says that in modern times he is robed in a leopard-skin—but in the ordinary course of events he did not wear these. (Language, 1941, pp. 119 ff. Cf. Schapera, 1938, pp. 59–60.) Doctors also wore special regalia in former times. (Cf. above, p. 33 n., and Brown, 1926, p. 127.)

CHURCH ORGANIZATION 91

the unmarried girls). The association is usually presided over by the wife of the senior church official, and the ranking of the wives of officials in accordance with the status of their husbands is evident in several of the churches, both Separatist and non-Separatist.[1]

Although these associations play a very important role in most churches, they do not dominate the churches to the same extent that the Leading Women do in the L.M.S. Further, although the members of an association are group-conscious and co-operate in various manners, the social cleavage between the association and the rest of the church is also not accentuated as strongly as in the L.M.S. These associations usually form the active force in the churches and are generally recognized as a great support to the church leaders. They help to organize church functions and collections, often make a separate contribution of their own towards some cause, and are held responsible when refreshments have to be served. They usually have their own funds to which they contribute apart from the ordinary church contributions. In most churches there is a weekly women's prayer meeting (almost always on Thursday afternoons), which is either attended exclusively by members of the association, or organized by them. The members are therefore often referred to as Prayer-women (*Basadi ba Merapêlô*). At these meetings the women also instruct each other in the Bible and about family relations, and discuss what business there may be on hand.

Nearly all the associations have uniforms for their members, which are worn for important festivals and gatherings of the association or of the whole church. They are often worn for funerals, especially those of prominent church members. The uniforms usually consist of a combination of a few garments of different colours, black, white, and red recurring most commonly. The black skirt, red jacket, white collar, and white hat of the Methodist women is well known. The women of the Ethiopian Catholic Church, e.g., wear a black skirt, blue jacket, white collar, and a leopard-skin cap. The women's association of one of the Pentecostal Separatist churches has a somewhat more elaborate uniform. It consists of a green skirt, a white blouse, and a white hat with a green star on it, and with it they wear a green cord around the waist and a band over each shoulder, one white and one green. This uniform is specifically worn in connexion with the women's association of this church, and is something apart from the robes and other garments worn by all the members of the church, as is the custom in some of the Pentecostal Separatist churches.

---

[1] Dr. Sundkler mentions this as a particular tendency in Separatist churches of the Ethiopian type. (*Op. cit.*, pp. 138, 141–142.)

92 RELIGION IN A TSWANA CHIEFDOM

Of his own accord a retired minister of the A.M.E. gave the following explanation of the colours of the uniform worn by the women of his church. The black spots of the leopard-skin cap, he said, show 'that we are black people; the black clothes show that this was a black country at first; and the white collar means that now we have come into the light'. However, I do not think this was more than his own personal interpretation, and it is doubtful whether such symbolical significance is commonly attached to the colours of the uniform.

In some churches there are girls' associations also, which are usually affiliated, or at least closely connected, with the women's associations. The male members of the churches are not organized in this way. Very few churches have any special men's or boys' associations, but often the church council, which usually consists of men only, is viewed as the men's parallel of the women's association. In the Native Independent Congregational Church men may become members of the women's association, but it must always be presided over by the minister's wife.

Before discussing possible reasons for the numerical preponderance of women and their general importance in church affairs, I wish to stress that I do not regard conversion as a process merely determined by social factors, but social factors often play a role and may make an individual receptive or unreceptive of an appeal for conversion. It is in this sense that I wish to discuss several factors which seem to be involved in the situation under discussion.

Labour migration, of course, causes a certain disproportion between the sexes in respect of the whole population in the reserve, but the degree of disproportion is much larger in the churches than in the population as a whole. Labour migration, however, is further of importance in that it exposes the men—more than the women, because the women migrate less—to the secularizing influences of the towns and industrial centres. On the other hand, as we have seen, it sometimes brings men in contact with the churches. We therefore have to find other explanations for the disproportion.

With reference to the Zulu, Dr. Sundkler ascribes the greater response of women to the message of the church to the fact that Christian ideals are not in accordance with the traditional Zulu ideal of manliness according to which the man is essentially a warrior. Moreover, the issue over polygyny is a stumbling block to many men, and further the herding of cattle, which is the work of boys, hinders them from going to Christian schools.[1] These factors were probably valid, at least to some extent, for the Tlhaping in the past,

[1] *Op. cit.*, p. 140.

CHURCH ORGANIZATION

but can hardly be held to be valid at present. If the Tlhaping male had a warrior-like attitude and bearing in the past, to-day he is a labourer and not a soldier, and he seldom has an imposing physique. Further the number of polygynists is small and there cannot be many who are to-day prevented by polygyny from joining the church. In Taung boys nowadays perform very little herding, probably because the reserve is not very extensive, and has for some time past been fenced in, so that herding has not been a hindrance to the younger generation of men and boys to attend schools. In spite of this, girls still constitute more than 60% of the children attending school in the chiefdom. We may accept, however, that in earlier stages of missionary and church activity among the Tlhaping, the traditional ideals of manhood, polygyny, and herding did indeed constitute stumbling blocks which prevented the men from joining the churches.

The predominance of women in Swazi churches has been explained by Dr. Hilda Kuper partly by reference to the inferior position of women in conservative Swazi society. Christianity has enhanced the position of women in various ways and has therefore had more attraction for them than for men.[1] This may be regarded as true of the Tlhaping as well, but this factor also is less important at present than in the past, since many other influences have come to join forces with the missions for the emancipation of women, and other avenues have opened up, providing women with opportunities for self-expression and for the widening of their sphere of activities. Particular mention may be made of the fact that they can now also go out as wage labourers and can be trained for and enter specialized occupations such as teaching and nursing. In tribal politics and jurisdiction they are, however, still subject to certain traditional discriminations.[2]

I think in Taung the initiation ceremonies constitute an important factor directly responsible for holding men back from joining the churches. Mere attachment to the ceremonies, of course, may also prevent some women from becoming full church members, but it is the manner in which the influential men of the chiefdom are connected with the ceremonies that is of significance to the problem. In organizing the ceremonies, the men take the initiative, and the girls' ceremonies only take place after the boys have been initiated. The men have to remind the chief of his duty to organize the ceremonies, and the ceremonies cannot take place without the chief's consent, while he also fixes the opening date. The headmen have to co-operate closely in organizing them. Further, the performance of rain magic,

---

[1] 1946, pp. 183–184.   [2] Cf. Schapera, 1953, pp. 37–8.

94 RELIGION IN A TSWANA CHIEFDOM

also plays a role, since the chief and headmen are expected to take the initiative in its performance (see p. 27 f.).

This means that it is difficult for the politically influential men to become church members. If they join the church, they can no longer fulfil the duties which a considerable proportion of their followers still expects of them. It is not strange, therefore, that neither the chief, nor any of his important advisers are church members, while only one of the headmen formally belongs to a church. Presumably the example of such leading men influences many others, and confirms the opinion that the churches are the concern of the women rather than of the men.

The prominent position that women have been given in churches has probably also become a deterrent to men. This is particularly obvious in the L.M.S. where the dominating position of the Leading Women cannot but discourage men who might wish to join the church. Moreover, since evangelistic campaigns are conducted by these L.M.S. women, it is likely that the appeal would carry less weight with men than with women. It appears, therefore, that to a large extent the predominance of women in the churches is a tendency inherited from earlier times. Because of the obstacles in the way of the men, and the enhancement of the position of the women through the churches, more women joined than men so that the church in time came to be regarded as a matter for the women rather than for the men. Although some of the actual hindrances in the way of the men have disappeared, the attitude which arose as a result of those hindrances, persists. This is consistent with the fact mentioned above, that the proportion of women in the churches introduced into the chiefdom in later years is not as large as in the older churches. If men have historical prejudice against the churches, it is to be understood that the prejudice would be stronger against the older churches in connexion with which the prejudice arose, than against the churches which have been introduced later. This would also explain why the proportion of male members is largest in Sabbatarian and Pentecostal Separatist churches, since they are all of more recent origin.

In any case there seems to be little doubt that the predominance of women in the churches is connected with certain aspects of the traditional background of the Tlhaping. Men were formerly less responsive to the appeal of the churches on account of their traditional role as warriors and herders (as boys) and because of polygyny. The part they play in connexion with the tribal initiation ceremonies and rain magic still seems to act as a deterrent. On the other hand, the women responded more readily because the church offered them a

CHURCH ORGANIZATION

position and opportunities which were denied them in traditional society and which compensate for traditional forms of discrimination to which they are still subject.

Church property and finance

By far the most imposing church building in the chiefdom is that of the R.C. Mission at Taung, which compares favourably with many churches of European congregations in the country. It is a neatly plastered cruciform building, with tower, clock, and bells complete. On the premises are a cross with an image of the crucified Christ, and an artificial 'grotto' holding an image of the Blessed Virgin. The interior of the church, which seats about five or six hundred people, is heavily decorated with flowery patterns in various colours, and the altar is not lacking in finery. In the same enclosure as the church there are also the cemetery, quarters for the priests and lay brothers, the school, hostel, and the building for the industrial department. Opposite are the modern hospital and African nurses' home. The latest addition to the complex is a sisters' home, which was nearing completion when I left the field. The Mission has its own electric plant.

It is a far cry from this large complex to the small mud-walled structures which serve as the places of worship of some of the Separatist churches. Let us take the little building of the African Catholic Church near to the Catechist's homestead. It is a rectangular building, about twenty by eight feet, with a flat iron roof and mud walls plastered on the outside in the customary manner. There is one door, and one or two small windows, which have only wooden blinds and no glass. It was originally built as a dwelling, but is now used only for church purposes. Inside is a table at one end, with some books and writing material on it, and an advertisement calendar hanging above it. Beside the table are two chairs for the church leaders, while two benches provide seating for about eight members of the congregation. The others sit on skin mats. In front of the table lies a black and white goat skin for the Preacher and Catechist to kneel on. The walls are a mud-brown colour below and painted light blue higher up; quaint figures, apparently representing birds, form a border half-way up.

A few Separatist buildings are somewhat more imposing than this one. The buildings of Protestant missions are on the whole larger and better built than those of the Separatists, but none of them even approximate to the buildings of the R.C. Mission at Taung. Even the R.C. buildings at their outstations are better than any of the others. The L.M.S. church at Taung is a sturdy cruciform stone-walled building, without a tower. It has a mud floor, but there is a wooden plat-

TABLE V.—CHURCH MEMBERSHIP—

	Churches connected with Europeans								
	GROUP	Name of church	Date of origin	Men	Women No.	Women % of Total	Total		Name of church
PROTESTANT	A	Methodist .	pre-1923	393	852	68	1,245		Nat. Ind. Cong. .
		L.M.S. . .	1830–40	97	1,100	92	1,197		A.M.E. . .
		Anglican .	1880–90?	128	265	67	393		Afr. Lutheran .
		Lutheran .	±1910	25	73	75	98		S.A. Nat. Bap. C. M.
		Bantu Bapt. .	1939	20	27	57	47		Bechuana Meth. .
		D.R.C. . .	1951	14	17	55	31		Afr. United . .
									Eth. C. of Afr. .
									Eth. Cath. C. in Z.
									Afr. Cath. . .
									Eth. C. of X. by Rel.
		Total for Group 'A'		677	2,334	78	3,011		
	B	S.D.A. . .	pre-1920	33	160	83	193		Witness of X. (Sab.)
									Ch. of the 1st-born
									Holy C. of X. .
		Total for Group 'B'		33	160	83	193		
	C	Full Gospel .	1947	33	56	63	89		New Ap. C. in Z. .
		Pentecostal .	1918	32	51	61	83		St. P. Ap. F.M.S. .
									Z. Ap. C. of S.A. .
									Holy Xian Ap. C. .
									Found. Ap. C. in J.
									Holy Gospel C. in Z.
		Total for Group 'C'		65	107	62	172		
		Watch Tower	1951	—	—	—	—[1]		
		Total for Protestants		755	2,601	77	3,376		
R.C.		R.C. Church .	1895	1,343	3,402	72	4,745		
		Total for all churches		2,118	6,003	74	8,121		

[1] The Watch Tower has only twelve members, the relation of the sexes is uncertain.

[2] There are three separate sections of this church in the chiefdom; for one small section I could not obtain information on the numerical relation of the sexes.

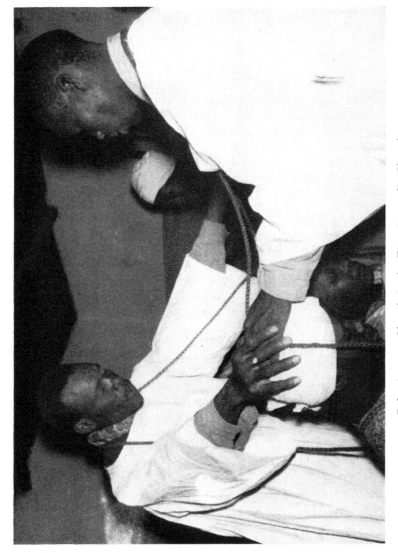

7. Laying-on of hands in the Zion Apostolic Church

8. Making list of donations at funeral night watch

CHURCH ORGANIZATION

Numerical Relation of the Sexes

	Separatist churches				All churches					
Date of origin	Men	Women		Total	Men	Women		Total (for which sex is known)	Sex un-known	Final total
		No.	% of total			No.	% of total			
1885 or '93	87	217	71	304						
1904–06	57	148	72	205						
1925	88	112	56	200						
pre-1947?	63	120	66	183						
pre-1914	29	93	76	122						
1919	34	66	66	100						
1943	23	73	76	96						
1944	6	33	85	39						
1947	15	23	61	38						
1951	9	9	50	18						
	411	894	69	1,305	1,088	3,228	75	4,316	—	4,316
1941	84	32	28	116						
1941	40	57	59	97						
1950	7	11	61	18						
	131	100	43	231	164	260	61	424	—	424
1950	58	51	47	109[2]					13[2]	
1944	—	—	—	—[3]					120	
1932	62	86	58	148						
1947	44	27	38	71						
±1949	13	27	68	40						
1945	12	21	64	33						
	189	212	53	401	254	319	56	573	133	706
	—	—	—	—	—	—	—	—	12	12
	731	1,206	62	1,937	1,506	3,807	72	5,313	145	5,458
	—	—	—	—	1,343	3,402	72	4,745	—	4,745
	731	1,206	62	1,937	2,849	7,209	72	10,058	145	10,203

[3] No particulars available; judging by attendance at services, the women form 60–65% of the members.

98 RELIGION IN A TSWANA CHIEFDOM

form in the chancel, on which there is a lectern and communion table, besides a few benches. This church makes a cold and bare impression. Other buildings of the L.M.S. at its head station are the old church, now serving as school, and the dwellings of the missionary and the African minister. The L.M.S., however, has more buildings at out-stations than any of the other churches. Only seven of the Separatist churches have special church buildings, while two more were erecting buildings at the time I was in the field. A few mission churches do not have any buildings in the chiefdom either. (See Table IV.)

The other side of the picture is that the Roman Catholic buildings are not seen by the members as being their very own to the same extent as the other churches, since they are not as directly responsible for them. In most Protestant churches the Bantu members are now altogether responsible for the building of new churches and the repair of old ones. A little Separatist church building may be simple and crookedly built but it is planned, built, and paid for by the people themselves.

The question of ownership of church buildings is not always clear, even in the case of one or two mission churches. In the constitutions of a few Separatist churches it is explicitly stated that buildings must be registered in the name of the church. One of these is the Holy Church of Christ which was formed as the result of secession from the Church of Christ, following a dispute about church property and funds. In the latter church all property is registered in the name of the Bishop, who is head of the whole church, and all funds are controlled by him. This is of more than usual importance, since various com-mercial activities such as farming, dairying, and trading are carried on in connexion with the church. When eventually some of the Bishop's followers tried to induce him to have the property registered in the name of the church, he was unwilling to do so, and the malcon-tents decided to form their own church. (See p. 55.)

The tribal authorities are in a dilemma about granting building sites to Separatist churches. Officially they have no power to grant sites for churches; these are supposed to be granted by the Government only, although the tribal authorities may make recommendations. The Government, however, only allows grants to churches which they officially recognize, and very few Separatist churches have been awarded such recognition.[1] Moreover, government officials do not favour the practice of conducting church services in homesteads. There are Separatist churches to which the tribal authorities would readily grant permission to build, and to others they have in fact

[1] See Sundkler, *op. cit.*, pp. 74–79.

CHURCH ORGANIZATION 99

given such permission (mostly for small buildings which are not very durable), but they are aware of the fact that they do not have the right to do so. The chief's chief councillor explicitly expressed their dilemma, after pointing out that only the Government could grant sites, by appealing to a tribal gathering with the words: 'Tell us what we should do; the church is a thing to be respected. . . .'

In practice none of the sites on which Separatist churches stand are registered with the Government, and this even appears to be the case with a few buildings of churches connected with Europeans. These churches have merely been erected with the consent of the local headman concerned, sometimes even without reference to the chief. As far as I know, no disputes about church property have ever come before the tribal authorities, but the men in authority seem to hold diverse views about the ownership of such church buildings which are not officially registered. One or two of the headmen who have such buildings in their areas, take the view that the buildings belong to the congregation and not to an individual. The chief's court official, however, when I confronted him with the case of a certain small church building which is part of the complex forming the leader's homestead, held that the leader is the owner of the building.

The sources from which church funds are derived are much the same as in Zulu churches.[1] The regular contributions required from members often consist of an annual subscription, and a quarterly contribution, usually given at the time of communion. Some people regard this fee as a payment for receiving communion. In a number of churches, mostly Separatist, a further monthly contribution is expected as 'Minister's support', the most common amount being 1s. per member per month. The total for these different contributions amounts to anything from 9s. to 15s. 6d. per member a year in Protestant non-Separatist churches, and from 6s. 6d. to 26s. in Separatist churches. On the whole they are considerably higher in the Separatist churches. In the Roman Catholic Church the only regular contribution expected of a member amounts to 4s. a year. Women are often expected to contribute less than men, and class members (noncommunicant members) less than full members (communicants). In several churches gifts in kind are given, often as an alternative to the cash contribution for the Minister's support.

A few Sabbatarian and Pentecostal churches (Separatist and nonSeparatist) expect their members to give a tithe from their income, in cash or in kind, but some of these have nevertheless fixed a minimum cash contribution as alternative. Excepting at concerts and

[1] Sundkler, *op. cit.*, p. 157–158.

100 RELIGION IN A TSWANA CHIEFDOM

drives (see below) where something of an exhibition is made of generosity, the idea of making voluntary contributions according to one's means is conspicuously lacking in all types of churches. It is true that a few churches have Sunday collections to which contributions are voluntary, and many special collections are made, e.g. for new buildings, contributions to functions of other churches, or for preparations for organizing a concert, bazaar, or other church function, but the contributions to Sunday collections are usually very small, and there is a general tendency to fix the amount to be contributed by every church member or household to special collections.[1] Contributing toward church work therefore tends to be considered as a duty concerned with one's salvation, rather than a voluntary expression of thanksgiving (cf. above, p. 81). This also applies to payments made in connexion with baptism and confirmation.

Mission policy has probably fostered this idea. In trying to develop the idea of regular and systematic contribution towards church work, many missions fixed amounts which members were expected to contribute. Apparently it was seldom understood that this was only a minimum and that those who had the means should contribute more.

It is difficult to say how faithful members are in paying their contributions in the different churches, but it seems that sometimes a considerable proportion of the members remains in default.

In mission churches a large portion of these regular contributions goes into central church funds, from which most of the trained church workers are paid. In the Separatist churches it is difficult to find out exactly how these funds are used. The most common explanation is that part of it, if not all, goes 'to pay the ministers', and into central funds. Since few of the Separatist church leaders in the chiefdom have the status of ministers, most of the money must be passed on to senior church authorities, and usually the leaders in the reserve know very little about the manner in which these funds are distributed. In the case of the Native Independent Congregational Church, however, it is known that such central funds have been used to send a member of the church to follow an Evangelists' course in Basutoland. A few churches also use part of the regular contributions for charity in respect of their own members and to help cover the expenses of funerals of church members or their children. A few churches have burial funds of which membership is voluntary.

Besides the special collections already mentioned, others may be made to cover the expenses of train tickets and food for preachers,

---

[1] The same procedure is followed by the tribal authorities when collecting money for tribal undertakings, such as the building of a new tribal office.

CHURCH ORGANIZATION 101

and for delegates to conferences and conventions. Of special importance are the collections held in connexion with the laying of corner stones or the consecration of church buildings. Contributions are then usually received not only from many different congregations of the same church, but also from other churches, as well as from interested persons, such as the headmen and storekeepers (also Europeans) of the neighbourhood. Such contributions are either formally handed over or are at least announced in public at the ceremony, and each announcement may be met with applause on the part of those present. The small Holy Church of Christ collected about £13 14s. in this manner at the laying of the corner-stone of its new church. The consecration of the new Lutheran church at Mocwedin was a much larger ceremony and the collection amounted to £64 1s. 3d. It included donations from Lutheran congregations as far afield as Bloemfontein, as well as a substantial contribution of £20 19s. 6d. collected by the local headman in his *kgotla*. Apart from collections, members sometimes give their labour towards building or repairing a church building.

Concerts for church funds usually take the form of an auction.[1] Usually one or more school choirs first deliver a programme, after which the bidding starts, mostly for items already rendered. Pentecostal Separatists sometimes organize a whole night service to which they invite other churches. The visitors are expected to bring a contribution to the collection which is held in the course of the night. Such a service I attended was held for the 'opening' of a new house—a small flat-roofed building which was a new addition to the Preacher's homestead and was used for household purposes, but which often served as a meeting place for his congregation.

The service started at about 9.15 p.m. and consisted of the usual singing, praying, scripture reading, preaching, and testimonies with all the interruptions resulting from the diverse manners in which members are moved by the Spirit. At about midnight a collection was held, but although the small room (hardly twelve feet square) was packed with about forty people, no more than 4/11¾ could be raised. A little later tough dough cakes and tea were served to all present, after which devotions were resumed. At 3 a.m., I returned home, utterly exhausted from all I had experienced, but my Pentecostal friends kept on until dawn. In this case the collection was made for the Preacher's personal benefit.

About six churches have formed an association called *Masincedane* (Xhosa: let us help each other)—the leading spirit is a Xhosa-speaking Separatist minister—for the purpose of jointly collecting funds, by means of regular all-night drives. Each member-church

[1] See Sundkler, *op. cit.*, p. 158, and Monica Wilson and others, *op. cit.*, p. 139.

102   RELIGION IN A TSWANA CHIEFDOM

takes turns to organize such a drive for its funds according to rules
drawn up by a representative committee, which also regulates the
dates of the drives and the order in which the churches take their
turns. The method of collecting money is organized on a competitive
basis, competition taking place between the organizing church which
acts as host, and each of the other member-churches. When one church
gives a drive, each visiting church brings a contribution of 10s., called
their 'bag' (*kgetsi*). When the members of a church produce their bag
they 'close' it by bringing further contributions. The hosts must then
'open' the bag by bringing contributions which exceed those put down
to close it. Sometimes the women's association of a visiting church
bring their own separate bag—which may consist of any amount. All
the proceeds from the different contributions go to the church which
acts as host.

The drive I attended was announced to start at 8 p.m., but it did not
actually start till after 9.30. Those present had already started singing hymns
beforehand, and several groups had arrived singing. Eventually Rev.
A——, the minister of the hosts (whom we shall call Church H) took his
place at the table on the low platform, wearing a clerical collar and a black
frock coat, and carrying a brief case. At his side was Rev. K—— of one of
the other member-churches, who was to assist him in receiving and counting
the money. Rev. A—— opened the meeting with a few words and announced
a hymn, after which Rev. K—— said a prayer, which was followed by a
chant by the congregation. While another hymn was being sung, the members of church X entered. In keeping with the rules of the association the
latecomers were promptly called upon to pay a fine of 2/6, which went into
the proceeds of the drive. This was done in good spirit, to the delight of the
audience. The roll of the different member-churches was called; two of the
six churches were absent.

While singing a hymn the members of church X now lined up and slowly
approached the table on the platform, moving with short steps and rhythmical movements of the arms and body. The leader placed their 'bag' (a
tobacco pouch containing their contribution) on the table, and started slapping a few pennies on the table one-by-one. Each member in the line
followed suit with his pennies, slapping them down to the rhythm of the
music, and each again lined up at the end of the line to produce a second
lot of pennies. When the line had passed the table several times, they stopped
and returned to their seats. The sum with which the bag had been closed
(about 12/–) was announced, and the hosts were called on to come and open
it. Following the same procedure, they contributed 13/8¼ to open the bag,
whereupon Church X again came to close it. When they had finished, Rev.
A—— announced: 'Those from Manokwane [referring to church X] say:
"Hey, Ethiopians [referring to the hosts]! One pound three and a penny!" '
Church H now finally opened the bag with £1.4.4. Now the women of Church
X came with their 'bag' and closed it with 11/–, and after it was opened and
closed twice in succession, Church H finally opened it with £1. 5. 6. The

CHURCH ORGANIZATION 103

announcement that the bag contained 7/– was met with the clapping of hands. It was now five minutes to midnight and only one church had completed its round! Church Y was now called upon to produce their bag but there was some delay and Rev. A—— announced that they were still 'digging for diamonds' and were fetching their bag, so Church Z was asked to come forward. They took part with less gusto and only opened their bag once. Church Y now repeated the same long process as Church X.

All this lasted till after 3 a.m., and all the while there was singing, the same hymn sometimes being repeated over and over, the singing only stopping when the announcements were made. Later some of the children turned over to sleep on the floor, and grown-ups would take short naps just as they were sitting, only to wake up and join in the activities refreshed. Although the same thing was repeated over and over the participants showed no signs of becoming bored. Above the singing could be heard laughter and shouts of enjoyment as people slapped down their pennies. Rev. K—— would occasionally encourage them with shouts of 'Beat it!', or would step about to the rhythm of the music, uttering shouts of enthusiasm. When a bag from the women was being opened (the contents being unknown), there was joking about the 'calf' which they had brought and that it was still unknown whether it was a heifer or a bull-calf. Sometimes when an uneven sum was announced, appeals were made to make it even, several people responding, and the total would eventually be uneven all the same. Once an old man put down a half-penny 'to ask the time', and he was formally informed what time it was. There was a pleasant spirit of competition, but all the same members of other churches often joined the ranks of those who were closing or opening the bag to help them, the hosts at times even joining the ranks of their 'opponents'. A few individuals returned to the table over and over again, with a few more pennies every time.

After the hosts had finally brought their own bag and opened it with the last 'drops', the total proceeds of the drive were announced to be £13. 16. 3. Ginger beer and cake were now served. It was 3.30 a.m. when I had to take my leave, but in accordance with the rules of *Masincedane*, refreshments were followed by devotions in which members of the audience were given the opportunity to deliver short sermons. This service, I was told, lasted till sunrise.

Such a drive illustrates the importance of the church group as a social group. The *Masincedane* drive is in the first place an activity to collect funds for church work, contains purely devotional elements, but also has high entertainment value, and through the strong competitive element partakes very much of the character of a game. Moreover, it offers the opportunity to the individual of gaining prestige through his economic resources. Even the outsider who does not belong to one of the member-churches, attends the drive and may join the rank and through his liberal contributions earn the appreciation especially of the hosts. The competitive element strengthens the bonds between members of the same church group, and the members of the

104   RELIGION IN A TSWANA CHIEFDOM

host-church are drawn closer together by their very role of hosts, while their activities and importance as hosts offer an opportunity for public expression and increase their self-esteem. Ample opportunity is also offered for new social contacts outside one's own church group, and the serving of refreshments heightens the social character of the proceedings. The minister of the host-church acts here, not so much as the leader of his flock, but as a social leader for a wider group representative of the whole neighbourhood.

A certain Separatist preacher said to me that the difference between his own church and the other churches is that those others are 'under the Government'. By this, it subsequently appeared, he meant that their ministers were paid by the Government, and he was reluctant to accept my explanation that in this country no ministers receive stipends from the Government. Foremost in this man's mind were probably the churches connected with Europeans. Apart from his statement I encountered no further evidence of suspicion about what becomes of church funds in these churches. In the L.M.S. churches, which are financially independent in the Taung district, the African leaders and the lay element have an ample share in controlling the funds contributed by the members. A certain sum is annually paid into a central fund from which the ministers are paid, but most of the money contributed from the churches in the district is spent in con-nexion with the administration and organization of the district churches, and accounts are placed before the district meetings in which the lay members outnumber the clergy. The missionary is the only European in this meeting. Moreover, the churches have recently decided, through their own district meeting, to increase the regular contributions so as to provide for a regular itineration fund for the African ministers, and for a building fund, both to be controlled by the district meeting.

It does not appear, therefore, that suspicion about financial matters is a significant reason for people to show preference for Separatist churches. There are, however, instances of trouble about financial issues within the Separatist churches themselves. Besides the split in the Church of Christ referred to above (p. 98) there are two instances in which local leaders changed their church affiliation as a result of a dispute about funds, and in one case the leader removed his flock to the other church as well.

Connexions with the church outside the reserve

None of the churches are purely local organizations restricted to the chiefdom or to the reserve. A few Separatist churches are restricted

CHURCH ORGANIZATION

to a relatively small area covering only a few magisterial districts, but the majority, even though some may not have very many congregations, are represented over a wide area. The Taung branch of a church is usually not of very great importance in the church as a whole. In the L.M.S., however, Taung holds an important position as the centre of a whole church district. The heads of two smaller Separatist churches live in the chiefdom, which gives it an important position in those churches also. Mostly the different centres of the church form a kind of hierarchy in which the Taung church shares a more humble status with other rural and semi-rural churches. The important centre for all these branches may be a large country town in the Northern Cape or the Western Transvaal, where a senior church official supervising the lesser churches in an area forming a district of the church, resides. The headquarters are usually on the Witwatersrand or in some other city or important town where the Founder or head of the church resides. A church in the chiefdom has regular contacts with the rest of the church through district and church conferences and synods, and through visits of senior church officials.

The older missions in South Africa mostly originated as rural missions and only started working in urban areas at a later stage in order to care for their members who migrated to the cities. In our area this is clearly illustrated by the L.M.S. which is essentially still a rural church. Such work as the Mission has on the Witwatersrand is a more recent development. In the Separatist churches the reverse of this process is now taking place and the cities and large towns are the strongholds from which their influence emanates to the rural areas. Most of the Separatist churches in the chiefdom have been introduced by influences coming from Kimberley, Bloemfontein or the Witwatersrand. When Rev. M—— and his flock seceded from their church, he went to Kimberley to find another church which they could join. Two other seceding groups wrote to church leaders in the city to establish new church contacts. The reverse also occurs, however. The Native Independent Congregational Church, for example, originated in the reserve and from there spread to the towns. On the other hand, some mission churches have moved the centres of their activities from rural areas to cities, and from the cities again have extended their influence to other rural areas. In Taung this seems to have been the case with the Methodist Church. Some Sabbatarian and Pentecostal missions, having entered the field in South Africa more recently, started working in the cities and from there spread their influence to rural areas.

It is especially in the Separatist churches that the city congregations

106 RELIGION IN A TSWANA CHIEFDOM

are of particular importance. Usually the city is the seat of the Founder of the church, the place where 'the important ministers' are. Often the local leader and other members made their first acquaintance with the church there. At a festival of a Sabbatarian Pentecostal church, the Bloemfontein Congregation was referred to as the place 'where all of us were born'. Messages from the Founder or Leader, brought personally by members returning from work in the city, or sent by letter, are received with interest by the rural church. Important activities are not undertaken without first consulting the superior authorities in the city. Members giving testimonies in Pentecostal churches add weight to their words by quoting the prophet of *Gauteng* (Johannesburg). In ritual and dogma that which has been learnt in the church of *Gauteng* is the norm. Visits of an Archbishop, a Bishop, or an Apostle from the city church are great occasions. Homesteads and churches are decorated and other preparations are made; the local church tries to do everything in the best style. Nevertheless, the uncertainty in the attitude of the more simple rural folk in the presence of the visitors betrays their awe of these self-assured men from the city and town churches.

In Zulu 'Zionist' churches the churches in the reserve stand in a more particular relation to the city churches. For them the reserve is the place where the pools and rivers are found which are most suitable for baptism and purification ceremonies, 'the only place where the essential business of the Church—healing—can be successfully performed'. Moreover, many of their leading prophets live in the reserves, rather than in Johannesburg.[1] In Taung, however, there was no evidence of the rural churches being so indispensable to any urban churches, but the dependence of the rural congregations on those in the city was apparent in all types of Separatist churches.

Interdenominational relations

There are numerous occasions on which contact and co-operation take place between the members of different churches, such as the night watches held after a death has taken place, and funeral services, prayer meetings for rain, concerts and drives for collecting funds. Co-operation of a more formal kind takes place on occasions such as the laying of a corner-stone or the opening of a new church, when representatives of different churches speak from the same platform, and different churches make official contributions to the building funds.

The European observer is sometimes surprised to find which

[1] Sundkler, *op. cit.*, p. 93.

CHURCH ORGANIZATION 107

churches do co-operate. For example, at the opening of a Lutheran church, donations were made not only by several Lutheran congregations, as well as by a number of L.M.S. and Methodist congregations and an Anglican church, but also by the S.D.A., as well as by a few Separatist churches, including a Separatist church which has split from the Lutheran Church. The *Masincedane* association, again, consists of a church from group 'A' connected with Europeans, two Separatist churches from group 'A', a Sabbatarian Separatist church, and two Pentecostal Separatist churches. In as far as there is awareness of interdenominational differences these do not result in such deep cleavages as are often found between Europeans of different denominations.

A typical example is provided by a woman who was an energetic member of the D.R.C. at the place she came from, and who, coming to settle at Buxton in Taung and finding that a branch of her own church did not exist there, promptly joined the Roman Catholics, in spite of the fact that there are several Protestant Separatist churches at Buxton, and other non-Separatist Protestant churches within fairly easy reach. However, when a congregation of the D.R.C. was formed at Buxton she returned to her original church.

The opinion is often expressed by Bantu church members that the differences between churches are not important, since they all worship the same God. On the other hand, there is little awareness in these churches of their connexion with the world-church, excepting the bonds that bind mission churches to their foreign missionary bodies.

Nevertheless, competition and petty jealousies also exist. On two occasions I heard people speak of this as the 'colour bar'—using the English term in Tswana conversation—between the churches. For example, the minister who is the leading spirit of the *Masincedane* explained that he wanted to wipe out 'this colour bar between the churches', so that there would be co-operation, and each one would not just say, 'I am London' (L.M.S.) or 'I am Wessel' (Methodist), and not want to have anything to do with the others. One does, in fact, find individual members who self-righteously exalt their own church as the only really important one. I have the impression that this is especially the case in the older mission churches, and is due more to a long-standing attachment, which has already become something of a tradition, than to convictions about differences in doctrine. Mention must also be made here of unfavourable comment which is often expressed by people inside and outside the churches about the multiplication of denominations, and the Separatists especially come in for criticism on this account.

108 RELIGION IN A TSWANA CHIEFDOM

Although interdenominational differences are not strongly accentuated, the awareness of such differences is not altogether absent from the churches. On the whole, it seems that on the level of the ordinary church members doctrinal differences are unimportant, and co-operation is easiest, but more importance is attached to the differences among superior church officials. The procedure at a night watch following the death of a child which had been baptized by the R.C. Church, illustrates this point.

The initiative was taken by a member of the R.C. women's association who was a neighbour of the bereaved household and an ortho-cousin (mother's sister's daughter) of the stepfather of the deceased child's mother. She asked her husband, a Methodist, to lead in an opening prayer, 'since a woman cannot open'. After a spontaneous prayer by the husband, the woman was joined by all present in saying the Lord's Prayer, after which she read several R.C. prayers, which many of those present said with her. Some hymns were also sung, all of them announced by her from the R.C. hymn book. Later on, however, she called on the members of other churches present to propose some of their hymns also, and added: 'We request the assistance of the other churches.' In the same connexion she also remarked that the death of the child had not bereaved one church only, but that all of them had been bereaved. Many L.M.S. and Methodist hymns were sung during the remaining part of the night, while all joined with enthusiasm when someone started a song very popular with some Pentecostal churches, which consists of a repetition of the words: 'Amen, Hallelujah!'

It is significant that, whereas the R.C. Church and its clergy seldom or never co-operate formally with other churches, and whereas the funeral service of the child was a purely R.C. rite, led by the Catechist and the priest, the members of the church readily co-operated with the other churches in the less formal religious activities of the night watch, even though the initiative was in their own hands.

Although there are no corporate groups in which different churches regularly co-operate on the basis of common teaching and ritual, the existence of elements common to a number of churches, especially common elements in ritual, does give rise to attitudes expressive of cohesions and cleavages. There is a fellow-feeling between all Sabbatarians and Pentecostals, in which the Baptist churches classified with group 'A' may also be included, because they are all united on the issue of adult baptism by immersion. Again, the Pentecostals, feeling that they are 'Apostles' all, are separated from the other churches by various customs such as speaking with tongues and being moved by the Spirit. The Sabbatarians, on the other hand, are aware that the observance of Saturday as Sabbath forms a common basis, separating them from all non-Sabbatarians. Cutting across these cleavages and

CHURCH ORGANIZATION 109

cohesions based on ritual and doctrine is the line between Separatists and non-Separatists. Although there is evidence of awareness of this cleavage in Separatist churches, it is more strongly stressed in churches connected with Europeans. These feel that their churches are just a bit more genuine than the Separatist churches; they reckon that the Separatists lack the proper background and connexions, and that their leaders are sometimes moved by ulterior motives. As one church leader expressed it: 'They lack *ditšó*'—a word used of lineages, totemic groups, and tribes, but also denoting traditional custom and history.

Between churches of the same type, minor differences are again accentuated at times and are important in creating solidarity within the church group by stressing its separateness from others of the same type. Thus one Sabbatarian Separatist church differentiates between itself and the S.D.A. by pointing out that the latter do not perform the laying-on of hands for people who have been baptized, whereas they do. One church which performs baptism by immersion may differentiate itself from others which also do, by immersing a person once only, instead of three times, or by baptizing in running water only, whereas others baptize in dams as well as rivers. These minor differences are of particular importance as integrating factors in the rural Separatist churches where groups of church members have seldom seceded *en masse* from one church to join a Separatist church, and where the integrative force of the secession crisis, as described by Dr. Sundkler,[1] is therefore rarely present. In the secession crisis highly emotional factors are usually involved, and these particularly tie leader and flock closely together. To the rural members of the church, however, who have joined it subsequent to its formation, the factors involved in a secession crisis, which might have taken place far away in the city, have little emotional content. Here these small differences help to convince the members that the church they have joined is different from others, thereby preventing their deserting it.

Several aspects of interdenominational relations emerge from the case of J—— S——, Bishop of a Sabbatarian Separatist church.

S—— told me that he used to be a 'Leader' in the Anglican Church, but later became Sabbatarian, because the Bible says you should baptize 'in the river', whereas the Anglicans do not; and the Bible says you should keep the Sabbath, but the Anglicans do not. He had been in contact with the S.D.A., and it was their influence that had made him feel that the Anglican Church was wrong. However, he did not join the S.D.A. because they do not allow attendance of initiation ceremonies (S—— is a Fingo), but he

[1] *Op cit.*, pp. 161–163.

110   RELIGION IN A TSWANA CHIEFDOM

joined the Separatist Sabbatarian Church of which he is now the Bishop. The foregoing information was given while I interviewed him about his church and his own life history. Before that time, on the way to his homestead, he casually told me and another man how the S.D.A. (before he had come to Taung) had invited him to join their ranks with his flock. To their invitation he replied that the coming together (*go kôpana*) of all the churches would only take place in the end. It is not time for it yet, but the end is near at hand and then all would come together. Nevertheless, if they wished to, they could rather join him. The S.D.A. would not accept this proposal and further pointed out that he was poor (meaning also that his church had little money) and that they could give him a salary if he joined them. This proposal he also declined, because he felt that they would dictate to him what to preach, and he does not like to be told what to say. He subsequently also told us that the first church ever to exist was Sabbatarian, and the second to originate was 'Roma' (the R.C. Church). 'Roma', however, killed all the others, including St. Paul, and then they told the people they were the first church. Later the Sabbatarian Church ('Sabbata') spread from the United States to other parts of the world.

Granted that all his facts or his interpretation of the facts may not be correct, S——'s statement nevertheless reveals the factors which to him constitute cleavages, on the one hand, and the basis of cohesions, on the other hand. In the first place, he has separated himself from his original church and other churches of group 'A' on the issue of baptism by immersion and the Sabbath issue. By accepting the Sabbatarian teaching about the Sabbath, he narrows down the group with which he feels closer cohesion by excluding the Pentecostal churches. The solidarity of all Sabbatarians is also stressed by the particular view he takes of history. Within the Sabbatarian group the issue about the initiation ceremonies constitutes the overt factor making for cleavage between his own church and the S.D.A. There is, however, also a covert motive for stressing the latter cleavage, namely his desire for the status and prestige he enjoys as the head of a church, which would largely disappear, were he to lose his independence. Interesting, also, is the manner in which he reconciles the numerous divisions between Christian churches with the idea of Christian unity.

It must be stressed, however, that these cleavages and cohesions are of a subtle nature and do not rule out easy contacts and cooperation between churches representative of widely different types. It cannot be denied, moreover, that the Bantu Christians often do not understand and appreciate the significance of the historical divisions between the different churches of European origin which are of the same type, but a new traditionalism seems to be arising in connexion with the divisions between the older churches, making the disappearance of these divisions improbable.

CHURCH ORGANIZATION 111

The churches and youth

Merely on the basis of general observation I received the impression that there is a tendency among the younger generation, among the young men and older boys rather than among the girls and young women, to disregard the churches. The figures which were obtained in the sample survey of the sixty-three homesteads in the two sample areas do show some consistency with this opinion. These are given below in Table VI. These are the same figures as those given in Table I, split up into a larger number of age groups and according to sex. All persons claiming official connexion with a church—members of Sunday Schools (SS) and catechumen classes (CC) and communicant or full members (FM)—are here grouped together.

As far as *males* in the sample are concerned, a clear trend is discernible. A substantial proportion of the males in all age groups have no church connexions, but the percentage is very distinctly highest in the age groups 15–19 (50%) and 20–24 (58%). Moreover, the percentage of males having close connexions with the churches (SS, CC, and FM) is lowest in the same two age groups—excepting in the 0–9 age group where one may expect that most are only adherents. In respect of *females* the trend is not so distinct. In all age groups the percentages of *females* with no church connexions are much lower than in the case of males. Excepting the 0–9 age group, the highest percentage with no church connexions is found in the 20–29 age group, the same age group in which the highest percentage of extra-church males is also found. On the other hand, the lowest percentage for females is found in the 15–19 age group. Furthermore, a very large percentage of the women in all age groups, excepting the 0–9 group, have close connexions with the churches, the percentage being even larger in the younger age groups than in the 30+ group.

Therefore, as far as the sample goes, we observe a conspicuous absence of church connexions among young men. A large percentage of young women have official church connexions but in as far as there is a tendency among them to disregard the churches, it is most conspicuous in the 20–29 age group (excepting the 0–9 group). On the whole this seems consistent with the opinion I formulated independently of these statistics, viz. that there is a tendency among young people to disregard the churches and that this tendency is more noticeable among males than females.

In assessing the significance of these figures it could be argued that the young men in the age groups 15–19 and 20–29 are probably involved in migrant labour more than the older and younger males and

TABLE VI.—CHURCH AFFILIATION—Sex and Age. (Sample.)

Degree of affiliation	0–9 years		10–14 years		15–19 years		20–29 years		30+ years		Total	
	M	F	M	F	M	F	M	F	M	F	M	F
Nil . . .	18 (33%)	13 (25%)	12 (44%)	3 (13%)	9 (50%)	2 (7%)	19 (58%)	7 (18%)	20 (37%)	10 (14%)	78 (42%)	35 (17%)
Baptized or blessed children, and adherents . .	33 (60%)	29 (56%)	5 (19%)	4 (17%)	5 (28%)	4 (15%)	7 (21%)	5 (13%)	14 (26%)	24 (34%)	64 (34%)	66 (31%)
SS, CC, and FM .	4 (7%)	10 (19%)	10 (37%)	16 (70%)	4 (22%)	21 (78%)	7 (21%)	27 (69%)	20 (37%)	36 (52%)	45 (24%)	110[1] (52%)
Total . . .	55 (100%)	52 (100%)	27 (100%)	23 (100%)	18 (100%)	27 (100%)	33 (100%)	39 (100%)	54 (100%)	70 (100%)	187 (100%)	211 (100%)

[1] I may draw attention to the fact that out of 155 persons having close connexions with the churches (SS, CC, and FM) 110 or 71% are females. This is consistent with the 72% arrived at on the basis of the actual numbers of communicant and non-communicant members of all the churches in the chiefdom. (Table V.)

CHURCH ORGANIZATION

the females, and that the unsettled pattern of their life at this age prevents them from taking a keen interest in the churches. This factor plays a role but I do not think it is all-important. Migrant labour certainly interferes with regular church attendance and the consistent attendance of catechumen classes in order to become full members, but it does not prevent men from occasionally attending services and from regarding themselves as adherents. I would suggest that the secularizing influences experienced by young migrants at the industrial and urban labour centres go further in accounting for the large percentage of young men without church connexions than the unsettled living conditions which migrant labour involves.

Further, I think this absence of interest in the churches is part of a wider process of secularization relative not only to Christianity but to religion in general, since these young people who are not interested in the churches can hardly be regarded as fervently adhering to traditional paganism. As paganism wanes and disintegrates, those who do not become Christians tend to take a secularistic and materialistic view of life. It is difficult to say how far young people whose families have been connected with the churches for a generation or more also tend to lose interest in the churches.

On the whole the churches do not show particular concern about youth and its problems, and in some churches there are factors positively discouraging to young people, especially if they are enterprising and idealistic. We have seen that this is so in the L.M.S., where the older women dominate the church. Nevertheless, most churches have Sunday Schools for the children, while a considerable proportion of the catechumen classes are made up of young people. There are several churches which have associations for girls, but there are none for boys. However, in the Anglican and R.C. churches they can become choir boys who assist the priests, and in this way play a prominent role in regular church activities.

Through their schools the churches have their widest opportunity of influencing youth. With the exception of the Secondary School and the Molala Memorial School (primary) at Matlapaneng, which are tribal schools, all the schools in the chiefdom are mission schools controlled by churches.[1] That these schools do have a certain influence on the religion of children is illustrated by the fact that children sometimes change their church affiliation to join the church which controls the school they attend. However, many churches, particularly the

[1] Mission schools are state-aided and subject to inspection by the Department of Education. (It should be remembered that fieldwork was undertaken before the promulgation of the Bantu Education Act.)

R.T.C.—9

114   RELIGION IN A TSWANA CHIEFDOM

Separatists, have no schools. The following is the distribution of mission schools and pupils among the different denominations:[1]

L.M.S. . . .	. 8 schools	: 1,122 pupils
L.M.S. and Anglican[2] .	. 1 school	: 198 „
Methodist and Anglican[2]	. 1 „	: 185 „
Methodist . . .	. 1 „	: 100 „
Roman Catholic . .	. 6 schools	: 1,054 „
TOTAL .	. 17 schools	: 2,659 pupils

The churches and political authorities

The dealings of non-Separatist churches with the Government are usually undertaken by the European missionaries or ministers. To the leaders of Separatist churches such dealings are tricky and difficult, since through their lack of educational background they often feel uncertain and ignorant about the requirements of the law and correct procedure. When representations are made to the Native Commissioner, a senior church official sometimes visits the reserve to conduct the negotiations. Only four of the Separatist churches in the chiefdom enjoy Government recognition.[3] The A.M.E. minister is the only Separatist minister in the chiefdom who has been appointed a marriage officer by the Government.[4] There is little evidence of openly 'seditious teaching' in the Separatist churches, and as far as the churches in the chiefdom are concerned, this characteristic which is often associated with Separatism seems to have been more evident in the past[5] than at present. The government officials authorized the expulsion from the reserve of a certain Separatist leader a few years ago, but in this action they upheld the authority of the chief and headman with whom he first clashed. In sermons and testimonies of the Separatists there may sometimes be subtle references to the inferior position of the Bantu in the country, but this is not an openly rebellious attitude. On the whole the Separatist churches show a desire to have the reputation of being law-abiding and therefore acceptable to government authorities.

[1] These figures show the position in September 1952. There were 312 pupils in the two tribal schools at the time which brings the total in all the schools of the chiefdom to 2,971. (See ch. I.)

[2] 'United Schools' in which different denominations co-operate.

[3] For an account of government policy concerning recognition, see Sundkler, *op. cit.*, pp. 65 ff. It has not changed substantially in recent years.

[4] The minister of the Native Independent Congregational Church at Manthe in the Maidi chiefdom is also one.

[5] See pp. 47 ff.

CHURCH ORGANIZATION 115

Although hardly any of the headmen and the men belonging to the chief's inner circle are active members of the church, the tribal authorities on the whole show the churches respect and appreciation. One sometimes hears the complaint, however, that the ministers are indifferent to tribal politics, that they do not pay due recognition to the tribal authorities but think only of increasing their own authority and being chiefs themselves. Complaints are also sometimes made about the churches being too many, and this dissatisfaction is particularly concerned with the Separatist churches.[1] It is a fact that few church leaders ever attend the general tribal assemblies at the chief's *kgotla* at Taung, but nevertheless they usually do express formal recognition of the tribal authorities, and sometimes expressly appeal to their followers to recognize them.

In two Separatist churches I attended, particular stress was laid on obedience to those in power. The following extracts are from a sermon by the Bishop of the Witness of Christ (Sabbath).

'... A person who believes must be cured [as a skin] and be soft. He should be a person of the law. The law protects one. If there is no law, anyone can murder you. Therefore one should obey the law. If I go to a place I do not know, but I know that the Government is there, it will protect me....' I Pet. 2:11–15 was read verse by verse, with comments after each verse: 'We must understand that the Bible shows that we should honour the Government. It is our great protector.... Do you hear, this verse speaks as I have told you. The Government is our helper. Those who are against the Government are against God because God has set up the Government....' Later the first verses of Romans 13 were read, and much the same type of comment was made. In this connexion he also pressed his congregation to love policemen because they are their helpers, and to pay their taxes.[2]

A church in which stress is also laid on obedience to the authorities, 'both black and white', is the St. Paul Apostolic Faith Morning Star. This was not only my own impression received at services, but the church also has this reputation among the people and with the tribal authorities. The leader and members sometimes voluntarily assist the headman in reaping and other work on his plot on the irrigation scheme. It should be noted, however, that this church lays stress on respect and obedience to one's superiors in general, not only in the

---

[1] The favour that the chief granted the 'Ethiopians' at one stage (see above, p. 50), does not appear to have been enduring.

[2] It is improbable that his sermon was preached expressly to make a good impression on the investigator since the preacher was not expecting a visit from me that day, and had just started his sermon when I arrived. The idea of submission and obedience is in keeping with the leader's personality.

116 RELIGION IN A TSWANA CHIEFDOM

political sphere, but also in the sphere of the church, as well as in the sphere of family and kinship relations and in respect of age. The tribal authorities on their part have respect for the leader and his church, and an informant in a gathering at the headman's *kgotla* contrasted him with other church leaders who, he said, were 'cheeky' (using the English word in a Tswana conversation). On one occasion, when he attended the general tribal assembly at the chief's *kgotla*, he made a speech illustrated by portions read from the Bible, against the drinking of beer. Although this was rather an unusual thing to do and many of those present were people fond of their beer, most of the men listened to him attentively and respectfully.

The Constitution and Canons of the Ethiopian Catholic Church in Zion state that: 'Holy Scripture teaches that the Kings are appointed for the Supervision of both the Ecclesiastical and the political or the temporal world by God Himself. . . . Wherefore all members and ministers of the E.C.C. in Zion are commanded to render all possible respect and honour to all such as are appointed for the said work of the Kings of the world, and such men are the Magistrates and the Native Commissioners, as well as many others akin to them. . . .'[1]

Particular mention must here be made of the relation between the L.M.S. and the tribal authorities. There was a stage, when, in spite of conflicts between the Mission and the chiefs, the L.M.S. tended to become a tribal or 'state' church, and although none of the chiefs have been members of any church, they have often performed at important church ceremonies. For example, chief Molala and the tribe officially assisted in building the present church building at the head station. Chiefs have performed the laying of corner-stones or the opening ceremonies in respect of various L.M.S. church buildings in the chiefdom, which, as far as I know, has not happened in the case of any other church.

Although the L.M.S. has lost its pre-eminence to-day, superficial observation leaves the impression that it is still the most important church in the chiefdom and is to a certain extent a 'state church'. Unfortunately the census returns on religious affiliation in the district are not available, but the Native Commissioner who held office at the time of the 1951 census, told me that he received the impression that the majority of the population of the district were returned as L.M.S. people. This goes to show that this church still has a large number of adherents, but the very fact that there are so many who claim adherence, but fail to join wholeheartedly, is typical of a state church. A

---

[1] *The Constitutions and Canons of the Ethiopian Catholic Church in Zion,* Bloemfontein (1919?), p. 56.

CHURCH ORGANIZATION 117

councillor of the chief, taking part in a discussion in a general tribal assembly, recently referred to the L.M.S. as 'the church of the chief'— although the present chief hardly ever appears in church. During the time I was doing field work, the annual prayer meetings for rain[1] were held in turn by the leaders of different churches at the headmen's *makgotla*, but at the chief's *kgotla* it was held by the minister of the L.M.S. every week. It is typical of the situation that in the L.M.S. church the benches in the chancel are reserved for the clergy (on the left) and for members of the chief's lineage and their families (on the right). However, that the L.M.S. has lost the favour of some members of the tribe, was illustrated by a remark made in a tribal assembly by a member of the chief's lineage, who is not a member of any church. He had a complaint about funerals, and said that ' "London" is not our church as it used to be our church formerly. . . It used to bury our fathers even though they had not been baptized.'

The tendency toward the acceptance of a particular branch of Christianity as an official 'state' religion is much more evident among the tribes of the Protectorate than among the Tlhaping. There, 'until fairly recently, many tribes had missionaries of one denomination only'.[2] The traditional social structure of the Tswana has undoubtedly been favourable to the formation of tribal churches. The concentration of the population in large towns and their highly centralized form of government were connected with a high degree of tribal solidarity, and these factors must have caused reluctance to accept missionaries of different denominations within a single tribe, since it would weaken tribal solidarity, and thus endanger the chief's influence over the tribe. This attitude was so much stronger if a chief joined the church himself.[3] Moreover, in spite of the lack of co-ordination between different denominations in their missionary activities in South Africa, most Protestant denominations would have been reluctant to open a mission in the same *town* in which another denomination was already working.[4] That there is to-day less evidence of a state church in Taung than in reserves in the Protectorate is in keeping with the differences in social structure between the Tlhaping and Tswana societies in the Protectorate, which are the result of social changes which have taken place in Tlhaping society. Since in Taung the power and status of the chief as well as the degree of tribal solidarity has long been declining—

[1] See ch. VI. [2] Schapera, 1953, p. 58.
[3] Cf. Schapera, 1936, p. 229.
[4] Now that the mobility of the Bantu population in any case tends to cause the multiplication of denominations in a given area (cf. p. 51), this is no longer the case.

118 RELIGION IN A TSWANA CHIEFDOM

much more than in the Protectorate[1]—there has been greater opportunity for the multiplication of denominations. This would also explain
why Separatist movements are so much less evident in the Protectorate.[2] Nevertheless, at an earlier stage, when tribal solidarity was still
stronger, and the L.M.S. more of a tribal church, these factors probably had a retarding influence on Separatism in Taung as well. On the
other hand, the fact that so many people had accepted Christianity to a
certain extent, without actually joining the church, prepared the way
for other churches, and it seems that, while the L.M.S. did not lose
many *members* to other denominations, the Separatist churches and
certain non-Separatist denominations, collected many L.M.S. *adherents* into their respective folds.

Attitude to Europeans

European members of the Roman Catholic Church sometimes
attend Mass at Taung, where there is a separate chapel for them in the
southern transept of the church. Other churches very seldom have
Europeans attending their services, although it does happen occasionally in connexion with some important activity, especially of churches
connected with Europeans. They are then usually given seats of
honour. I tried to make my visits to churches as casual as possible,
but the Separatists were even more emphatic than the others in
requiring that I should take a seat of honour on the platform, or at
least in the front row. In their churches a visit from a European is a
much rarer experience than in churches connected with Europeans and
is probably regarded as adding a little to their prestige. The Europeans
living in the reserve who are active church members (i.e. Protestants)
attend separate services which are occasionally conducted by the
L.M.S. missionary and European ministers from neighbouring areas.
In church matters there are therefore very few contacts between Bantu
and European Christians. In the churches which have mixed congregations at some places outside the reserve, or mixed conferences or
synods, some of the members in the reserve would at least be aware
of this, and some may also have taken part in such gatherings.

In sermons and prayers in the Bantu churches direct references to
the relation between Bantu and Europeans are seldom heard (i.e.
judging by the services I attended). On a few occasions reference was
made to the equality of all people before God but in no church could
I observe expressions of direct hostility. The Pentecostal Separatist
leader who stresses the principle of obedience and submissiveness to
one's superiors, also teaches his people to apply this to their relations

[1] See pp. 5 ff.   [2] See Schapera, 1953, p. 58.

CHURCH ORGANIZATION

with European employers. With reference to the history of Joseph in the service of Potiphar and Pharaoh (Gen. 39 ff.) he entreats them to be trustworthy even when they are sent to the bank with 'papers', or when they are left alone to take care of the house or farm in the absence of their employer. When they are called by the farmer, the Magistrate, or the Agricultural Officer (in connexion with the irrigation scheme), they should go immediately, without delaying. When they see a European woman having trouble with a bicycle with a punctured wheel, they should go to her assistance.

The same leader, who is held in high esteem inside and outside his own church, also tends to idealize the European and hold him forth as an example to his audience. He praises him for his wisdom and zeal and for the care he takes of his stock, and encourages his followers to do likewise. On one occasion he idealized an aspect of the moral behaviour of the European, but at the same time, perhaps without intent, pointed to a moral weakness on the part of Europeans. They do not make a public scene of drunkenness, he said, but cover it up. If you went to the house of a European and asked to see a certain member of the household, and that person was drunk, it would not be openly said so, but you would be told that the person you wished to see was ill. From this he proceeded to recount the episode of Noah's drunkenness, and showed how Ham made fun of his father, while Shem and Jafeth, respectfully covered him (Gen. 9:20–23).

Illustrations used in sermons also show indirectly how the European way of life, especially on its material side, is held as the ideal. In the following example it is the parallel of Paradise.

A well-educated Separatist minister in a church of group 'A' preached a sermon on the Fall and the subsequent expulsion of Adam and Eve from Paradise. He compared their acts to that of a girl employed in domestic work under favourable conditions. One day her employer left on a journey and gave her the freedom of the whole house during his absence. He[1] handed all the keys to her and granted her permission to eat any food that was in the house, to drive about in his motor car, even to sleep in his bed. However, before he left, he made a box in which he imprisoned three mice, without the girl knowing it, and told her that the one thing she was not allowed to do was to open the box. After his departure, she took the motor-car and drove to town, came home and ate of all the food, and then went into the employer's bedroom and took a rest in his bed. After that she went for a drive in the other car, but on her return the 'dog' (i.e. the devil) got inside her and approached her soul with the question: 'What is inside the box? You could just open it slightly and peep.' She immediately drove off in the car again, but as soon as she returned, Satan got busy with her once

---

[1] The sermon was given in the vernacular which does not define the gender.

120 RELIGION IN A TSWANA CHIEFDOM

more. . . . So the story wound on in great detail, and, of course, the mice escaped from the box and the girl was dismissed from service on the return of the employer.

It is evident that the employer was envisaged as a well-to-do European. There is no hint of open opposition to him, and he is pictured as being unusually liberal to his employee, but the expression of a desire to partake of his material prosperity is unmistakable.

The idealization of the European pattern of society and behaviour is also illustrated by the pattern of organization followed by some Separatist churches, especially those of group 'A'. Some of the constitutions of these churches are close copies of the constitutions of the European parent churches, even though they are never really put into practice in that form.

The question of the bearing which interracial relations have on Separatism can be better discussed in a broader context along with other aspects of Separatism which will emerge in the course of subsequent chapters.

Summary

In this chapter we have observed the importance of the church, particularly the local church group, in present-day society. It presents numerous opportunities for joint activity, and on occasions such as concerts or drives for funds offers entertainment to a much wider circle than the members of the church. It also provides abundant opportunity for exercising leadership. Further examples of the importance of the local church group and church activities will be met in the following chapter.

Secondly, the structure and organization of the churches has been influenced by traditional patterns of social structure and organization. We observed this in respect of the relation of the local church group to the important groups in traditional Tlhaping society. It is also shown in the general pattern of church offices which reflects the pattern of traditional political organization, and in the procedure followed in connexion with church discipline which is similar to the procedure in traditional courts. Further, we have seen that the predominance of women in the churches seems to be connected with certain traditional values and patterns of organization.

While the traditional pattern of concentration of the population, connected with strongly centralized authority and a high degree of tribal solidarity still existed, it was favourable to the development of a 'tribal' church and prevented the excessive multiplication of denominations in the chiefdom.

CHURCH ORGANIZATION 121

I may here also point out that where the church has opposed traditional customs it has not always been able to wipe them out, not even among church members. In spite of stern opposition in some churches some of their members still adhere to the initiation ceremonies, the giving of *bogadi*, and the consulting of native doctors.

The churches are not only affected by traditional patterns, but are also involved in the processes of change to which the society as a whole is being subjected (apart from the fact that the church itself is a force making for change). The scattering of the population, decentralization of authority and weakening of tribal solidarity has caused the pre-eminence of the 'tribal church', the L.M.S., to wane considerably and may also be related to the multiplication of denominations in later years. Another example is the effect that labour migration has on religion. The unsettled living conditions resulting from it make it difficult for migrants, mostly younger males, to enter actively and regularly into church activities, and it is also a force making for secularization among them. It has compelled the older mission churches, which started as rural churches, to extend their activities to the towns and cities, while it is an important factor in the spreading of Separatist churches.

Finally, a few points must be mentioned here in connexion with the Bantu Separatist churches. In respect of church organization there are no radical differences between the churches connected with Europeans and the Separatists. The former are usually more efficiently organized and controlled than the latter. The Separatists tend to require a shorter period of instruction for converts and discipline erring members for shorter periods than the others. They do not approve of polygyny but tend to be more lenient to men who were polygynists before their conversion than the churches connected with Europeans. The basic patterns of organization of the two types of churches are much the same. Both tend to follow a pattern of church organization that reflects traditional patterns of political organization. In both the wives of office bearers tend to form a hierarchy (parallel to that of their husbands) in the women's associations. In both types of churches we find leaders who joined their respective churches as a result of crises in connexion with which they received visionary and/or audible revelations.

We have noted a drift from churches connected with Europeans to Bantu Separatist churches, but there is also a drift from one type of church connected with Europeans to another (e.g. from type 'A' to Sabbatarian or Pentecostal churches). The Separatists do not seem to attract communicant members from the other churches on a large

122   RELIGION IN A TSWANA CHIEFDOM

scale.[1] It does not seem as if suspicion about the distribution of funds collected from the Bantu members in mission churches constitutes an important factor making for secession from these churches. In this connexion we may note that contributions which members are required to make are often considerably higher in Separatist churches than in those connected with Europeans. Nevertheless, the feeling Separatists can have of managing their own affairs, of having their own buildings, built by themselves and with their own funds, probably has a particularly gratifying effect. I have not found evidence of strong hostility among Separatists to the Government or to Europeans in general.

[1] The only instance I came across of apostacy on a large scale was in connexion with the Native Independent Congregational Church in the Maidi chiefdom.

CHAPTER V

THE PATTERN OF CHURCH ACTIVITIES

In this chapter I shall describe the general pattern of church activities, and in the next deal with various aspects of ritual and revelation in detail. Whatever is dealt with in that chapter will here only be mentioned in passing, to show its position in the general pattern of activities.

The general pattern of life in the churches

In the life of active members the church and its activities takes a very important place. Of primary importance are the Sunday, or Sabbath services, which, apart from their religious character, offer opportunities for social contacts, especially before and after services. In some churches every Sunday has a full programme and many hours of the day may be spent in devotions.

Most churches have at least one or two gatherings during the week also, and in some there is activity almost every day of the week. The L.M.S. at Taung has the following weekly programme:

Monday afternoon: a service, led by one of the women Deacons. After the service two women go out to visit the sick.
Tuesday: confirmation class.
Wednesday: a service at which only men preach.
Thursday: a Bible Class for the Deacons, led by the African minister.
Friday: a service in the afternoon at which the women Deacons preach again.
Saturday afternoon: Deacons' meeting.

The *Holy Church of Christ* meets every evening of the week as follows:

Monday night: instruction in the Bible, and teaching illiterate members to read.
Tuesday night: general prayer meeting.
Wednesday night: as on Monday.
Thursday night: practising of hymns.
Friday night: evangelistic processions to preach at different homesteads.
Saturday: Sabbath services.
Sunday: as on Friday.

Besides such regular activities, special services are conducted on particular occasions such as the termination of a mother's confinement, marriage, and death.

124 RELIGION IN A TSWANA CHIEFDOM

Where special associations exist in connexion with the churches these account for some regular activity. In most churches, however, these are confined to the women's and girls' associations. The R.C. Church, however, has a general association for men, a Burial Association, a Catholic Teachers' Association, besides the three associations for women and girls (see ch. IV). The different associations are affiliated to the Catholic African Union, each being represented in a council which forms the local branch of the Union.

In some churches baptism and communion services come fairly regularly, once a month, or once a quarter, whatever the case may be. In the L.M.S. these take place over the first weekend of every month, when the general meetings of the whole sub-district take place at Taung. Many people travel to Taung from the outlying areas to attend these monthly gatherings. In smaller churches the administering of the sacraments often coincides with the visit of a superior church official. It calls for extraordinary preparations, is the occasion for much activity, and is in general an important event in the life of the church. In the Roman Catholic Church, most of the annual Christian festivals are observed, and are the occasion for activities typical of the church, such as special masses, processions by day, or candle-light processions at night. In other churches at least Christmas and Easter receive particular attention, and are usually observed by holding special night services. The whole community, both Christian and non-Christian, views the time of Christmas and New Year as a festive season. There is general cleaning and decorating of homesteads before the time, and there are reunions of friends and relatives: migrant labourers try to be back home before Christmas, or those preparing to return to work postpone their departure till after New Year, while friends and relatives from the towns pay visits to the reserve. In the L.M.S. a service is held in the church on New Year's day, which is followed by a service at the chief's place, conducted by the Leading Women.

Activities organized for collecting church funds provide pleasant diversion for church members as well as outsiders. Among the most festive occasions in the life of churches are the special activities when a church is opened or a corner-stone is laid, when members from distant congregations of the church, perhaps as far off as Kimberley, arrive by bus, motor-car, or mule wagon or in other ways. Although the religious activities of the day are not considered unimportant, the social character of the occasion is unmistakable.

As regards evangelistic work, baptismal services of Sabbatarian and Pentecostal churches usually draw many spectators, providing a useful opportunity for making propaganda for the church. On one occasion

THE PATTERN OF CHURCH ACTIVITIES 125

when I was present, the congregation moved in procession to the river, singing as they went, while several men branched off to the homesteads in the neighbourhood to preach to the inhabitants and exhort them to be converted and to come to be baptized. Similar short sermons were also delivered to the spectators at the river. Mention has already been made of special attempts at evangelization made by the L.M.S. (see ch. IV), and also by the Holy Church of Christ (see above, p. 123). Several churches occasionally have processions which move about between the homesteads while hymns are sung and evangelistic sermons are preached. These attempts all bear a general and communal character, and little seems to be done to confront individuals with the gospel in a more particular and personal manner.

Sometimes members of a single household act as a religious unit in daily devotions, especially when the father is a devout church member. Such devotions may consist of a hymn and a prayer, and occasionally also of the reading of a portion from Scripture. However, the homesteads in which such devotions are held, seem to form only a small minority. This is perhaps partly to be explained by the fact that often only a part of the family are Christians. Some individuals also say their own private prayers every day.

The preceding paragraphs illustrate the fact that the church group is the important unit in present-day non-pagan religion, and not the family or kinship group. Through its numerous activities the church provides more occasions for group activity and social contacts than any other institution in Tlhaping society. The strong social character of church activities is illustrated by the fact that hardly any important religious activity is complete without a meal or at least some form of refreshments being served. Funerals, memorial services, 'bringing out a child', night watches, drives for funds, the laying of a corner-stone or consecration of a building, and some baptismal services—all these are accompanied by eating and drinking at the end or half-way through the proceedings.

The pattern of church services

The following discussion of the pattern of church services is almost exclusively based on the field-worker's own observations. During the first period of fieldwork I attended a service of the L.M.S. almost every Sunday, but during the second visit to the field attended as many different churches as possible. On the whole, church leaders very readily gave me permission to attend their services and the participants fulfilled their parts without seeming to be very conscious of my presence. Nevertheless, it was often taken for granted that I was

126 RELIGION IN A TSWANA CHIEFDOM

a government agent, and I sometimes had difficulty in convincing them of the contrary. On one occasion, when I had explained my position, a preacher came to the conclusion: 'Then you have been sent by God only, to travel through the country ... just like St. John and the other Apostles.' My goings about were often thus interpreted in Biblical terms.

Excluding the L.M.S., seven services of churches connected with Europeans were attended, representing six different denominations, and twenty-five services of Separatist churches, representing sixteen different denominations. The services attended represented all types of churches, excepting the Watch Tower movement. The local leader told me that they make 'house-to-house' visits on a Sunday morning and have a meeting for Bible study at his home on a Sunday afternoon. Roman Catholic services are not described here; these adhere to the pattern universally followed in this church. Sunday services and Mass are conducted by one of the Priests at the Taung church every Sunday, and once a month at each of the important outstations. There are also simpler devotions at all the outstations every Sunday, led by a Catechist or Elder.

In describing the pattern of services in Protestant churches I shall deal with each of the three types of churches separately, but I shall also draw attention to common characteristics. We may start with a description of a Sunday service of the Bechuana Methodist Church, a Separatist church of type 'A' with an episcopal form of church government.

At present the senior church official in Taung is Deacon J—— M——, who lives at Modimong, near the church building. This is also near the homestead of the Deacon's late father, who used to be the local leader. The church is an unimposing rectangular little building which, for the lack of necessary materials, is still incomplete. A number of old roofing-irons cover part of the building, but the top ridge is closed up with sacking. No door has been fitted in the entrance yet, neither any form of window nor the usual wooden blind in the two small openings in the side walls. (See illustration 13.)

Outside hangs the inevitable piece of iron—the surest evidence that this is a church—in this case a length of metal rail. Although it is a sultry December day, it is 11.30 a.m. before the sexton rings the first bell by beating the piece of rail. A few people start arriving at the old homestead where they sit chatting. At five-to-twelve the second bell rings, and the women and children present start moving to the church where they seat themselves on the mud floor and start singing. There are about fifteen women, seven girls, two young boys and three small children present. (Two other girls come in at a later stage.) A table with a white tablecloth and a few chairs have been brought from the homestead to implement the solitary bench in the church. The sexton now also takes a seat in front and is soon followed by

THE PATTERN OF CHURCH ACTIVITIES 127

the Deacon, the Evangelist, and two Preachers, who fill the remaining seats. No other men attend the service. The Deacon is wearing a clerical collar with a black stock and a greyish sports coat, on the lapel of which he has the small badge of his church: a round button with the image of a long Zulu-type of shield with assegai and stick, surmounted by a small cross, and with the letters B.M.C. below it. The Evangelist is wearing an old black frock-coat which he has closed up at the neck. The two Preachers wear no clerical clothes but one also has the small badge.

When the singing stops, the Deacon opens with a spontaneous prayer and then starts the Lord's Prayer, which the congregation says after him, only a few syllables at a time, at a fast tempo, producing a striking rhythmical effect. When he starts reading Psalm 122 the congregation rises, and after he has read a verse or two they respond with the next verse, and so on through the whole Psalm, which is followed by a chant in Tswana. The whole service is conducted in Tswana, except for a few S. Sotho hymns. Announcements follow, in which the Deacon also includes a short reference to the Annual Conference of the Church, which he recently attended, and to the Night Watch that was held on Christmas Eve. He gives a reminder of a coming Church meeting and finds occasion to mention his appointment to the Church at X (a large mining centre in the Transvaal), which is still being delayed by a dispute between the inhabitants of the location and the Town Council. He further explains my presence to the congregation, announces that the Evangelist will preach, and announces a hymn from a Methodist hymn-book. When he asks me to say a few words I explain the purpose of my visit and the nature of the work I am doing. The Deacon starts a hymn without announcing it—something I should have done after speaking!

The Evangelist rises and immediately announces another hymn, after which he reads Matthew 7:13-14, and starts yet another hymn. He starts preaching, and although he has probably had very little school training and certainly no theological training, he is self-assured. His sermon lasts only about five minutes and consists of a chain of rather incoherent statements about the broad and the narrow way, and the kinds of people that follow each of them, and their respective destinations. At the end of the sermon he announces a hymn during which he and the Deacon change places, after which the latter starts another hymn. He starts speaking about Christ's mission into this world to redeem us, but soon takes up the topic of the narrow and the broad way, much in the same trend as that in which the Evangelist spoke, though perhaps speaking with less self-assurance but more coherence. After speaking for about six or seven minutes, he announces a hymn and then one of the Preachers says a prayer. The Deacon again asks me to say a few words after the singing of another hymn. It seems to be expected that I should also speak about the text. Another hymn follows.

After the benediction the women leave the building first, and to the singing of a hymn move in procession to the old homestead. They form two parallel rows, the men following the women, and the Deacon taking up the rear. Near the homestead the two rows move apart and the Deacon passes between the ranks, followed by the men. He leads the congregation into the hut where the singing continues. Another benediction follows and two more

128   RELIGION IN A TSWANA CHIEFDOM

verses are sung. When the singing dies down the people begin to chat. A few soon leave but many remain and carry on the conversation inside or outside in the homestead enclosure. The service has lasted about an hour.

The general pattern of this service is typical of the churches of type 'A': the first part consists mainly of hymns, prayers, and liturgical formulae, and is followed by a Scripture reading and one or more sermons. Announcements may find a place anywhere, before or after the sermon. This service was relatively short. In churches of this type a Sunday morning service usually lasts about an hour and a half. In churches of the Anglican type one finds a good deal more of liturgical formulas. Few church leaders pronounce these in a dignified manner: often they go by jerks and jolts for lack of efficient reading ability, or else a leader may race through a formula at a speed which makes it completely unintelligible.

Some aspects of the service described here are typical of all types of churches. Services are often conducted in a relatively informal and familiar manner, even though they may bear a strongly liturgical character. It is common for a preacher to relate some of his recent personal experiences, either at the beginning of the service or of the sermon. Even the Archbishop of a certain Separatist church, on a visit to the Taung church, looking extremely dignified in his robes with mitre and crook complete, started his sermon by relating his recent journeys, and adding: 'But only, I have a cold. From Johannesburg I went to Bloemfontein, and from there to Petrusburg, etc., etc.—but I have a cold.' Sometimes these personal anecdotes are connected with a greeting to the congregation. Different steps in the service may be linked by the preacher's own little remarks. Members of the congregation are often requested to lead in prayer. All this again illustrates the intimacy of relations within the church group. A service by a European missionary or a trained African clergyman usually bears a more formal character. The formality and 'efficiency' of a service led by an R.C. priest contrasts most strongly with most other services.

In all types of churches a large number of hymns are sung and processions to or from the church are common. At the close of the service the whole congregation and the leaders often greet each other with a handshake. This is usually done in a formal manner: with the singing of the hymn the congregation starts filing past the leader, shaking hands with him as they pass. The first person in the line takes his place beside the leader and is also greeted by the next one in the line, after the latter has greeted the leader. The second one also takes up

THE PATTERN OF CHURCH ACTIVITIES   129

position beside the first, and so on, until each one has greeted everybody else. They usually file past in the following order: first the office bearers (often they are the only men present), then the older women, and after them the young people and children.[1]

The pattern of services in *Sabbatarian churches* does not differ radically from the service described above, although Sabbatarian sermons have a style of their own (see below, p. 138). Sermons and prayers are sometimes punctuated by a soft exclamation or a mere assenting 'mmm' but in spite of this the services are very orderly. Services of the S.D.A., are even simpler and less liturgical in character than those of the churches of group 'A', which are of the 'free' type. Their neat and well-built church hall at Taung is a reminder of the fact that they receive financial aid from European sources, while inside the building posters of American origin testify to their foreign contacts.

The services of Sabbatarian Separatists are not as bare of liturgy as those of the S.D.A., and two of them hold special prayers and anointment for the sick at the end of the Sunday morning service. A particular characteristic of these three churches is that they do not sing any rhymed hymns, but only a number of portions from the Bible, in prose form, to tunes of their own. This custom seems to derive from the church from which all three of these are 'descended'.[2]

Services of *Pentecostal churches* all conform to a distinct pattern, although there are differences, e.g. in the degree of intensity and violence of actions and utterances. I first give a description of a service of the Pentecostal Holiness Church, which is an American mission church, representing the moderate type.

The Evangelist who is the local leader was absent, but there was to be a Sunday service at his homestead all the same. He had recently changed the site of his homestead, and everything was still makeshift, the homestead consisting of only one small single-roomed building. This had been cleared for the service: one corner was screened off by some blankets, and on one side was a rather ancient side-board, stacked with household utensils. The room also contained a table and a few chairs. There were about eight women and girls, a few small children, and two men, besides two Preachers, to whom I shall refer as A and B.

B asked the Evangelist's daughter to start a hymn, and while the congregation was singing, A looked for an appropriate passage from the Bible. While waiting for him the congregation sang a few more hymns. In between he made a few remarks, all the while still looking for his text. Eventually

---

[1] The Methodists close their class meeting in this manner. Perhaps the other churches have adopted the custom from them.

[2] Cf. p. 44.

R.T.C.—10

130 RELIGION IN A TSWANA CHIEFDOM

he rose and read the first portion of Matthew 12. He started speaking: 'I cannot preach, I am only a thing. Moreover, I am not feeling well. . . .' His sermon consisted of a series of remarks, some connected with the passage he had read, some not. Occasionally he interjected an 'Amen!', 'Halleluya!' or 'Peace! Apostles', to which the congregation all together reacted with an 'Amen' every time. After a few minutes he stopped preaching. A few hymns were sung and then the congregation was asked to join in prayer and to pray for all, for ministers, for travellers, as well as for their visitor. One of the Preachers started praying aloud and immediately the congregation joined in, each one saying his own prayer and his own words aloud. They produced a considerable volume and confusion of sound but no one actually shouted, and they were just kneeling calmly. Eventually some of the voices became quiet, till only the two Preachers were still praying. When A also stopped, B continued for a few moments and then closed, but immediately intoned the Lord's Prayer, which all said after him in unison, in the same manner and with the same rhythmical effect as described above. A concluded his sermon.

After a good deal of singing, B rose and read I Corinthians 6:7 ff. with some difficulty, before proceeding to preach for a few minutes. Before closing he intimated that he could not preach, for if he were to preach, he would be a minister. An old woman who spoke Southern Sotho was asked to say a closing prayer. After another hymn the service was over, having lasted about an hour-and-a-quarter. The hymns often had a lively, 'swing' type of rhythm, and the people sang heartily, clapping hands to the rhythm of the hymn they were singing.

On another occasion, during a week-end of important activities, I attended part of a service of the same church on the Saturday morning, where a visiting African minister and his wife were the preachers. Here more emotion was displayed. Both preachers spoke with fire and dramatic effect. One woman appeared to be sobbing, softly repeating the name of Jesus all the time. After the sermons the whole congregation filed past the preachers to receive the laying-on of hands and to be prayed for in respect of their health. While uttering petitions to God for their well-being, the minister and his wife put their hands on the chest, shoulders, and head of every person. Later on the minister merely kept on repeating the words 'in the Name of Jesus Christ', as he laid his hands on each one. When eventually a blind woman came, they prayed for her longer than for the others and also placed their hands over her eyes.

The typical Pentecostal service falls into two parts of which the first part consists of singing and prayer, and a series of sermons, while the second part consists of special prayers for individual persons, accompanied by the laying-on of hands, for the purpose of improving or sustaining their health. The service described above was short, but in several of the Separatist Pentecostal churches an ordinary Sunday

THE PATTERN OF CHURCH ACTIVITIES   131

service may easily last as long as four hours. They seldom use liturgical formulas in their regular services. Other characteristics of Pentecostal services are the type of prayer in which all pray together, each
uttering his own prayer, the exclamations of 'Amen', 'Halleluya',
'Peace . . .', etc., the clapping of hands when singing, the preference
for 'swing' melodies, and the interruption of the sermon by singing.
In some churches the last happens much more frequently than in
the service described above, and often members of the congregation
just start a hymn when they wish to, while the preacher is speaking.
One is struck by the display of emotion in all Pentecostal churches,
but that referred to above is mild in comparison with what is displayed
in the more violent types of churches. The latter usually have special
church apparel for all the members.

We may now proceed to an extremely violent type of Pentecostal
service. The setting for the service is at Buxton, where the atmosphere
is very much that of a town location. The building in which the
service takes place consists of a number of small rooms next to each
other, and it has a low, flat, iron roof. It is inhabited by members of
the church. The service takes place in one of the rooms which does
not seem to be used for domestic purposes regularly. An asterisk-like
figure, the recognized symbol for a star, is painted on the door. Inside
a picture calendar, a hand-broom and a cord are the only objects hanging from the smeared walls. The mud floor is sprinkled with water
before the service starts. A few benches are placed along the wall, and
a small table in one corner.

All the members attending the service wear special robes consisting
of a long cassock or dress, over which a long, loosely flowing cloak is
worn. Cords are tied round the waist and across the shoulders. Various
forms of headdress are worn by the men, such as bands around and
across the head or a high four-sided cap. Women's headdress somewhat resembles a nurse's veil. Some people also wear cords or bands
around the ankles and wrists. Shoes must not be worn to church.

The various garments are adorned with coloured figures, mostly the
star-symbols and crosses, while crescent moons and rings also occur.
White is the most commonly occurring ground-colour of garments for
both men and women, but blue, red, and yellow also occur, while some
garments are made of sackcloth. A larger variety of colours is used
for the figures and cords. Some members wear only part of the outfit.
There is no clear distinction between the garments of leader and other
members.

A staff usually completes the outfit. The men who hold the more
important positions in the church have metal staffs, others have wooden

132　　RELIGION IN A TSWANA CHIEFDOM

staffs, or bundles of sticks. The metal staffs are surmounted by stars or crosses, to which other figures are attached; one or two of these attached figures represent birds. The wooden staffs are sometimes in the form of a cross, while the top of a bundle of saplings is bent round, somewhat in the fashion of a shepherd's crook.[1]

At the best of times it is difficult to follow everything that is said at a service such as the one described here. Moreover, at this service Xhosa was spoken most of the time, and only some of it was interpreted, into Southern Sotho, not Tswana, although a Tswana Bible was used. In the following description therefore the stress will be on action and general behaviour.

The Leader of this church, H—— G——, is of Hlubi (Nguni) descent. Both his father and mother were born in Taung, but his grandfather came from the south-east to settle in Taung. He is young, tall, and thin, with large eyes, a slightly nervous type, but not extremely so. When all are settled in the little room for the service, he says a few words and announces a hymn. A drum beats out the rhythm of the hymn which is sung with enthusiasm. The women on the one side of the room stand still, only clapping hands, but the men make steps and contort their bodies. Some of them sing with eyes closed, another sways back and forth in a stooping attitude, while his face is strained, with eyes wide open, like a person who is afraid. Another inclines his head to one side with both hands to his cheek. Occasionally one gives a loud and wild shout, or another blows hard. These actions and attitudes recur throughout the service. The whole procedure is reminiscent of some Bantu dances in which the men perform the movements and the women form a chorus to provide the accompaniment.[2]

Presently the tempo of the singing increases, and a few start walking in a circle in the middle of the floor. The room is no more than twelve feet square but so far there are only about twelve persons in the room so that one can still easily move about! The tempo of the hymn increases still further and those in the circle almost break into a trot. One man's knees suddenly give way under him and he nearly falls, shouting wildly. On a sign from the Leader the roundabout stops and all kneel, completing the verse they are singing. Then all break out in loud prayer, causing a terrific din.[3]

The service proceeds more or less according to the general Pentecostal pattern already described. An unusual feature is the reading of the Ten Commandments. H—— reads a few verses in Xhosa, and after all have joined in singing a series of 'Amens', he reads a few verses in Tswana. So the reading continues, interrupted by the 'Amen' song several times.

Besides the leader, four other men deliver sermons, punctuated by the

---

[1] The significance of these robes and accessories is discussed in ch. VI.

[2] This is the pattern of dancing and singing followed by the Tswana bridal party. The *mohobelo*-dance of the Southern Sotho is also of this nature. (See Ashton, 1952, pp. 96, 97.)

[3] In one Separatist Pentecostal church they always face east—'from where the light comes'—when praying.

THE PATTERN OF CHURCH ACTIVITIES 133

customary interruptions. One of these is caused by the arrival of a group of about ten church members, who are heard outside as they approach singing and beating a drum. (My enquiry later on reveals that these people have been to the river 'to wash off the *sehihi* of death'. Cf. ch. VI, pp. 191, 194.) The last preacher, with his luxuriant beard—the men abstain from shaving their beards in this church—and longish hair, and with his flowing robes and staff looks as though he has just stepped out of an old-fashioned Bible picture. He speaks with prophet-like fervour, but is soon stopped by a man (X) who starts telling something in a soft but urgent voice. Another man (Y) to whom he has pointed, also rises and speaks quickly but quietly. Later I find out that X was 'prophesying' about possessions of Y that had been 'taken'. These were 'taken in the night by things—things with which people perform sorcery'. Y was sleeping as if dead. When Y spoke, he was acknowledging that he had experienced such deep sleep. It was further explained that Y had not been aware of what had happened, because the things were returned before he awoke, though only after they had been 'worked', i.e. with medicines.

When I have also spoken by request, H—— announces that 'we are now closing the preaching. All things have their proper time . . . [reference is made to Ecclesiastes 3]. . . . We shall now open the work of intercession.' In this connexion he refers to Mark 16:15.

Before observing details of the last part of the service, we may briefly note the general procedure. Accompanied by the singing of the congregation, a number of people move in a circle (as before), and inside the circle one or more people pray for those who come forward to be prayed for individually. The praying is done by special 'Prayers' or other more senior office bearers who are sometimes also referred to as Prophets. Those members who feel the need for such prayer, come forward. They kneel down for a moment before the prayer commences. The prayers contain many sounds which do not form part of everyday language and the laying-on of hands is rather violent at times. Occasionally a short conversation takes place between the one who prays and the person who is prayed for. During these conversations the 'Prayer' prophesies to the 'patient' what course the latter's ailment is taking, and perhaps also what garments the latter should wear to be healed. All the while the roundabout continues, and those moving in the circle only turn about occasionally. Some of them are relieved by others, but a few seem to keep on most of the time.

Before the intercession starts, all furniture is removed from the room, the floor is sprinkled again and the roundabout starts. Those who are not in the circle—and it must be remembered that by now there are about thirty people in this small room!—crowd into the corners and against the walls. Soon a young 'Prayer' or Prophet (A) goes to the middle of the circle and starts praying. Someone takes up a position behind him, but A first joins

134 RELIGION IN A TSWANA CHIEFDOM

the roundabout for a few moments, then returns and starts praying with his hand on the man's shoulder. He draws the man's arms forward, manipulates his hand, and then feels over his torso, praying all the while. Fortunately it is not extremely hot to-day, but it is November and the heat is bad enough at the middle of the day. The door is closed—as is the custom during prayers in all churches—and there are only two small windows. Dust soon rises from the floor. Everybody sweats freely. Under the low flat roof the atmosphere in the small room is 'thick' beyond description. When later three men are praying simultaneously, prayer and song combine to produce a deafening confusion of sound, for 'Prayers' shout at the top of their voices and singers sing with lively spirit, '*Amen, Jesu, Amen*', the same short refrain over and over again, while at times the singing is distinctly guttural.

When another young man (B) enters the circle a young girl comes to him to be prayed for. Occasionally he utters a buzzing sound. First he takes hold of the girl's arm, then places his hands on her forehead and goes on to feel and press her shoulders and over the upper part of her body rather roughly. A has now swung his short sackcloth cloak over the person for whom he is praying. A stout, middle-aged man (C) is also praying now, holding a baby in his arms which has been brought by its mother. I notice one girl whose nerves seem to be strained, and she looks as if she might be pregnant. She also comes for prayer and eventually starts crying under the tension. Many people show excitement, but to most it is an excitement they seem to be enjoying thoroughly. They run in the circle till they are quite out of breath, and then still keep on, and still gasp '*Amen . . . Jesu . . . Amen*' with the other singers. '*Amen, Jesu, Amen; Amen, Jesu, Amen . . .*' —it goes on for ten minutes, fifteen minutes, twenty minutes, and then to my relief the words and the tune change, but the action remains the same.

A small digression comes when H—— hands a bottle of water to C, who prays over it, handling the bottle as he prays. Towards the end A and C are literally beating their patients and they utter high-pitched shouts at the top of their voices. When there are no more people to be prayed for, the singing and roundabout is stopped. The benediction follows a few words by H—— and the congregation files out and suddenly everybody is quite calm and normal again, as if all this that has been going on was nothing but a dream.[1] The whole service has lasted close on four hours, and there has been no pause, although individuals occasionally leave the room for a few minutes. On returning, each one makes a small curtsey (without crossing himself), as all also do when entering for the first time.

The intercession part of the service, the individual movements and shouts, as well as the wearing of special garments by all members, and the taking off of shoes, are closely connected with topics which will be treated in the next chapter, and their significance will be discussed there. A few other matters touching the churches in general must still be discussed here.

[1] In a description of an American 'White' revival service Dr. Hortense Powdermaker (1939, ch. 12), also mentions a similar instance of a striking contrast between the behaviour during the service and immediately after.

THE PATTERN OF CHURCH ACTIVITIES   135

Singing is the only form of music in church services, drums being the only instrumental accompaniment ever used, and that only in one or two Pentecostal Separatist churches. On the whole the congregations join in the singing with enthusiasm, and it provides pleasant listening, but in a few instances it is very poor. The churches connected with Europeans mostly have their own hymnals and use these exclusively. The music and words of most of the hymns are based on the lighter type of European hymns. One or two Separatist churches have their own hymnals. The others use hymn-books of the mission churches, and hymns from books of several different denominations are often used in the same church. The Pentecostals tend to have certain favourite hymns from these books. They appear to be favoured mainly on account of their tunes, the popular tunes being those that have a lively, swing rhythm. Often Separatist Pentecostals sang the hymns to different tunes from the ones in the hymn-book. They also sometimes sing short refrains which have probably arisen spontaneously in these churches. Besides the *'Amen, Jesu, Amen'* already mentioned, there are others such as *'Basione, tlang, loo dumedise'* ('Zionists, come and greet'), *'Hoza Moya o Incwele'* ('Come Holy Spirit'—this Nguni refrain was heard in an exclusively Tswana church), *Johane Mokolobetsi* (3x), *a kolobetsa mo letsheng ja Joredane* (John the Baptist (3x), he baptized in the water of Jordan), and *'A re kubameng ka mangôle'* ('Let us go on our knees'—sung before praying). Not only these refrains, but also hymns or verses of hymns are often repeated over and over again.

The music to which the portions from Scripture are sung in the three Separatist Sabbatarian churches has originated within the churches. I lack the technical training to describe and analyse these tunes, but to me they were reminiscent of traditional Bantu music. Some of the tunes of the Pentecostals also reminded me of the rhythm of Bantu music, but on the whole I would still have interpreted them in terms of certain types of 'Western' music. One must add here that the rhythm of some 'Western' hymns is changed so as to make the melodies almost unrecognizable. In mission circles an attempt at 'indigenization' has been made in a new little book of children's hymns recently published by the L.M.S. for their own use, in which use has been made of some traditional Tswana melodies. In liturgical formulas which have recently been introduced, some of the responses of the congregation are also set to traditional music.

In spite of the existence of several Tswana hymn-books, one of the most widely used volumes is in Southern Sotho, and, like the other, is a mission publication. There are other examples of Southern Sotho lin-

136   RELIGION IN A TSWANA CHIEFDOM

guistic influence in the churches also, especially among the Separatists. It emerges in the institutionalized shouted responses of Pentecostals, in a baptismal formula, and in the terminology of some preachers who are themselves altogether Tswana, born and bred in Taung. I have even noticed many Southern Sotho words and expressions in the everyday conversation of such men. This is not a common phenomenon among the population at large and therefore cannot be ascribed to the general contact of migrant labourers with the foreign language at the labour centres. What apparently happens is that Taung men at the labour-centres join churches in which Southern Sotho is used and not Tswana. When they return to Taung and establish local branches of their churches, they impart to their congregations the foreign lingu-istic influence they have acquired. Thus the church acts as an agent of contact between different Bantu cultures.

In the churches connected with Europeans the official dress for clergy generally follows fairly closely the pattern in the parent churches. Outside those Pentecostal churches in which all the members wear special church apparel, it is difficult to generalize about the clerical dress of Separatists. In churches of the Anglican pattern, the apparel of the clergy is usually an imitation or attempted imitation of vest-ments worn in the Anglican Church. With several church leaders the clerical collar is very popular, and is worn with various combinations of clothing. Some favour black suits with ordinary ties and occasion-ally one sees a frock coat. In two churches the church officials wear white laboratory coats. In one of the Pentecostal churches the mem-bers wear ordinary clothes, but the leaders wear white tunics with green cords round their waists, which are untied and serve a special purpose when they are praying for the sick (see ch. VI).

Attention may be drawn here to the attitude of the Bantu to time, as illustrated in the activities of the churches. Many people possess watches and clocks, and when in employment keep to their working hours with a considerable degree of punctuality. When engaged in their own activities, however, time still seems to be of little impor-tance. Most churches usually have an official time at which services are supposed to start, but it is common for a service to start half an hour or an hour later, while another day one might arrive on time and find the service well in progress. Functions advertised for a certain time invariably start a good deal later. Moreover, activities sometimes proceed with extreme monotony and repetition.

The general pattern of church services undoubtedly makes for group cohesion, which adds to the importance of the church group in the present structure. Besides the social intercourse before and after a

THE PATTERN OF CHURCH ACTIVITIES 137

service and the setting it often has in the homestead, informality in style and handshaking after the service foster intimate in-group relations.[1] The high degree of participation of ordinary members, especially in Pentecostal churches, is also important in providing opportunities for self-expression, which increase the value of group membership. Examples of this are processions, preaching by ordinary members, responses and shouted reactions, and especially the violent type of healing ritual of Pentecostals. The latter at times almost partakes of the character of a game. The robes worn by members of some of the Pentecostal churches also contribute to group cohesion. While the general appearance of these robes may be alike in different churches, there are differences in the figures which adorn them, a particular church tending to concentrate on particular figures or symbols.

Preachers and their sermons

Although preachers often take little trouble to prepare a sermon, the majority speak with great ease and without self-consciousness, seldom lacking words. Often their eloquence is combined with much gesticulation and a dramatic way of speaking, and Pentecostal preachers especially tend to use artificial vocal effects. One preacher often dramatized activities about which he was speaking. However, one also finds monotonous and unenthusiastic delivery.

Different types of sermons corresponding to the different types of churches (A, B, and C) are discernible, although not all sermons conform to type. In the typical sermon in churches of type 'A' a single verse or portion from Scripture serves as text, and a certain theme, either expressed in the text or associated with it, is discernible. The main theme does not necessarily run through the whole sermon, but often merely recurs here and there. When the text is from a portion describing some episode or happening, the whole episode is usually first related in detail in the first part of the sermon, easily accounting for as much as a third of the whole. The sermons of trained preachers, as well as teachers and other men with a similar standard of education, usually exhibit a much higher degree of coherence and continuity of thought than others.

The following gives the trend of a sermon by a teacher in the L.M.S. church on an ordinary Sunday morning. It lasted eighteen minutes.

[1] Some of the churches carry some of their particular customs into everyday life. One day while I was sitting talking to a Pentecostal Separatist Preacher in the enclosure of his homestead a woman passed along the path nearby and the following remarks passed between them without her stopping. She greeted him with 'Peace! father', to which he replied with an 'Amen!' 'Halleluiah!' 'Where do you come from?' 'I visited . . . at . . .' 'Yes?' 'I went there in the morning.' 'Amen!' 'Halleluiah!'

138 RELIGION IN A TSWANA CHIEFDOM

The text was from the Sermon on the Mount, Matthew 7:21: 'Not every one that saith unto me Lord, Lord, shall enter into the Kingdom of heaven; but he that doeth the will of my Father which is in heaven.' The preacher began by pointing out that one lives by working with one's hands: by taking up employment with Europeans, or by farming with stock or ploughing the earth. If one merely talks, without working, it is of no avail. A field does not plough and cultivate itself.

'All things on earth come to an end: even a rock, and grass just the same. . . . But more than all this—seek first the kingdom of heaven, and all other things will be added.

'It is no use that we merely talk with our mouth and do not do the will of God. We should confirm our words by our works. St. Paul writes to St. James [sic] that if faith is not accompanied by works, the faith is of no avail. Faith should be confirmed by the works. The saying that I belong to the Lord and the Lord belongs to me should be confirmed by my doing what God desires.'

The preacher went on to refer to the insects and their activities, and to the ants which meet each other on the way. 'They take their food into their store-rooms, knowing that the time of famine, namely winter, is coming. . . . Seek the Lord while there is still time.' There was reference again to the grass 'that is seen in the veld' and to the young of birds which are fed from their 'store-rooms'. 'Where have we stored our faith? . . . Let our faith be evident as well as the works which testify to the true faith.'

In the typical Sabbatarian sermon, instruction predominates, and the sermon is of a fragmentary nature. A series of texts relevant to a particular theme are read and discussed in succession, each text being discussed separately before proceeding to the reading of the next. A sermon by a Deacon of the S.D.A. (untrained) at an ordinary Sunday afternoon service was delivered more or less as follows:

The first portion read was from Genesis 2, about the blessing and sancti-fication of the seventh day, after God had created the heavens and the earth. After speaking about the duty to keep holy the seventh day, the preacher proceeded to read the first four commandments from the Decalogue (Ex. 20) and found occasion here to speak about the Egyptians who were heathens and worshipped other gods, the sun amongst others. Now followed various portions from the Old Testament, all containing injunctions to observe the Sabbath, and about each portion a few remarks were made. The last two Scripture readings (from Ps. 95 and Heb. 4) both contained references to entering into God's rest.

After the sermon the preacher, who is well on in his sixties and has had only enough school education to enable him to read and write, told me that the texts were his own choice, and that he had not pre-pared his sermon beforehand, since he knew these texts by heart.

It is difficult to analyse the sermons of Pentecostals, since these are

THE PATTERN OF CHURCH ACTIVITIES 139

the most incoherent, and usually lack a central recurring theme altogether. Perhaps we may say that each Pentecostal church has a few favourite themes and that some or all of these occur in nearly every sermon. There is, however, one pattern which does recur, especially when there is a whole series of sermons by a number of people. The introductory sermon by the leader then usually consists of a repetition of thoughts contained in the Scripture reading, and subsequent speakers repeat these thoughts but add something here and there, some of which may not be contained in the Scripture reading, but may be associated with it. An example of such a series of sermons is given below. The service in which these were delivered, was held in the leader's homestead, and was of the violent type, being interrupted by hymns and the customary shouts. It is not possible to give more than mere extracts from these incoherent sermons.

After the introductory part of the service the local Preacher greets the congregation with exclamations of

'Peace be with you!'—'Amen!'
'The peace of Jesus!'—'Amen!'
'The peace of God!'—'Amen!',

and utters some sounds. He remarks that 'these times are pressing; it is now already November, and in December the ministers [from Johannesburg] are coming'. After announcing the Scripture reading and commenting on John the Baptist and Jesus, he reads Matt. 3 (the teaching of John the Baptist and Jesus' baptism) and Mark 1:1–16 (a shorter version of the same subjects, with a short reference to the temptation in the wilderness and the calling of the first disciples). After some more sounds, the Preacher starts his sermon by relating in a high-pitched, shouting tone details of the life of John the Baptist. He speaks about John's preaching of judgement that is at hand, about being baptized and bearing fruit. 'To bear fruit is to fulfil the law of the church'. . . Then again about the clothing and food of the Baptist '. . . and he did not drink beer and *khadi* [a highly intoxicating native drink], neither did he smoke tobacco. He ate only two things: locusts and honey' . . . He continues the narration, repeating again some of the matter already mentioned, and describes how the Spirit took Jesus into the wilderness after his baptism, and how He was tempted. . . . 'And Satan said to Him: "Look at all my farms, look at my cattle, look at that village. If you worship me, all these will be yours" . . .' After the Preacher, the Evangelist takes his turn and after greeting with peace, he expresses his thanks to God for various things, repeats the announcement about the expected visit of the ministers, and then turns to the actual topic—'the son of Zacharias'. He repeats almost eveything the previous speaker has said about the coming judgement and the Baptist's customs. He tells how the Baptist preaches: ' "You say that you are children of Abraham. But I tell you that God is able to produce children of Abraham from stones. . . . The axe is already laid unto the root of the trees. . . . Leave the things of yesterday—beer,

140   RELIGION IN A TSWANA CHIEFDOM

and tobacco . . ." The son of Zacharias announced that Jesus was coming and that He would light a fire which no one could quench.' The Evangelist tells about Jesus' corn which He will gather in his store-room, proceeds to the 'son of Zacharias whose voice is that of one crying in the wilderness. . . . Matthew and Mark are witnesses. Mark testifies to Matthew.' Again he deals with the baptism of Jesus and proceeds to the temptation. 'Jesus was in the wilderness, amongst the animals. He had no food, but the angels served Him. . . . When He was hungry, the devil came to Him and addressed Him: "Hey, man Jesus! . . ." ' After relating the different temptations, he proceeds to new material: the arrest of John the Baptist, his death at the hand of Herod, and the presentation of his head '*mo pitseng ya mahura*'.[1] '. . . The time is near. . . . Believe in me. . . . Believe in my Father [these words seem to be placed in the mouth of St. John] . . . Jesus came to heal the sick, the deaf, etc. . . . "I go . . . to be the last sacrifice" . . . Jesus died for our sins.' In closing, the speaker returns to the calling of Christ's first disciples with the challenge to leave their nets and be fishers of men. Almost the whole sermon has consisted of narration and there has been hardly any exhortation.

The third speaker is a young man who speaks so fast that his speech is hardly intelligible. Again it is all about John the Baptist, and the Baptism and temptation of Jesus. With reference to His baptism he says that He is the 'Foundation' (using the English word)[2] and all are built on Him. About baptism he says that it 'means the confession of sins. It knows *kotsi* . . .[3] Baptism means *kotsi*.' He closes with a reference to Moses and the third heaven. The next speaker is an old man who besides repeating some thoughts, also tells how John the Baptist sent some of his disciples to Jesus to ask whether He was the one that was to come, or whether they should look for another, and how Christ sent them back with a report of the healing and other miracles He was performing.

Two older women then speak without saying very much, and a third also intimates: 'I do not stand up for anything', but nevertheless carries on for quite a time. As a new element she relates how the people took their horns and threw them into the river under the influence of the Baptist's preaching. (My first thought on hearing this was of the snuff containers made from the horns of cattle, but on my enquiry after the service several people joined in explaining that the reference was also to medicine horns.[4]) A youth and

[1] It is difficult to know exactly what is envisaged by this term. Literally it could be translated as 'on a pot of (or for) fat'. In this and other Pentecostal churches it recurred very often in narratives of the Baptist's death. Neither in the Tswana nor the Southern Sotho translation of the Bible is this term used.

[2] The name of the church is Foundation Apostolic Church in Jerusalem.

[3] A Southern Sotho word meaning 'accident, harm, damage' (Mabille, A. and Dieterlen, H. (revised by R. A. Paroz); *Southern Sotho English Dictionary* (Morija, 1950)). A Tswana informant who is an ex-teacher recognized it as a Southern Sotho word and said that it denoted 'danger'.

[4] What they actually said was *dinaka tsa boloi*, lit., horns of sorcery, which, as I understand it, refers to the horns of which the contents are used as protection or antidote against sorcery and other evils (see p. 27). I do not think the reference was to medicines used to perform sorcery.

THE PATTERN OF CHURCH ACTIVITIES 141

three young girls now speak, each one repeating what has already been said. One of the girls cannot be older than thirteen. She is a leading spirit in the singing, often starting a hymn on her own during sermons. Her version of the events described in Matt. 3 is remarkably near to the original words of the Bible, perhaps more so than any of the other sermons. Finally, the Evangelist thanks God for all the witnesses and announces the next part of the service. It may be pointed out here that nearly every speaker—there were eleven of them altogether—opened with wishes of peace and of thanksgiving, while most of them closed with an expression such as 'The time is past, it is time for me to sit down'. The preaching, with all the interruptions, lasted over two hours.

In all the churches the Bible takes a prominent place: usually there is Scripture reading, or the reading of the text for the sermon, and quotations from and references to Scripture in the course of the sermon. An analysis of all the verses or portions used as texts for the sermons I attended, and other quotations from or references to Scripture, of which I made notes during services, reveals the following.

(i) A distinct majority are from the New Testament, both in Separatist churches and those connected with Europeans. A number of the portions used from the Old Testament deal with fulfilling the law in general, keeping the Sabbath, pure and impure animals, and with the evils of wine and what is interpreted as referring to tobacco. These latter texts are mostly used in Sabbatarian and Pentecostal churches.

(ii) By far the most popular portions in Pentecostal Separatist churches are those dealing with the activities and preaching of John the Baptist.

(iii) The most popular single pericope is the parable of the vine and the branches, and Christ's exhortations connected with it (John 15:1 ff.). It recurred mostly in Pentecostal Separatist churches, but also appeared in sermons of churches of group 'A'.

(iv) Another passage recurring in references and quotations is the first two verses (one or the other or both) of John 14.

Before discussing the significance of these points, we should also take note of frequently recurring topics. The necessity of fulfilling 'the law', doing right, bearing fruit, and being diligent (either in general or in respect of 'good works') is frequently mentioned. This moralistic tendency is particularly evident in Pentecostal and Sabbatarian churches, and often the main content of 'the law' is interpreted as being baptized, avoiding certain things and (with Sabbatarians) keeping the Sabbath. Although one encounters a greater variety of themes and topics in sermons of type 'A' churches, a general moralistic tendency is nevertheless also observable in the sermons of some preachers in these churches. It is not that preaching about Jesus

142 RELIGION IN A TSWANA CHIEFDOM

Christ, faith, and forgiveness is absent, and I must point out that in some sermons the moralistic tendency is in the background or even absent, but on the whole more stress is laid on the conduct of the individual than on the acceptance of grace through faith. In a Separatist Pentecostal church the leader had spent a long time in talking about the law and doing what is right, so that when I was asked to speak I felt urged to point out that faith in Jesus Christ and forgiveness in his Name is the essence of our salvation. The leader's wife, who was the next speaker, thereupon explained that 'forgiveness is when we behave well' (*tshwarêlô ke ha re itshwara sentlê*).[1] The expression 'faith is works', which I heard in several churches, is perhaps the most explicit expression of this tendency. An old Evangelist of a type 'A' Separatist church, when chiding the congregation because of the small collection they had given, also said that 'faith is works' and as he held up the two coins I had put into the collection plate, made quite a fuss of the amount I had contributed and added: 'It shows that he is a believer.'[2]

It is also common for preachers to remind their congregations of the future: of the end in general, of death, of future judgement, or of heaven and future blessings. In this connexion the idea of future judgement is most common, and is connected with the thought, expressed or implicit, that one should prepare for it by being converted, or by doing the right things referred to above. In connexion with the coming judgement reference was often made to different passages from Matt. 25, and the parable of the sheep and the goats particularly recurred in several sermons. The predilection shown for John 15 (the vine and the branches) is to be seen in the light of the moralistic tendency and the connected thought of future judgement. It is not the idea of the mystic union between Christ and the believer that is important, but the expectation that the branches should bear fruit, and the fate of the unfruitful branches which are cast forth, wither, and are thrown into the fire.

We may refer to a few points Dr. Sundkler makes in connexion with Zulu Separatist churches. In respect of the 'Ethiopian' sermons, he points out that 'the racial emphasis gives peculiar bias to the interpretation of the text, which is often chosen from the Old Testament'.[3] In another context he says of the 'Zionists': 'Obviously the

---

[1] The fact that the words for 'forgiveness' and 'behaving' are derived from the same verbal stem (*go tshwara*, to take hold of) perhaps helps to make the statement more acceptable.

[2] *Modumedi,* 'believer', may also mean 'Christian' or 'full church member'.

[3] *Op. cit.,* p. 191.

THE PATTERN OF CHURCH ACTIVITIES 143

Old Testament forms the foundation of the belief of these churches. A common argument in all *materia theologica* is: The truth is to be found in *"u Dutelonom"* or *"u Levi"* (Deuteronomy or Leviticus). Moses is the central figure in their Bible; Moses, leader, liberator, lawgiver; Moses overcoming the dangerous waters of the Red Sea; Moses fixing detailed prescriptions or taboos.'[1]

Both Taung and Zulu Separatist churches therefore show the same tendency toward moralism or legalism, but the churches from our area do not show the same preference for the Old Testament,[2] neither is Moses given such a central place in their teaching. Although reference was once made to working for Europeans in one breath with Israel's servility in Egypt, this cannot be said to be representative of a general trend.

According to Dr. Sundkler ideas about heaven and the 'Gate of Heaven' are very prominent in the theology of Zulu Zionists and he describes a distinct 'Zulu version' of the blessed hereafter,[3] which is obviously biased by the racial issue. In contrast with this the future judgement is much more prominent in Taung churches than the expectation of future salvation, nor did I come across any notions representative of a distinct version of heaven influenced by the interracial situation. The nearest to this was the thought expressed by one preacher that all, rich and poor, would enter at the same gate.

The frequent use of John 14:2 ('In my Father's house are many mansions') in Zulu Separatist churches is also related by Dr. Sundkler to the interracial situation, in that it is taken by the Zulus 'as a charter and guarantee that there will be, possibly, a separate mansion for them'.[4] Although there were often references to or quotations from the first verses of John 14 in Taung churches, the first verse was often quoted alone. In the few instances in which the second verse was quoted, it was connected with the idea of being strangers on earth, having no home or heritage here. The speaker who connected this verse most distinctly with the subordinate position of his people, was an L.M.S. Leader, speaking at a funeral. Another speaker had already introduced John 14:1–2, and had also referred to Heb. 13:14 ('For here we have no continuing city . . .'). The L.M.S. man spoke in the following vein:

[1] *Op. cit.*, p. 277.

[2] Dr. Van Antwerp says of Separatist churches in general that they appear to have a particular liking for the Old Testament and the old Jewish ceremonies. (Van Antwerp, C.M., 1938, p. 85.) Dr. Hilda Kuper (1947) draws attention to the preference for the Old Testament in Swazi Separatist churches.

[3] *Op. cit.*, pp. 289 ff.

[4] *Op. cit.*, p. 276.

144   RELIGION IN A TSWANA CHIEFDOM

'Christ has gone to prepare a place for us. Everyone has his own chair. Prepare yourselves. . . .' At a later stage he said: 'To-day it is thus: we buy our water, we buy our wood. Our houses have been given [to others?]. . . . The land is not ours, it belongs to another. The land belongs to strangers. Only the Father is alone, He is in heaven. Our Father has waited for us. We are ploughers, we are a garden.'

It may be that we should see in these remarks a reference to the land on the irrigation scheme in particular, about which the opinion is sometimes expressed that it no longer belongs to the Tlhaping. It is significant that these were the words of a simple mission church leader who had little about him of the political agitator. I must make it clear, however, that this does not represent a common trend in sermons.

In the churches studied in Taung, awareness of the subordinate position of Africans is occasionally expressed, both in Separatist churches and churches connected with Europeans. However, they do not seem to be as consciously concerned with the interracial situation as those described by Dr. Sundkler, and it has not biased their teaching to the extent that this has happened in Zulu Separatist churches.[1]

In the prominence they give to John the Baptist, the Taung Pentecostal churches resemble the Zulu Zionists. In Taung this tendency is to be understood in the first place because of the importance of the rite of baptism in these churches. Moreover, his asceticism, his preaching of conversion and bringing forth 'fruits meet for repentance' (Matt. 3:8), and his warning against the coming judgement, fit in well with the general moralistic trend.

A final remark concerns the manner in which the subject material is treated. Although interesting illustrations and comparisons were often used by preachers, sermons did not abound in figurative language.[2] Many illustrations are taken from the Bible, and of these some are drawn from nature (e.g. the tree with branches and fruit, the diligent ants) or from rural activities (the shepherd and his flock). Some of these involve material that is foreign to the indigenous culture. Thus, joining the church is likened to Noah's entering the ark, or the grave is likened to the Red Sea: as the Israelites were allowed to pass through unharmed and the Egyptians were caught by its waters

---

[1] It should be remembered, of course, that Dr. Sundkler's study involved a much larger number of churches than my own. I can merely state in negative form that in the restricted area I covered I did not witness such distinctly biased notions as Dr. Sundkler describes.

[2] In everyday conversation and public speaking generally the use of metaphors, comparisons, and proverbs did occur, but they were not as striking a feature as I expected in a Bantu language.

THE PATTERN OF CHURCH ACTIVITIES   145

and perished, so the believers pass through the grave unharmed, but the unbelievers are caught in it. Some illustrations are from nature (i.e. apart from those which have a precedent in the Bible). Very few are from the traditional culture. On the other hand, illustrations and comparisons from the sphere of contact with Western civilization are numerous: the policeman, the school, the time-table, the pass system, the wedding ring, the railway, the office-stamp—all these provide material for illustrations or metaphors. Thus the pilgrimage to heaven is likened to a train journey, and every Sunday service to a station along the line. Or death is likened to reaching the station and catching the train (the implication is, of course—to heaven). Another again explains that when death comes, you have to go, there is no chance of staying longer, 'your pass is up'.

The sermons I heard did not produce much evidence of the Bible being interpreted in terms of traditional culture, although a few such examples occurred. We have already seen how John the Baptist's abstinence was expressed in terms of the native drinks, beer, and *khadi*, and how the Jews who were converted by his preaching were attributed with having possessed snuff and medicine horns which they threw into the river. Or again, when the Magi arrived at Herod's court and enquired after the place where the King had been born whose star they had seen, Herod, amongst others, called doctors who threw the dice (Tswana style) and revealed that the King was born in Bethlehem! Or when Christ says: 'I am come to set . . . the daughter-in-law against her mother-in-law (Matt. 10:35) it is explained in terms of traditional relationships between in-laws. On the other hand, when Christ, speaking about John the Baptist, says: 'Behold, they which are gorgeously apparelled, and live delicately, are in Kings' courts' (Matt. 7:25), it is explained in terms of modern conditions: in terms of the 'suits' and 'shining furniture' of the kings.

The relative unimportance of material from the traditional culture is consistent with what I shall attempt to illustrate in connexion with ritual, namely, that it is not the external forms of the indigenous culture that have been carried over into Christian ritual and teaching, but the magical nature of the rites and religious dogma.

R.T.C.—11

CHAPTER VI

RITUAL AND REVELATION
IN THE CHURCHES

IN this chapter we shall be dealing with present-day ritual and with beliefs and avowed experiences connected with revelation, that is with such of these as are regarded as Christian and not pagan rites. We shall see that elements of traditional ritual and belief have found their way into the churches, but I shall try to show that ritual and belief in the churches do not resemble traditional ritual and belief so much in respect of external form but in respect of their magical character.

It is necessary, therefore, first to make clear what I understand by magic and beliefs and ritual which bear a magical character.[1] I take for granted that it will be agreed that what we are dealing with here belongs to the domain of what is usually described as magico-religious, and that the ceremonies described may be regarded as ritual. What we are concerned with, is to find a criterion to distinguish what is magical within the magico-religious sphere. The description of magic[2] as ritual and belief which do not presuppose the existence of spiritual beings, as opposed to religion as beliefs and ritual which do pre-suppose such beings, is not sufficient. Rites which do not presuppose such beings are indeed magic, but rites which do presuppose such beings may also sometimes bear a magical character. Perhaps we should say that the former type of rites constitute pure magic, but that there is no absolute division between magic and religion, and that magic often enters into the sphere of what according to the above-mentioned distinction is regarded as religion.

A few examples may help us to formulate a workable definition of magic.

(1) When a native doctor smears medicines in the corners of a hearth to ward off sorcery, and believes that the medicine possesses the intrinsic power of making the sorcerer's medicines harmless, it is magic.

(2) When a child dreams of a deceased father, some earth is taken from the grave of the deceased and (perhaps together with some medicines) is added to water with which the child is purified to drive away the shadow or

[1] Since anthropologists have not yet formulated a generally accepted definition of magic I take the liberty of using my own definition. It is not offered as a definition in respect of all magic but as a tool for explaining my own material.

[2] Cf. *Notes and Queries on Anthropology*, Sixth Edition, 1951, p. 174.

RITUAL AND REVELATION IN THE CHURCHES 147

the *sehihi* of the deceased. The rite is connected with a spiritual being but the fact that it is believed to be in *itself* effectual to bring about the desired result gives it a distinctly magical character.

(3) When a prayer is said over a stick or a staff and God is asked in the prayer to bless the object and thenceforth that object is believed always to be imbued with a power or influence it did not possess before, the action ascribed to that power or influence of the stick is magical even though it may be thought to have been given by God.

(4) When the rite of baptism is in itself nothing more than a symbolic representation of an inner cleansing, the rite is non-magical. But when the performance of the rite in itself is believed necessarily to have a beneficial influence, whether of a spiritual or physical nature, it bears a magical character.

(5) When a prayer is said petitioning God to grant healing, it is a purely religious activity if it is said with the expectation that God will grant healing, but with the realization that He is free to do so or not. However, if it is believed that the prayer must necessarily result in the recovery of the patient, it bears a magical character, even if the recovery is thought of as being caused by God.

The important point in deciding whether ritual is magical, is whether it is believed that it must *necessarily* have a particular super-natural or mystical effect. Even when a spiritual being enters the chain of thoughts and is thought of as causing the effect, the ritual may still be magical if it is thought of as *necessarily* resulting in that effect, as if the spiritual being is *compelled* by the ritual to react in a particu-lar way. When it is believed that a rite or an object *may* have a particular effect but that the outcome ultimately depends upon the decision of a spiritual being in which that being decides according to his own free will, it is non-magical. Ritual is also non-magical if it is merely a symbolic representation of a mystical belief, but as soon as such symbolic ritual is thought of as necessarily having a particular effect, it bears a magical character.[1]

This does not imply that non-magical ritual is devoid of all mystical effect. A particular rite may be connected with a particular mystical effect but if the connexion is not thought of as absolute, and is seen as depending in the last instance on the free decision of a spiritual being, it is still not magical.[2]

I have already pointed out that magic may penetrate into the sphere of religion. We should also note that the extent to which magic enters the field of religion varies in different religions. In other words,

[1] I am indebted to the Wilsons for some of the ideas used in connexion with magic. (See Wilson, Godfrey, and Monica, 1945.)

[2] This point has particular significance in respect of the view which different churches take of the sacraments.

148   RELIGION IN A TSWANA CHIEFDOM

different religions may be characterized by varying degrees of 'magi-cality'. Some religions may be purely or almost purely religious and therefore non-magical. In other cases again, magic may penetrate into the field of religion so deeply that there is almost nothing that can be regarded as purely religious. Such religions may be said to bear a highly magical character.

Christianity, as I understand it, is essentially non-magical. The revelation contained in the Christian Scriptures, stressing God's abso-lute freedom and man's complete dependence on God's grace, does not leave room for the possibility of man exercising compulsion over God.

What is actually practised and believed by Christians and their churches, is, however, a different matter. In fact, in the sense in which magic is used here, ritual and belief in churches may also bear a magical character, depending on the value that is attached to ritual acts. This is not only the case where pagan ritual has been incorporated in the churches, but magical value may also be attached to such essentially Christian rites as baptism and holy communion. More-over, this phenomenon is not confined to churches existing in societies in transition from 'primitive' to large-scale: not only is it found among individual 'Western' Christians, but the ritual and doctrines of differ-ent churches in Western society may reflect varying degrees of magicality. On the whole, however, I think the magicality found in Western churches is of a lesser degree and of a more subtle nature than that reflected by the ritual described in this chapter.

Before proceeding to a discussion of ritual in the Taung churches, it is necessary to show what role magic played in the traditional magico-religious system of the Tlhaping. We observed in chapter II that the remnants of paganism among the Tlhaping consist mostly of beliefs and ritual connected with medicines, doctoring, and divining, and with purification from 'heat', *dibêla, sehihi*, 'shadow', and breach of taboo. A great deal of these remnants may be regarded as pure magic, but a religious element does sometimes enter, e.g. when the doctor's abilities are ascribed to the ancestors or God, or when the falling of his dice is believed to be controlled by them; when *sehihi* or 'shadow' is connected with an ancestor spirit or when the purification of *dibêla* by means of medicines is accompanied by a prayer to God for rain. Nevertheless, magic, the belief in the inherent efficacy of medicines, treatment, and dice, predominates in all the important remnants of paganism.

It is difficult to assess the degree to which the ancestor cult itself was penetrated by magic, since so little of it is left. It is clear, how-

RITUAL AND REVELATION IN THE CHURCHES   149

ever, that prayers and sacrifices to the ancestral spirits were often accompanied by the use of medicines, and I suspect that generally magic played an important role even in connexion with ritual that was concerned with the ancestors.

In this connexion I refer to the account an old informant, who was a native doctor, gave of a rain rite which he remembered to have been performed in the time of chief Mankurwane. It involved the slaughtering of a black beast (bovine) in the chief's *kgotla* as a gift to the ancestors (*badimo*). Young immature girls had to bring water and driftwood from the river. The driftwood and the contents of the slaughtered animal's stomach (*mošwang*, an important element in some purification rites—see p. 37, n. 3) were burnt. The water, over which a prayer had been said for the help of God and the 'fathers' of the officiating rain-maker, was sprinkled on the fire to produce clouds of smoke. In the light of the discussion of the ritual concept of 'heat' given in ch. II, I suggest the following explanation: water and also driftwood (because of its connexion with the river) are used for their 'cooling' properties, and the same applies to *mošwang*; young girls must bring the materials required, because they are still 'cool', have not yet become 'hot' through sexual intercourse and will not impart defiling heat to the cooling agents. All these factors are involved in a magical process expected to produce the condition of coolness associated with rain. The smoke clouds symbolize the desired rain clouds, but probably are regarded as being in a sense also effective in producing those clouds. In the rite as a whole the sacrifice and prayer to the ancestors is intimately tied up with magical measures and in fact seems to be less important than the magic.

Taking all into consideration, I think we may say that traditionally magic predominated and penetrated deeply into the field of religion, i.e. the ancestor cult, among the Tlhaping. It is against this background that we should consider the role of magic in the ritual of the churches.

Ritual of childhood and youth

Reference has already been made to the 'bringing out' of a baby and its mother on the termination of confinement. It consists of a feast which is an occasion for bringing together the child's paternal and maternal kin, and for announcing the child's name. The feasting is commonly preceded by a short service. In former times, I was told, the ceremony of bringing out the child was not accompanied by feasting, and the Christian service, of course, is also an innovation. I give a few particulars of a ceremony I attended.

150   RELIGION IN A TSWANA CHIEFDOM

On the afternoon before the ceremony I visited the homestead where the woman (*d*) was confined in one of the two small flat-roofed buildings which made up the homestead. It was the homestead of her father (*A*) and mother (*b*); she was not living there but had come specially for her confinement. In the other building a few relatives of *A* were gathered, pleasantly conversing over some beer after having assisted in preparing for the ceremony. The following relatives of *A* were present: his wife; his daughter (*d*'s younger sister) and her husband; his father's younger brother (actual) and the latter's wife; two young women both of whom *A* called 'my elder brother's child', and a woman who was called a 'sister' of *A*.[1]

The following morning guests started arriving before 9.30. At about eleven o'clock a service was held in a small room and nearly all the people inside who were not engaged in conducting the service were relatives of the baby's father (*C*). *C* himself could not be present but was represented by his elder brother. The service was conducted jointly by two old women of the L.M.S. who were accompanied by a few younger female members of the church. During the singing of the first hymn, *d* emerged from the other house, wearing a long dress and hat (the 'change' costume which she had worn at her wedding). An older woman carried the baby and conducted *d* to the room where the service was held. The woman was a 'cross-cousin' of *d*'s mother. She told me that by right this should have been done by a woman belonging to the baby's father's lineage.

The service lasted half-an-hour. Besides singing and prayer, a portion was read from Matt. 3 (the wise men from the East) and one of the old women delivered a short sermon, connecting what had been read about the birth of Jesus with the birth of the child. At the end of the service *C*'s brother announced the child's name, after which a collection was made for the baby. *A* and *b* were not present at the service, but a younger sister of *d* was.

After the service the church leaders were served with refreshments at a nearby homestead. The child's paternal relatives remained in the room where the service had taken place, and were given tea and cakes. *A*'s son-in-law, who is a prominent official in a Separatist Pentecostal church, later served beer. He was assisted by a younger sister of his wife and one of the guests. Later on beer was also served to casual visitors outside. A young man started playing an accordeon and *b* and her daughters (including *d*) danced a little.

According to one of my most reliable informants on traditional matters, the traditional 'bringing out' ceremony was not accompanied by ritual, but as we have already observed, Rev. W. C. Willoughby describes a rite which was performed on the termination of the period of confinement (see ch. II, p. 15). We have here, then, either an instance of a Christian rite supplanting a pagan rite, or being added to

---

[1] This collection of relatives does not constitute a specific regularly co-operating group. However, it is important to note that they are all maternal relatives of the baby, i.e. relatives of the people at whose homestead the ceremony is to take place.

RITUAL AND REVELATION IN THE CHURCHES 151

a traditional ceremony which did not formerly bear a religious character. It remains an occasion on which the ties between husband's relatives on the one hand, and wife's relatives on the other, are reinforced. The wife's parents act as hosts and are assisted in particular by their other daughters and some of the wife's paternal relatives. The husband's relatives are the guests of honour and are treated with more formality and less familiarity than the other guests. On this particular occasion I received the impression that the hosts were more concerned with treating their guests in an appropriate manner, than they were with the service. It is important to note, however, that the women who came to conduct the service received particular treatment as a separate group.

When one or both of a baby's parents are church members, the child is usually baptized soon after the 'bringing out' ceremony. Roman Catholics hold a small feast at the 'bringing out', when the name of the child is also announced. On the subsequent Friday it is taken to church by its mother 'to be blessed' (*go segohadiwa*) and is baptized on the Sunday. The Constitutions and Canons of the Ethiopian Catholic Church in Zion lay down that 'no woman, whatsoever, shall after childbirth come to Holy Communion or partake in any Divine Service prior to her being churched by a minister in Holy Orders. . . .'[1] In practice the 'churching' of the woman amounts to much the same as the 'bringing out' ceremony described above.

The churches which do not perform infant baptism usually perform a rite to 'bless' (*segohatsa*) the new-born infants of church members, with reference to the blessing of the Child Jesus by the prophet Simeon (Luke 2:28 ff.). I attended such a rite of the St. Paul Apostolic Faith Morning Star which followed a baptismal service.

The reading of the formula appropriate to the occasion was followed by a warning by the minister that parents would be judged by their children, with reference to Eli and his sons (I Sam. 2 and 3). A list of the names of the children was read and the minister proceeded to bless each of them with a touch of the hand, taking the small babies in his arms. The blessings varied, and included expressions such as the following: 'So-and-so, I bless you by the charge (*ka taelô*) of Jehova the God of Israel, by the name of the Father and the Holy Spirit. . . . May God give you a wise spirit . . . a good (pure) spirit . . . a God-fearing spirit . . . a spirit of lowliness . . . a respectful spirit. . . . May He make you increase in his knowledge and love. . . .' The portion from Luke 2 about Simeon's blessing of the Holy family was read, after which the minister blessed the parents 'because Simeon also blessed the parents of Jesus'.

[1] *Op. cit.*, p. 45.

152 RELIGION IN A TSWANA CHIEFDOM

The minister proceeded to exhort the parents to instruct their children, 'because tomorrow you will find them playing dice'.[1] He also spoke of 'the law' which requires that parents should instruct their children and that they should punish them (lit., beat them) if they do not heed. After announcing that he would now 'produce the law' (*ntsha molao*), he read Prov. 3:11–12 and added: 'The law of God permits that one should punish one's child if it does not listen. . . . Pray for it; if you pray, the rod will help you. . . . Teach it to fear God and respect the chief. . . . If it honours God and the chief it will be saved. . . .' A prayer was said for the parents and children.

Certain Christian denominations have introduced the general pattern for this kind of rite, and to this extent it may be regarded as an element of Christianity as a 'foreign' religion. In some of its details, however, it reveals aspects which are typical of the Bantu Separatist churches. The tendency to back ritual with Biblical precedents which are followed literally and as closely as possible is clearly revealed: the blessing of the children is not sufficient; to be in full harmony with the particular passage of Scripture on which the rite is based, the parents must also be blessed.

The blessings and the instruction given to the parents reveal the values which are important in this church: wisdom, lowliness, respect of authorities and one's parents and seniors, and doing what is right according to the law generally. The importance of filial obedience, and strict discipline enforced by corporal punishment which constitute traditional values, are re-stated in Biblical terms and with Biblical sanction, in reaction against the disintegration of society as observed in the lawlessness of present-day youth. The moralistic tendency which has been shown in the previous chapter is also clearly illustrated.

In spite of the missions' strong opposition to tribal initiation ceremonies, no purposive attempt seems to have been made to develop a Christian ceremony that could take their place. One might have expected that some Christians would regard confirmation as the Christian counterpart of traditional initiation, but I found no evidence of such a parallel. On the contrary, as we have observed, some Christians hold that young people should first undergo the tribal initiation and then join the catechism classes and be confirmed.

Marriage rites

All churches insist on their members being married by Christian or civil rites. Since many churches, especially the Separatists, do not have church officials locally who are recognized as marriage officers by

---

[1] Playing dice is the symptom commonly referred to to denote the corruption of the present generation of young men and boys. It is regarded in this light by older people generally, not only church people.

RITUAL AND REVELATION IN THE CHURCHES 153

the Government, many couples of church people get married by civil rites in the Native Commissioner's office, and then attend a service in church for the consecration of the marriage. At such a service in a Separatist Pentecostal church those present brought their wedding gifts forward at the end of the service and a prayer of thanksgiving was said in respect of the gifts. Besides the following of the bridal couple, very few people usually take the trouble to attend the rites in church. Often short services are also held at the respective homesteads of the couple's parents, where the feasting takes place.

A number of conventions have developed in connexion with the wedding outfits. The bride invariably has a white sunshade, and bride and bridegroom have a wedding as well as a 'change' outfit and they change from one into the other several times in the course of the three-day celebrations. The bridegroom usually wears white gloves and his best-man carries a clothes-brush in his pocket which is used on the bridegroom at unexpected moments, for example when the couple emerge from church. A veil is usually considered part of a complete bridal outfit, but at least one church has made the rule that 'a girl or a woman who has fallen in sin [this usually refers to extramarital pregnancy] cannot use a veil for her wedding'.[1] The important point in connexion with Christian marriage rites is that in many cases these rites are performed beside pagan rites such as those described in chapter II. At one wedding I attended, the church leader who said the prayer in the services at the homesteads and the doctor who performed the pagan ritual was one and the same person. Here paganism persists side by side with Christianity in the lives of the same people. In this connexion it is important that the Roman Catholic Church encourages the pronouncing of a blessing by the priest over the food for the wedding feast as a substitute for the pagan rites.

Death and its ritual

The idea of going to heaven when one dies is held not only by church members, but also by many outside the churches, although people do not seem to have a very clear picture of what heaven is like. At funerals one often hears references to 'arriving at the other side', or 'arriving there'. A Separatist Pentecostal leader once demonstrated to his people how they should walk when arriving at the gate of heaven: upright and straight, not staggering and reeling. An old man spoke of the long distance behind him, and pointing upwards, he

---

[1] *Minutes of the Twenty-Ninth Session of the South African Conference of the Pentecostal Holiness Church.* A trader's wife who sells many wedding outfits every year maintains that this is a widely recognized convention.

154 RELIGION IN A TSWANA CHIEFDOM

added that he had only a short distance to go still. An old woman, who is a prominent Leading Woman in the L.M.S., informed me of the recent death of her husband by saying: 'The old man has gone there' (pointing upward). The dead are sometimes thought of as becoming angels after death. At a night watch on the occasion of the death of a little girl (see p. 108), a Roman Catholic woman said that it was not necessary to spend much time in praying, because it was only a child that had died: 'A child has not got sin. . . . It is an angel now.'

Although the idea of future judgement is prominent in sermons, there does not seem to be a clear notion of the nature of the punishment to be meted out to those on whom adverse judgement will be pronounced. References to hell are seldom heard. An informant who was well versed in traditional matters and who had once also temporarily attended a catechumen class, when questioned about the activities of the spirits of the dead, referred among others to the belief in *dipoko* (sing., *sepoko*, from the Afrikaans, *Spook*, a ghost).[1] A *sepoko* is something which produces a flame (*se tukisa molelo*), he said. 'It is said that they (*dipoko*) are the spirits of the dead (*badimo*). They are dead people. It is said that it is the spirit (*môya*) of one who does not go to heaven. The ministers tell us so.' He explained further that the spirit of a rich man who is very much attached to his riches (such as money and cattle), cannot go to heaven. 'God does not accept his spirit, because he desires to go [to heaven] with his riches, whereas he cannot go with them. Neither can he sell them and buy life.' The cattle and small stock of such a man die before him, in the year of his own death. 'And when he dies, we will say: "He has departed with his goods (belongings)." '

People do not show extraordinary fear of death and are not afraid to speak of it. One often hears of old people who had a premonition of their death, and who foretold the time when they would die. During the preparations for a funeral a number of people are often gathered in or around the homestead, and the conversation is pleasant, not as boisterous as it sometimes is under normal conditions, but not different in content from normal conversation. People are particular, however, to keep on good terms with each other at a funeral and any complaint that is raised or a reference to any dispute, is immediately snubbed.

The following text illustrates the ideas held about death. At an A.M.E. memorial service for a deceased woman which is described later, a close friend of the deceased related the circumstances of her

[1] Cf. Schapera, 1953, p. 61.

RITUAL AND REVELATION IN THE CHURCHES 155

death. I took a few notes at the time, but afterwards asked the speaker to tell me the particulars again, and then took down this text.

'Before her death she told me that the sickness was severe in her. "But I, as I am ill here, I see myself, that I am not an inhabitant of this earth." She said: "On this earth we have been placed just like seed. Now it is observed that we should return to where we come from, for we have been placed on this earth to be sheep that are tended. Now I leave this earth for good. But I would be glad if my children could know something about the church and God." Then she strengthened herself with John 23 [sic]. "May my children die in faith."

'On Friday she said: "Saturday at three o'clock in the night I shall depart from this earth." She said: "It pleases me to call L—— M——," so they came to call me. Then she told me: "I am leaving." She spoke to me for two hours, and when it was the third hour, she said: "I am going now; say a prayer for me." I prayed for her; I sang the hymn which says: "Ha le mpotsa tsepo ea ka, ke tla re ke Jesu."[1] She prayed herself. She gave [me] her hand and greeted, saying: "Do not let my children grow weary in the Transvaal; may they behave; they must not prevent me to die. Be greeted, congregation. My secretary, L—— M——, hold fast your faith." '

At the memorial service L—— had spoken about a cart. When I questioned her about this, she said:

'When she spoke about her hour [i.e. the hour of her death] she spoke about the cart of heaven. It came to fetch her. The cart was brown, just like the horses. She was shown by God that she would die.'

Questioned about a reference to Jordan, the informant explained:

'She said: "I have passed through sin; I have crossed the river [Jordan], now I go to heaven." We do not know what kind of a river it is, because it is seen only by the dead. . . . Those who are in their sins cannot cross this river.'

The reference to the children in the Transvaal is not quite clear. Possibly the dying woman meant that her children who were away in the Transvaal—probably working—should not grow weary of behaving in the right manner. According to traditional belief, if a person dies in discontent, or his children quarrel after his death, or his successor treats his juniors unfairly, then the deceased comes to trouble the living in dreams or similar appearances, and does not 'rest' before the wrong is righted or before a purification ceremony is performed.

In this case the premonition of death came to a woman who was seriously ill, but I have also heard of it being experienced by old people who were in relatively good health. The text also illustrates

[1] A Southern Sotho hymn of which the initial words mean: 'If you ask me my hope, I will say it is Jesus.'

156   RELIGION IN A TSWANA CHIEFDOM

the realistic ideas people have about the passage from this world into a future life and the judgement it implies—in this case visualized as being able to pass through the river or not.

One cannot distinguish between two distinct types of funerals, viz. pagan and Christian. All follow approximately the same pattern. The activities following the death of a person are not organized according to a customary pattern whereby kinship decides which person is responsible for a particular activity. Near kinsmen and immediate neighbours are expected to refrain from working as far as possible and to render assistance to the bereaved in preparing for the funeral. If more people are present than are needed for the actual work, some just sit about talking 'to keep them (the people of the homestead) company'. More distant relations and people from the more distant neighbourhood usually also try at least to attend the funeral service. A large attendance at the funeral service is particularly valued. At the funeral of a widow, her brother with whom she had been living and who had organized the funeral, related that the previous Thursday she seemed to be dying but improved again. There was an age-set feast on the Friday and Saturday and God had seen this and decided that she should not die yet, because of the feast. However, on Sunday, when the feast was over, she died. If she had died on the Thursday 'she would not have been buried like to-day [because less people would have been able to attend]. To-day she has seen people'.

The master of ceremonies or organizer of the funeral is usually a close male relative of the deceased. For the funeral of one old man it was his younger brother, for another it was his father's elder brother's son's son, who is a headman, and for a third it was his elder brother's son. For one child it was its paternal grandfather's younger brother, and for another child its father's mother's brother.

Close relatives of the deceased are immediately summoned, and sending telegrams to those some distance away, at labour centres for example, forms part of the preparations for almost every funeral. When enquiring after the time a funeral is to take place one often hears that the arrival of a child or a sibling or a parent of the deceased is still awaited. The presence of these relatives is not indispensable though. Close relatives who cannot come in time to attend the funeral, are expected to come home on a visit as soon as possible after the funeral.

The most important preparations for the funeral include digging the grave, preparing the coffin and slaughtering one or more animals, all of which are done by the men. The women prepare food and, if the deceased is a woman, lay out the corpse. In the course of the preparations most of the people present contribute food or cash to help cover

RITUAL AND REVELATION IN THE CHURCHES 157

expenses. Coffins are made of inexpensive wood and are either bought ready-made or else planks are bought and made into a coffin. The coffin is covered with black cloth in the case of adults, with white for children. Sometimes a cross is fashioned on the lid. The corpse is dressed in a garment of the deceased, and new white cloth or paper, into which patterns are cut, is placed over the chest and shoulders and around the head. When the corpse has been placed in the coffin it remains in a hut or a room in the homestead, with the lid half open, leaving the face exposed. A woman who is closely related to the deceased, such as a child's mother, or a man's wife, has to sit beside the coffin all the time until the funeral. Others may also keep her company, but one in particular must always remain sitting there.

At least one night usually intervenes between the death and the burial. Relatives, neighbours, and friends gather at the homestead of the bereaved family and a night watch (*tebêlêlô*) is held the whole night. Inside the homestead, sometimes in the same room as the corpse, they all gather. Prayers may be said and someone might make a short speech early in the night, but most of the time they just keep on singing hymns. In the middle of the night food and drinks are served. Candles are usually burnt beside the coffin. The purpose of the night watch, it is said, is to keep the bereaved company and console them.

The actual funeral consists of a simple service which starts at the homestead. Before proceeding to the grave, all of those present file past the coffin, taking a last look at the face of the deceased, before a few men finally nail down the lid. As many men as possible take turns as bearers. Some churches have a special graveyard for church members. Others, some church members also, are buried in the stock pen of their homestead (cf. pp. 21 f.) and others are buried some distance from the homestead, usually in a place where there are already a number of other graves. At the grave the service continues, a formula is read and on the words 'ashes to ashes, dust to dust' the church official conducting the service throws a few handfuls of earth into the grave. The grave is closed up during the singing of a hymn and again all or most of the men take a turn in handling one of the spades. The closing benediction is not given until the grave is finally completed.[1] When the coffin is closed, or when the grave is filled up, one sometimes hears a woman giving a few short moans, but for the rest there is little display of emotion and those taking part appear calm and controlled.[2]

---

[1] At a funeral conducted by an R.C. priest, this was not the case.

[2] I did not have the opportunity of attending a funeral of a member of a Pentecostal church, so that I do not know whether, perhaps, there is a greater display of emotion.

158 RELIGION IN A TSWANA CHIEFDOM

Food is served at the homestead after the washing of hands and speeches by the men (see pp. 22 f.). The food is supposed to be in the first place for those who have come some distance, but usually all the people present are served. No definite order is followed, but church officials are sometimes served separately in a hut or a room, whereas the other people sit about outside. At this stage the proceeds of the contributions made toward the funeral expenses are announced. Sometimes a smaller and shorter night watch is held on the evening after the funeral.

Some churches deviate somewhat from this general pattern. If a person is buried in the R.C. graveyard a very short ceremony is held at the homestead, from where the procession goes to the church. In the church as well as at the grave the ritual includes the burning of incense over the coffin and the sprinkling of holy water. We should note here the close resemblance in morphology between these church rites and the burning of medicines and sprinkling of medicated water by the native doctor. To this we shall refer again later.

In some churches the baptismal certificate, other certificates or tickets and receipts of church contributions are formally placed in the coffin before it is closed. If the deceased was a member of the women's association or a Leading Woman in the L.M.S., one of the garments of her uniform may also be placed in the coffin. On one occasion an old L.M.S. church leader had spoken about the parable of the labourers who had been hired at different times of the day (Matt. 20), and when the time came for closing the coffin, he held up the papers before placing them beside the corpse in the coffin and said: 'I shall now give [her] her certificates (*ditšhupô*).' Referring to 'the one Who called: "Come and work . . . I shall give you reward," ' he added: 'The charge (*taêlô*) for which she has been engaged is these. . . . These are the certificates with which she will arrive in heaven. . . . She will be able to say: "I have done my work." ' Not all people see the placing of these objects in the coffin in this light. Some explain the custom by saying that these objects can not be inherited by the children of the deceased.

A certain Sabbatarian Separatist leader told me that his church has the custom of fashioning a chamber in the side of the grave where the coffin can fit in. It is then closed up with a piece of roofing iron before filling up the trench, so that the earth does not fall on to the coffin. He said this is his traditional custom (he is a Fingo), which he has introduced into his church.[1]

The St. Paul Apostolic Faith Morning Star Church has a few rites

[1] Among the Tswana this type of burial was also known. (See Brown, 1926, pp. 67f.)

RITUAL AND REVELATION IN THE CHURCHES   159

peculiar to it. If the funeral takes place at the main centre of the church
at the leader's homestead, the service starts in church. From there they
proceed to the 'holy place' where the coffin is placed on the coffin-shaped
concrete block, and where the service is continued, until they finally
proceed to the grave. The coffin is covered with blue material, instead
of black. On the words 'ashes to ashes', real ashes from the hearth are
thrown into the grave. (Some informants said that on the words 'dust
to dust', dust from the sweeping of the house is thrown in, but others
spoke only of ashes.[1]) They do not allow the cooking of food at the
homestead of the deceased. Another Pentecostal Separatist leader also
said that in his church they do not make a feast in connexion with a
funeral as other churches do, but he added, nevertheless, that something could be slaughtered and eaten. They do not eat during the night
watch either, because 'men shall not live by bread alone'. The St. Paul
Apostolic Faith Morning Star, as well as some other Pentecostal
Separatists, have particular rites of purification which have to be performed after a funeral. These will be dealt with in the section on
purification.

A grave in a cattle kraal or a stock pen is not covered with a mound.
A slight rise marks the place of the grave after the funeral, but this is
soon levelled by the trampling of the animals, and nothing remains to
betray the presence of a grave. Graves out in the open are covered
with large stones and an upright stone is placed at each end. In grave-
yards crosses or tablets are sometimes placed on graves, or initials or a
cross may be marked out with small stones. Objects such as glass
dishes or jars, a small glass doll, a plate from a toy tea set (on a small
grave), and a cup with an odd saucer have also been seen on graves
in a graveyard.[2] Apart from the activities at All Saints which is
observed by the Roman Catholics (and perhaps some others) little
attention is paid to a grave subsequent to the funeral.

The remnants of pagan ritual described in chapter II are often
integrated into Christian burial rites, even in the case of funerals
conducted by officials of churches connected with Europeans. I refer
to burial in the stock pen, the taboo on entering at the regular entrance
and on returning by the same way as the corpse was taken there, the
careful scraping together of all the earth from the grave, the washing
of hands by the men, the speeches of consolation and instruction to
the children of the deceased, and the pagan rite of purification per-

[1] In view of the particular difficulties experienced with this church, some of the
information could only be obtained from outsiders.
[2] In an African graveyard at Kimberley I observed a much wider range of household
utensils and childrens' toys (or remnants of these) on graves.

160   RELIGION IN A TSWANA CHIEFDOM

formed by a native doctor. The necessity for avoiding disputes referred to above is probably also connected with the traditional belief that discord among the relatives of the deceased may cause him to return and trouble them.

In many different ways a funeral strengthens the bonds between neighbours, relatives, and friends. The obligation to visit the bereaved homestead, to assist in the work that has to be done, and to contribute to the collection act as so many ties that draw these people together. The avoidance of disputes and the communal meal add to make it an occasion for the expression of solidarity between them. As already pointed out, this takes place across the lines of denominational differences (ch. IV).

Several churches, both Separatists and non-Separatists, some time after the funeral conduct a memorial service, which is sometimes called *matshedišô* (sympathizing with the bereaved, cf. ch. II, p. 23). Usually it is held only for prominent church members or leaders. I attended such a ceremony held by the A.M.E. Church for a prominent member of the church and the women's association. It was held about a year after her death and took place at her homestead where some of her children were still living. The Local Preacher and some other members of the church came to conduct the service.

The service consisted of a series of speeches, with hymns in between and a prayer for the people of the homestead. Besides the Preacher a few members of the men's 'Allen League' and the women's association spoke, as well as the local headman, who is not a church member. In the speeches the children were comforted and were also exhorted to be of good conduct. The greater part of the speeches, however, dealt with the deceased, what a virtuous woman she was and what the circumstances of her death were. (Cf. above, p. 155) One speaker expressed disapproval of the people who follow new customs, and the headman, amongst others, spoke of the old days, when there was still respect and fear, whereas to-day neither chief nor minister is respected.

At the end of the service a collection was held for the children of the deceased (who were already grown-ups). The contributions of the men and the women were kept apart and announced separately. The Preacher, his 'assistants', and the headman, were taken into a separate room in the homestead where they sat down to a meal. The others present were mostly served outside. That evening there were still a number of people who sang hymns for some time.

In the L.M.S. it is also customary to hold a special *matshedišô* service for ministers, local church leaders and Leading Women. The time between the funeral and the *matshedišô* is usually about three months. The service is a usual Sunday morning service at the church

9. The action referred to as 'tress' (running in a circle)

10. St. Paul Apostolic Faith Morning Star: 'the holy place'

RITUAL AND REVELATION IN THE CHURCHES 161

where the deceased officiated, and is preceded by a night watch in his or her homestead.

At the service 'the works of the deceased' are related. It is followed by a meal at the homestead.

The traditional *matshedišô* which the Tlhaping know seems to refer to mere visits of condolence which were not accompanied by any religious rites. Some people consider the rite of slaughtering the *mogôga* animal (see pp. 23 ff.) as the traditional *matshedišô*, but some of these also maintain that slaughtering something as *matshedišô* is actually a custom of the Southern Sotho and Nguni peoples, not of the Tswana. A leading church official of the Methodists, a well-educated man, held that the *mogôga* ceremony is performed in memory of the deceased, and that for this reason his church is opposed to it.

The most direct linking of a church ceremony with the rite of slaughtering the *mogôga* animal was encountered in a Pentecostal Separatist church. The leader described to me how they perform it themselves. 'About a month after the funeral we call all the people. We slaughter a head of cattle; we pour out the blood; we cook it. We do not eat blood.' The significance of the rite 'is to tell him the way, the one who has died, so that he should not be troublesome here on earth, but may remain in heaven'. He said that the deceased could trouble like ghosts (*dipoko*, cf. above, p. 154) and also referred to Lev. 2 and 7: 'There you will see (about) sacrifices.'[1]

Here we have the old cult of the dead pure and simple, with only a slight modification to bring it in line with Old Testament ritual, although the Biblical significance of the sacrifice is neglected altogether. However, this is a unique example, and although there is a tendency to consider the memorial services as a substitute for a traditional rite or custom, the connexions with tradition are usually vague and varied. Moreover, the ideas that Christians have of the traditional performances with which they connect it, are confused, as our material above shows. This can be understood and explained not only by the impact of Christian teaching on traditional belief and custom, but also by the contact with traditions of non-Tswana Bantu peoples, especially the considerable Nguni element in the chiefdom.

On the other hand, some people connect these memorial services with, or compare them to, European customs such as putting up a tombstone, or putting off mourning (dress). One Separatist church

---

[1] The chapters referred to deal mostly with sacrifices of which meal (flour) is the basis. Lev. 7 does, however, contain references to sacrifices of flesh and a prohibition on the eating of blood. Cf. also Deut. 12:16, where there is reference to the 'pouring out' of the blood.

R.T.C.—12

162   RELIGION IN A TSWANA CHIEFDOM

leader explained that the *mogôga* known in the church is the putting up of a tombstone, as for a church leader or minister. The different congregations are invited and something is slaughtered.

Baptism

In the churches of type 'A', with the exception of the two Baptist churches included in the group, the rite of baptism is not as important as in Sabbatarian and Pentecostal churches. The children of full church members may be baptized in infancy, but it is still quite common in these churches, also, to see grown-up people, some of them quite old, receiving baptism. Incidentally, this shows that the stage has not yet been reached where new accessions to church membership are confined to young people who have grown up in full connexion with the churches. Baptism is performed either by sprinkling or by pouring.

The two Baptist churches included in group 'A', in common with Sabbatarian and Pentecostal churches, are opposed to infant baptism and insist that it should be by immersion only. In all these churches which recognize only one form of baptism, the performance of the rite is an event of outstanding importance, and teaching about baptism figures prominently in sermons. It is most strongly accentuated in the Pentecostal Separatist churches. In the following paragraphs we shall be dealing more particularly with churches which recognize only adult baptism by immersion.

The tendency toward a fragmentary and literal application of portions from Scripture, to which we have already referred (p. 83), is particularly evident in the teaching about baptism. It is held that baptism must be accompanied by the confession of sins (cf. Matt. 3:6). With some Separatists a public confession has to be made at baptism. It is argued then that since small children cannot confess their sins, they cannot be baptized. Others, again, argue that children have no sin to confess, and should therefore not be baptized. The idea of the sinlessness of children, which was also expressed by a R.C. woman (see above, p. 154) has a precedent in traditional ritual: in the traditional rain rites immature children had to perform a part of the ritual (see above, p. 149). My own informants did not state in so many words that such children were held to be pure, but it was implied in the explanation that adults were not fit for the task because they might have committed adultery or performed sorcery.

Much stress is also laid on Christ's own example: He was baptized as an adult, not as a child, and He was baptized 'in the river', which in Baptist terminology is synonymous with being immersed. An S.D.A.

RITUAL AND REVELATION IN THE CHURCHES 163

preacher pointed out that instruction and faith must precede baptism (cf. Matt. 28:19 and Mk. 16:16), which implied that small children could not fulfil this requirement. More explicitly he stated that a parent cannot fulfil the responsibility of believing in the child's stead.

To give weight to his argument a Separatist Bishop had portions from Mark read from three different translations of the Bible, Xhosa, Southern Sotho, and English. He pointed out that all the Bibles say the same thing, that Jesus and the other people were baptized as adults. He offered to give two pounds 'pasella'[1] to anybody who could bring him a Bible with a single verse stating that Jesus or the apostles baptized children.

The necessity of immersion is explained with reference to the Biblical comparison of baptism with burial (cf. Romans 6:3, 4; Col. 2:12). The whole body should be baptized, not only the head, because one buries the whole body, not only the head. A preacher in whose church candidates for baptism are immersed once only, instead of three times, defended their particular practice by reference to the fact that Christ died and rose only once, not three times. Or again, from the connexion laid between baptism and 'putting on' Christ (as clothing, cf. Gal. 3:27) it is argued that just as one would not think of dressing the head only, so baptism which involves the head alone is not sufficient.

There is a tendency to consider baptism—i.e. the correct form of baptism, of course—as an important condition of one's salvation. 'Be baptized like Jesus, and see your salvation', one preacher said. It is not merely regarded as a symbol of the purification which consists in the putting away of sin and evil (cf. the element of confession), but as a rite which in itself cleanses from sin. The Bishop already mentioned above, explained to his audience, how, according to 'the law of Moses', animals had to be sacrificed on account of the transgressions of the people, and that the blood of the animals cleansed them of their iniquity. However, so he continued, in the time of Christ, as to-day also, not everybody possessed animals to sacrifice. For this reason baptism instead of sacrifice now constitutes the cleansing from sin. On the other hand, there were preachers who stressed the fact that baptism is not significant if the convert does not fulfil the law. Others, again, see in baptism the fulfilment of the law *par excellence*.

This type of reasoning is, of course, found not only in Bantu churches, but at a later stage I shall try to show that it has particular significance in the society with which we are concerned.

---

[1] A term used both by Europeans and Bantu, denoting a free gift, especially that made by a trader or storekeeper to a client.

164 RELIGION IN A TSWANA CHIEFDOM

I attended four baptismal ceremonies of churches of types 'B' and 'C', of which two were in Sabbatarian churches (the S.D.A. and a Separatist church). These two ceremonies followed much the same simple pattern: the congregation going to the river in procession, singing hymns; preaching on the river bank, followed by the baptism at a place of the right depth. Baptism consists in a single total immersion of the candidate, accompanied by the utterance of the trinitarian formula of baptism.

In the Pentecostal Separatist churches the rite is more elaborate.[1] The other two ceremonies were both of the St. Paul Apostolic Faith Morning Star, and one of these is described below. The ceremony was performed in a small rectangular reservoir at the leader's homestead, about fifteen by twelve feet in size. The reservoir is also used for irrigating the garden, and is filled from a well. (Some other churches insist that Baptism should be performed in a river not in a dam.)

The ceremony[2] was preceded by a service in church, which lasted about an hour. After the service nearly everybody first went to change, putting on clothes that would not be spoilt by the water. At about 11.30 a.m. the women had taken up their position on one side of the pool or reservoir, and the men on the other. The minister stood on top of the wall in his white dust-coat, with a red cord round his waist, Bible in hand. A hymn was sung to the accompaniment of a drum and the clapping of hands. Occasionally a woman would twitch her body or fling her arms into the air, or just produce a hissing sound, but such actions were few and did not interrupt the performance. Having read two Bible portions about baptism, the minister preached on the same topic. He also announced that those who had tobacco with them, or wild hemp (*dagga*), or horns (cf. p. 140), or those who wished to anoint themselves (with medicines?) should go and sit at the flag-post (some distance away). They would be given a chair, or a mat, or a cushion, in order to rest, he said. Nobody went there.

The woman and two men who were to be baptized, had taken up position on the steps leading up to one end of the pool. With each of the candidates the same activities were performed: first the minister announced the name and told the candidate to confess his or her sins. The sins confessed were mostly smoking, drinking, and eating of animals that had died (not having been slaughtered). If the candidate found difficulty in enumerating sins, the minister suggested a few things he might have done. Utterances of amazement were elicited by the confession of a young man that he had 'killed' a man in Johannesburg. (The verb for 'killing' is commonly used for actions other than actual killing. An Evangelist later explained that by saying he had 'killed' a person, the young man meant that he had attacked and robbed him.) At the second ceremony I attended one woman confessed the attend-

[1] I did not witness a baptism of a Pentecostal church connected with Europeans.

[2] The description given here is based on my notes of the first ceremony I attended. I was able to verify these at a second baptismal ceremony where I was present.

RITUAL AND REVELATION IN THE CHURCHES   165

ing of dances, and another said that she had 'transgressed' (the verb *leoha*) with someone in her youth. (Illicit sexual intercourse is commonly implied by such a vague term denoting sin or transgression.) After each confession, all joined in prayer for the candidate, all praying together after the customary fashion. There was a fourth person in the line, a woman, who, the minister explained, was not being baptized, as she had already received baptism, but she was a 'lost sheep' that had been found again. The congregation was asked to pray that she should not sustain any injury when passing underneath the water. Occasionally the water was referred to as the cloud into which they were entering.

While the congregation was singing again, the minister, walking stick in hand, gradually descended into the water by a few steps. With his stick or staff he churned up the water, and then threw it aside where it sank to the bottom. (At the second ceremony I noticed that he spoke while churning the water, uttering a wish or prayer that all those who were to pass through the water should be blessed. On this occasion two dishfuls of sandy earth were thrown into the water.) Thereupon he went down on his haunches, drawing his whole body and head under for a moment. A few men took up position on either side of him in a line across the length of the dam. They helped the people through the water and when children came later, passed them from hand to hand. The women all came carrying blankets on their heads. As a woman descended into the water, her blanket was passed from hand to hand and kept in readiness at the other end, where someone threw it over her to cover her up the moment she emerged. Apparently it was considered unseemly for a woman to be seen with the wet clothes clinging to her body.

The candidates for baptism descended into the water one by one. After reading the name of each, the minister immersed the person's head three times, while pronouncing the trinitarian formula. The 'lost sheep' was put under only once while the minister uttered only the words 'in the name of the Father'. The singing was resumed now, and a whole number of women lined up and started entering the pool. Each was immersed by the minister twice, but no formula was pronounced with the act. Those who twitched their faces or bodies seemed to be kept under a bit longer than the others. (At the second ceremony a woman and a girl who acted in similar manner were detained in the pool and immersed after all the others had been through.) A few women appeared to have no control over their bodies, and had to be firmly held by the men to prevent them from sinking. One was carried away in her blanket. The women were followed by a large number of children, some still infants in arms wearing diapers, three of them very small limp babies who were held only partly in the water and had water poured over their heads. The men went through last. Nearly all present passed through the pool. From the time the first four people had passed through the congregation kept on singing. As soon as a woman had been through the water, she immediately went to put on dry clothes, soon to return and join the singers again. When all had been through, the minister's staff was fished out and the benediction pronounced.

The whole atmosphere toward the end of the baptismal ceremony re-

166 RELIGION IN A TSWANA CHIEFDOM

minded one of a large picnic at a watering place: children standing about half-naked with their little bodies glistening in the sun, others dressing themselves in public; grown-ups looking clean and fresh, carrying wet clothes or hanging them out to dry; and small bundles of personal belongings scattered all about the place. A further ceremony followed a little later at the 'holy place' for which most of the people had now dressed in special uniforms.[1] (When I attended a baptism a second time, the blessing of the children and their parents[2] intervened between the baptism and the performance at the 'holy place'. When all the performances were over, food was served to a large number of people, including visitors who were not church members.) This and the festive picnic atmosphere referred to above are instances of church activities bearing a distinct social character.

Because of the unwillingness on the part of the superior officials of this church to allow the minister to discuss church affairs with me, I lack explanations for some parts of the ceremony. A few explanations emerged from statements made in the course of the activities, or could be given by outsiders who had an intimate knowledge of the Church and had casually picked up some explanations.

The staff used by the minister to churn the water has been blessed by a church official and always accompanies the minister when he is engaged in church activities. Undoubtedly it is regarded as imbued with particular powers.

The reason for everybody's entering the pool (including members previously baptized and children still unfit for baptism) is that going through the water is an act of healing or of safeguarding good health. Whether the rite of actual baptism is also regarded as an act of healing, or whether the fact that baptism has been performed in the water imbues it with healing power, is difficult to say. In another church which baptizes in the river, healing power is attributed to the water collected from the bottom of the stream at the place where baptism has just been performed. The manipulation of the 'holy' staff and the prayers and utterances over the water probably contribute to its healing powers. I think it is clear that this ritual bears a distinctly magical character.

It is interesting to note that this church has a particular rite for reinstating an erring member, which consists of 'partial' baptism—a single immersion 'in the name of the Father' only. Why she particularly had to be prayed for that she should not sustain injury, I do not know. In another church which performs baptism in the river I heard a reference to dangerous 'things' which may be in the water where they

[1] These are not the same as the robes which are worn in some Pentecostal churches for all church activities. In this church such robes are not worn.
[2] The ceremony is described above on pp. 151 f.

RITUAL AND REVELATION IN THE CHURCHES 167

baptize. In connexion with a purification ceremony performed after death by one church, an informant stated that a prayer is said before entering the water, so that the water should be 'good', as there could perhaps be a snake in the water. This informant undoubtedly had in mind the *phikakgolo* of tradition (see ch. II, p. 38).

It is not only the particular ceremony described here that bears a magical character, but the magical element is revealed in the whole dogma on baptism in all the churches which lay so much stress on adult baptism by total immersion. All the stress is on the correct performance of the rite: for adults after confession of faith only, by total immersion only (and for some: in a river only). Undergoing the rite in this form is thought of as necessarily bringing salvation, or at least putting one on the way to salvation. But the rite is not valid if it is not performed in the correct manner, just as it was done by John the Baptist.

Even in non-Baptist churches there are traces of a tendency to attach magical value to the rite. Special allowance is sometimes made for 'emergency' baptism of the sick in that church officers who are ordinarily not allowed to administer baptism are allowed to do so in the case of unbaptized people who are seriously ill. Bantu Christians often regard baptism as having healing power or consider it an indispensable requirement for the salvation of the soul. I have no direct evidence of this manner of thought among Taung church people, but an informant who is not himself a member of any church, in explaining the significance of the rite of the cradle-skins (*dithari*, ch. II, p. 17) compared it to baptism and said that a child attending the initiation ceremonies without having had the rite of *dithari* performed, would not propser, just like a child that has not been baptized.

Mass and Holy Communion

In churches of type 'A' Holy Communion or Mass is usually celebrated on much the same pattern as in European churches. It is often preceded by a church meeting at which disciplinary matters are first settled. In Separatist churches of the Anglican type church members are enjoined to abstain from various things before receiving the sacrament. According to one church constitution 'Christians shall not at all, at all, at all, and yet at all, *eat*, *drink*, *smoke*, or be engaged in *unnecessary conversation* until the Mass is over, this being quite an irreverent and unbecoming habit'.[1] The fast is said to last from Saturday night till Sunday noon or afternoon. In another church which also requires members to abstain from smoking in the morning before

[1] *Constitution and Canons of the Ethiopian Catholic Church in Zion*, p. 86.

168   RELIGION IN A TSWANA CHIEFDOM

going to Holy Communion, communicants have to swill their mouth and wash their hands before attending the sacrament. I was told that a cup of water and a basin of water are placed in readiness in an appropriate place for this purpose.

There is a tendency to make of Holy Communion a secret into which only the 'initiated' are admitted. In at least two churches of type 'A', both non-Separatist, only full church members may be present when Holy Communion is administered. Outsiders and even catechumens are not permitted to attend. In one case the church doors are closed during the sacrament—something which otherwise only happens during a prayer. In one instance this secrecy was consciously connected with the secrecy of the tribal initiation ceremonies. A leading councillor of the chief who occasionally attends a church service, but is not a member, is said to have asked an African minister what takes place at Holy Communion. The minister replied that if the councillor told him what they did at the initiation ceremonies, he would tell him about Communion! The councillor would not divulge his secret, so the minister kept his also. I suggest that the secrecy about Communion is a kind of compensation for having to remain outside the tribal initiation ceremonies, of which the secrecy of some aspects is still guarded very closely.

In Sabbatarian and Pentecostal churches Communion is not as important as baptism. In all the Separatist churches of these two types, as well as in the S.D.A. a ceremony of feet washing takes place before the actual Communion. Some of these churches administer the sacrament in the evening and one Sabbatarian Separatist church has it on Friday night 'when the Sabbath has started'. Here again, we see the insistence on following the Biblical description of the rite in all its details as closely as possible.

In a constitution in use in one section of a Separatist church which is a split from the L.M.S. and follows the Congregationalist pattern of church organization we find the following statement of faith: 'We believe that the bread and wine that we use for the Sacrament when used by faith turn into true Flesh and Blood of Jesus Christ. In use therefore we eat the true body of Jesus Christ.' Why this element of Roman Catholic dogma in a church which has its roots in 'free' Protestantism? I suggest that the explanation is the same as for the general appeal that Roman Catholicism has, which will be discussed later.

In the L.M.S. a non-alcoholic drink with fruit flavouring is used instead of wine in the celebration of the sacrament, presumably from temperance motives. A Sabbatarian Separatist leader told me he uses

RITUAL AND REVELATION IN THE CHURCHES 169

'grape juice, not wine that is bought from a bar, because that is mixed with spirits'.

Ritual avoidance

Apart from the fasts in connexion with Holy Communion or Mass, ritual avoidance is not very important in churches of type 'A', but injunctions about avoidance loom large in the teaching of all Sabbatarians and Pentecostals, both Separatist and non-Separatist. We should consider this trend against the background of such of these churches as are connected with Europeans, in which avoidance has two aspects. On the one hand, it is part of a legalistic tendency according to which various ritual prescripts from the Mosaic law, such as those about pure and impure food, are considered as being still incumbent on Christians. This is particularly stressed by the Sabbatarians who also adhere to the Old Testament Sabbath. On the other hand, a type of avoidance is practised which follows from a mechanistic notion of the Christian doctrine of sanctification. Certain activities are classified as 'worldly', and to be sanctified the Christian must abstain from these. A 'Committee on Morals' of one such church enjoins: 'That all our members follow the injunction to come out from the world and to refrain from evil and doubtful works such as attending bioscope (theatres), beer drinks, dances or smoking in any form, reading foolish and harmful literature, and the use of bad language.'[1] In the Sotho version of the church laws, football games, picnics, circuses (*papali tsa liphoofolo*), and dances are added. This type of avoidance is particularly stressed in Pentecostal churches, and is more oriented to the New Testament than to the Old.

Both these types of avoidance have found considerable application in Separatist churches, particularly in Pentecostal and Sabbatarian churches. In all these members are expected to avoid tobacco and alcoholic drinks, and one or two also add dancing. The most common food prohibitions from the Mosaic law are those on pork—some even prohibit keeping pigs—and the meat of 'dead things' (carrion), while eating blood is also explicitly mentioned in one or two instances. Two church leaders made a general reference to all the animals prohibited 'by the Bible' and particularly mentioned several from Lev. 11 and Deut. 14. Another quoted Gal. 5:19 ff. where the 'works of the flesh' are listed. (See Table VII.)

There are, however, other types of avoidance of which there are not

---

[1] A further illustration of the mechanistic character of notions about sanctification is provided by the type of statistics given in the same report 'Converted 810, Sanctified 557, Baptized with the Holy Ghost 259, etc.'

170 RELIGION IN A TSWANA CHIEFDOM

such clear precedents in teaching and practice of European missions. In several Separatist churches the men abstain from shaving their beards. In some Pentecostal churches the shoes are removed when a church service is attended. This is considered necessary when going into the presence of God, with reference to Moses' experience at the burning bush. One church leader thought of the noise made by shoes as unbefitting God's presence. Another, when speaking of Moses, said he might have trodden in some dung and it would have been unbefitting for him to stand on holy ground with shoes thus defiled. He also held that if they were to go into church with their shoes on there would be no agreement amongst them. The disorderliness of some people at a night service I attended he ascribed to the fact that one of the visitors was wearing shoes.

The Church of St. Paul Apostolic Faith Morning Star has a 'holy place'. It is the custom in this church for women and girls to wear long dresses, reaching to the ankles, and no woman wearing a short dress may go on to the holy place. The same applies to menstruating and pregnant women, and people who have not finally been purified after taking part in a funeral service (see p. 192). People with impurity from a funeral must also abstain from active church work until they are purified. In this church shoes are worn to ordinary services, but they must be removed before going on to the holy place.

The fact that traditional belief involved many rules about avoidance is probably responsible for a particular receptivity on the part of Bantu converts to the type of Christian teaching which lays stress on the avoidance of certain objects and activities. In a few cases the rules of Separatists about avoidance are also comparable to particular traditional taboos and rules. Avoidance of the holy place by menstruating and pregnant women may be related to the traditional taboos encumbent on such women. The same rule applying to persons who are ritually impure through contact with death may be connected with the traditional beliefs and usages referring to impurity resulting from death (ch. II, pp. 23 f.). There is also some resemblance between the prohibition on meat of impure animals and the taboo on eating the meat of one's totem. The breaking of this taboo traditionally had to be followed by a purification ceremony.[1] From these examples it appears that avoidance in the churches is also connected with traditional notions of impurity such as 'hot blood' and *sehihi* (see ch. II, pp. 33 ff.). This aspect will be discussed in greater detail in connexion with rites of purification.

The breach of rules of avoidance does not appear to be regarded as

[1] Schapera, 1953, p. 35.

RITUAL AND REVELATION IN THE CHURCHES   171

resulting in immediate and particular misfortune. The nearest to this
was the explanation that the wearing of shoes in church causes dis-
agreement among the members. The same leader explained the rule
about the avoidance of smoking by pointing out that if you smoke
'you are burning the Spirit of Christ now. You are lighting a fire
toward Him' (*o gotsa molelô mo go Ênê*). Of beer he said that if
you were to get drunk, you might blaspheme in church, therefore you
should abstain from drinking altogether. The idea of some misfortune
following the breach of these rules of avoidance is not altogether
absent, as I shall presently show. The misfortune is of a more distant
nature, and the connexion between breach of rule and misfortune is
more general and less particular than is usually the case with taboo.

Besides the connexion between traditional beliefs about taboos and
church rules of avoidance, we should also see avoidance within the
wider context of the moralistic tendency. In moralism it is the doing
of works, the observance of rules of right conduct, of what should be
done and what should not be done, that is stressed. Rules of avoidance
are the negative aspect of moralism, the rules about what should not
be done. Those who keep these rules will attain eternal life in heaven;
those who do not heed them will be excluded from heaven. That is the
misfortune which follows a general breach of these rules. In chapter
VII, I shall try to show that this moralistic tendency of which we have
had evidence in previous chapters (ch. IV, p. 81, ch. V, pp. 142 ff.)
is connected with the tendency toward ritual that bears a magical
character.

It should be made clear that ritual avoidance in the churches does
not necessarily imply a glorification of the Old Testament above the
New. When asked what things are avoided in his church, a leader
referred to the list contained in Gal. 5:19 ff. side by side with
Deut. 14. So also the avoidance of pork is explained by stating that
'a swine is the habitation of evil spirits', with reference to Matt.
8:28–34, beside various Old Testament references. To prove that the
consumption of tobacco is an evil reference is often made to Ezekiel
8:17, but 1 Cor. 3:16 is also quoted in this context.

Illness and healing

The native inhabitants of the reserve on the whole do not strike one
as having a robust physique. Complaints of ill-health are numerous,
especially in winter, when more or less everybody seems to complain
of *sehuba* (chest trouble). It is probable that in many cases the complaint is genuine, and local medical authorities are inclined to think
that tuberculosis of the lungs is increasing in the reserve. Venereal

172 RELIGION IN A TSWANA CHIEFDOM

diseases are also common. It is held that malnutrition lies at the root of much ill-health.

Most of the medical services available, if not all, developed after 1930, mostly as part of the local Roman Catholic Mission enterprise. The St. Konrad's Mission Hospital provides accommodation for 123 African or Coloured patients, and 10 Europeans. The doctor attached to the hospital is also district surgeon. Besides the European Sisters, there are 2 African staff nurses, and 34 probationers. During 1952 the hospital admitted 1,198 African in-patients, of whom 200 were non-paying, the others being either part-paying, or full-paying patients. In the out-patient department 850 persons were treated.[1]

There are four clinics in the reserve, which the district surgeon attends once a week. During 1953 treatment was given to 1,129 V.D. cases (primary, secondary, and tertiary). Besides these, other patients are also treated at these clinics on an average of about 70 to 80 per week.[2] Two of the clinics each have an African maternity nurse attached to it. The housing, transport, and equipment of these nurses are financed by the Local Council, but their salaries come from other sources. The Local Council usually also donate £100 a year to the hospital.

The attitude of the Tlhaping to these medical services is reflected by the statistics given above, which show that good use is now being made of them, in spite of the unwillingness of some people to do so in the earlier stages. They are to-day recognized institutions in the life of the tribe. Extensive use is also made of patent medicines which are on sale in the traders' stores. Nevertheless, a considerable number of 'witch-doctors' continue to exist. Many ailments, such as those attributed to sorcery, are held to be outside the domain of European doctors and medicine. One of the native doctors told me that in the case of 'illness of God' he sends patients to hospital, but when it is 'poison', he treats them himself.

In addition to this, ritual of healing and maintenance of good health plays an important role in some of the churches, so that there is a notable increase of the institutions concerned with the health of the people.

The question arises whether this points to a deterioration in the health of the population. Statistics to prove that the present poor health conditions are the result of a deterioration during the past forty or fifty years are not available. However, considering the trend which characterized the economy until a few years ago, it seems feas-

[1] Information provided by the matron, St. Konrad's Hospital, Taung.
[2] Information provided by the district surgeon.

RITUAL AND REVELATION IN THE CHURCHES 173

ible that health conditions until recently have been on the downward grade. Although sorghum was the main crop of traditional Tswana economy, other food crops such as millet, melons, pumpkins, sweet cane, and beans were also cultivated.[1] These, together with the meat of animals that were occasionally slaughtered and milk in its various forms, made possible a relatively varied diet, even though the variety did not last all the year round. In Taung, however, the severe droughts of the 'twenties and early 'thirties caused grave deterioration in the local production of food. Locally produced cereals were substituted by maize and sorghum obtained by reaping on farms or through purchase from traders, but this was not the case with the other food crops. The droughts also diminished the stock so that less meat was available. Hunting has long ceased to be a possible source of food. Since cattle are seldom kept for milk nowadays, and many households do not even possess cattle, milk in its various forms has disappeared from the diet of the bulk of the population. Thus, whereas the Tlhaping used to have a relatively varied diet, deteriorating farming conditions have resulted in starchy foods constituting a larger proportion of the diet of the population as a whole than seems to have been the case in former times. Such a development may be expected to have had detrimental effect on the health of the population.

It may be that conditions will now improve as a result of the irrigation scheme. At present it is still of too recent origin to have had a marked effect on any large proportion of the population. Moreover, production on the scheme is mainly concerned with cash crops, and the small vegetable gardens that have been provided have not proved a great success. I do not doubt that in a small number of households the diet has again increased in variety as a result of the irrigation scheme. Some households also have a varied diet by purchasing a variety of foodstuffs. Nevertheless, the general situation seems to support the suggestion that the health of the population as a whole has deteriorated during the last half century. This would partly explain an increased concern with healing.

The economic situation must, however, not be considered in isolation from general social conditions. Weakening of family ties, lawlessness of the younger generation, weakening of the chieftainship, and the disappearance of many traditional institutions and values may be expected to produce the feeling that everything is going wrong, a feeling which is bound to result in lack of vigour and the absence of a feeling of general well-being. This can easily be associated with the

---

[1] *Schapera*, 1951, p. xx; cf. Schapera, 1953, p. 21.

174 RELIGION IN A TSWANA CHIEFDOM

feeling of ill-health and may thus also be responsible for the increased concern with healing.

We are primarily concerned here with the part churches play in connexion with illness and healing, but we have to pay attention to the churches' attitude to other institutions of healing first. In discussing this, I distinguish between native doctors and native medicines on the one hand, and secular techniques which are of 'European' origin, which include not only the services offered by trained doctors and nurses in hospitals and clinics, but also the use of patent medicines. For the sake of brevity, I refer to the former as traditional techniques and to the latter as European techniques.

Churches of type 'A', both the Separatists and those connected with Europeans are not opposed to the utilization of European techniques of healing. As we have observed, most of the medical services offered are connected with the R.C. Mission.

On the whole, type 'A' churches do not favour traditional techniques (Table VII), but the attitudes of individual church leaders vary. The catechist of a certain Separatist church is a traditional *ngaka*—one of the few whose performance I personally witnessed. Rumour has it that the Evangelist of a non-Separatist church is also a native doctor, while I know for certain that he had his house ritually purified and 'doctored' (pagan style) after it had been struck by lightning. A number of church leaders with whom I discussed the matter were not totally opposed to traditional techniques, and distinguished between some that were permissible and others not. Thus a trained African minister held that 'medicines' (*mereo*), charms (*dipheko*), and the throwing of dice are not allowed, but 'things that help' were permissible. Another approved of the use of 'herbs' but expressed opposition to 'other things like dice which are heathenish'. An office bearer in another church said that there was no objection to 'good doctors using herbs', but objected to 'witchcraft'.[1] An Evangelist whom I asked what things are 'avoided' (*go ila*)[2] in his church mentioned first of all sorcery and 'doctorhood' (*bongaka*), but added: 'If a person is ill, he must seek a doctor [native or European] for himself. He will heal the flesh. God will heal the spirit (*moya*).'

The four quoted so far were all leaders in churches connected with

[1] The two informants who mentioned herbs were interviewed in English. Both were well-educated men. The one who spoke of witchcraft probably meant sorcery, not being aware of the technical difference between the two. There is hardly any belief in witchcraft among the Tlhaping, except among the people of Nguni (and perhaps also Southern Sotho) stock and those who have been influenced by the beliefs of these people.

[2] Cf. p. 169 ff.

RITUAL AND REVELATION IN THE CHURCHES   175

Europeans. A Bishop of a Separatist church of type 'A' also approved of medicines which he referred to as being 'good' or being a 'help', specifically mentioning leaves and 'the little things which you dig up in the veld, you mix them, boil them, and throw them into a bottle— they are good. They are just like a chemist's medicines.' Those to which he is opposed are medicines connected with sorcery, horns, cross-marks put on doors as part of the process by which a doctor treats a homestead (ch. II, p. 27), doctored pegs (*ibid.*), and incisions. Another Separatist leader said that there was no objection to a native doctor 'because he helps the people'. He was opposed to those that provide medicines with which to perform sorcery, but approved of divining to discover agents of sorcery. Two leaders of different Separatist churches said that traditional techniques of healing are allowed in their churches, without further qualifying their statement.

Sabbatarian churches. The S.D.A. are opposed to traditional but not to European techniques. They are known to do medical work in connexion with their missions, and although they have no permanent medical mission at Taung, funds are sometimes collected by their Taung church for such work elsewhere. Of the three Sabbatarian Separatist churches two also do not object to European techniques but are opposed to traditional ones. The third discourages the use of medicines and doctors altogether, and upholds only healing practised in church. Some people, however, are said to be still 'weak' and do consult doctors, without being censured for this.

In the *Pentecostal churches* there is a general tendency to favour the exclusive reliance on the techniques of healing practised in the churches. The leaders of three Separatist Pentecostal churches were emphatically opposed to the utilization of other techniques of healing. The other Pentecostal leaders said it was permissible to consult European doctors and use European medicines, although not favoured. Pentecostals are unanimous in their opposition to traditional techniques.[1]

Throughout the churches, then, there is a tendency to disapprove of traditional techniques of healing. In a number of instances, however, leaders had some reservations, and did not condemn native doctors and their medicines altogether. It is difficult to see what is the underlying principle of distinction between permissible and non-permissible techniques. One needs to know much more about the traditional attitude to traditional techniques, and more intensive investigation is

---

[1] A minister of a Pentecostal church connected with Europeans said that he used to be a native doctor. He has parted altogether with traditional techniques of healing, but he said it was very hard to give up his doctorhood.

176   RELIGION IN A TSWANA CHIEFDOM

needed about particular medicines and their uses, about present-day
beliefs about the causes of illness and the medicines and treatments
appropriate to their cure. What follows cannot be regarded as more
than a suggested explanation.

In their terminology the Tlhaping do not distinguish different categories of medicines and medical techniques which would coincide
with our notions of 'magical' and 'non-magical'. All medicines are
ditlhare, or *meriane*, or *melemo*. The different words are used interchangeably and do not denote different categories of medicines. So
also the verb *go alaha* covers all healing or preventive techniques. The
terminological distinction that is made, is that between sorcery (*boloi*
—the verb *go lowa*), and magic which is made for purposes which are
socially approved.

So also the term *moleko* denotes a medicine used for sorcery
(although the names *ditlhare*, etc., also include such medicines).[1]

What appears to be important, however, is that treatment is sometimes in terms of symptoms only, and not in terms of causation. Here
are a few examples. A certain doctor uses the bulb of a plant known
as *hôkôhôkwane* to treat a child whose fontanelle had stopped pulsat-
ing. Or, again, one hears of medicines for the head, for the stomach,
or for a pain on the pit of the stomach. These are examples of treatment in terms of symptoms, without reference to causation. But if a
doctor divines the cause of illness and reveals that it is caused by
sorcery, then the counter-magic that he performs against the sorcery
is treatment in terms of causation.

This distinction between what one might call 'symptomatic' treatment and 'causation' treatment—which, of course, does not coincide
with the distinction between magical and non-magical—is not reflected
in terminology either, and is based merely on empirical observation.
It does not seem to be consciously made by the average Tswana, nor
does he seem to regard the material and techniques used in symptomatic treatment to be of a different order from those used in causation treatment. However, unconsciously, I think, the difference
between the two types of treatment influences his attitude to European
techniques, while it also affects the Tswana churchman's attitude to
traditional techniques.

I suggest that the Tswana sees European techniques in much the
same light as traditional symptomatic treatment, and regards them as of

---

[1] Prof. Schapera points out that 'some types of magical activity are more specifically distinguished, e.g. *go thaya*, to "fortify" . . . *go upa*, to expel or keep away
garden pests, *go fetlha pula*, to make rain, and *go lowa*, to bewitch' (1953, p. 62).
These activities, except perhaps *go lowa*, are also covered by the term *go alaha*.

11. Laying-on of hands, causing unusual movements said to derive from the action of the Holy Spirit

12. Members of the Holy Christian Apostolic Church in Zion after a service

RITUAL AND REVELATION IN THE CHURCHES 177

the same order, particularly when the latter involves drinking infusions, applying ointments, or taking powders. For this reason the acceptance of European techniques is not so difficult, and to the Tswana does not seem incompatible with continued adherence to traditional techniques.

Although European techniques are probably more particularly associated with traditional symptomatic treatment, this association seems to be effective for the whole traditional medical system, since the latter does not involve an overt distinction between the two types of treatment as different categories.

On the other hand, this bridge between European and traditional techniques makes it difficult for the Tswana churchman to see why he should altogether denounce traditional techniques in favour of European techniques as some European missionaries want him to do. Nevertheless, he is more or less vaguely aware that traditional notions of causation often involve concepts which are incompatible with Christian teaching (e.g. *dikgaba*, sorcery, action of the ancestor spirits). Thus he is left with an ambivalent attitude to traditional techniques, on the one hand regarding it as of the same order as European techniques, which mission teaching teaches him to accept as substitute for all traditional techniques, and on the other hand aware of a certain undesirability because of the incompatible notions of causation sometimes involved. He cannot dissolve his dilemma because he does not consciously distinguish between symptomatic and causation treatment. Because the latter distinction is not consciously made, the distinction that some church leaders do make between desirable and undesirable traditional techniques is still vague and uncertain.

I must add that this does not imply that traditional beliefs about the causation of illness are repudiated by all church people. In some churches, e.g. the belief in sorcery as a possible cause of illness, receives open recognition, even in 'official' circles. In such cases, however, it is usually only the belief in the existence of sorcery that is adhered to, whereas traditional techniques of counteracting it are strongly repudiated and are substituted by new ones.

We may now turn to the actual rites of healing in the churches.

Public and private prayers for the sick by office bearers of the church are said by all churches, and in most churches of type 'A' are the only form of ritual of healing observed. Laying-on of hands with prayer is common with Sabbatarians and Pentecostals, and is also observed by a few Separatist leaders of type 'A' churches. Most Sabbatarians and Pentecostals also recognize a rite of unction which

R.T.C.—13

178   RELIGION IN A TSWANA CHIEFDOM

is sometimes combined with prayer and laying-on of hands, while the
Roman Catholic Church, of course, observes the rite of extreme
unction. In Sabbatarian and Pentecostal churches these rites often
form part of ordinary Sunday services, although they may sometimes
also be performed for patients at their homes. Unction and laying-on
of hands are often connected with James 5:14 and Mark 16:18.

Mention may here be made of the fact that in a few churches of
type 'A'—those that I knew of are not Separatist—special allowance
is made for administering Holy Communion to sick church members.

A remarkable elaboration of ritual of healing is found in the
Pentecostal Separatist churches, and it is to this phenomenon that we
now turn our attention. These churches have a number of rites not
found in other churches, while they also observe elaborations of the same
types of rites as those performed by the others. The more violent the
nature of the service, the more elaborate are usually the rites of healing.

In these churches the rite of prayer and laying-on of hands is performed only by church officials such as Preachers, Evangelists,
ministers, and 'Prayers' or 'Intercessors' (*Barapedi, Barapeledi*).
The latter have been ordained to perform these rites particularly, and
their status and authority is less than that of Preachers, although in
the absence of a Preacher, they may also conduct a service.

The nature of the laying-on of hands varies. In one other church it
was almost as violent as in the one described in Chapter V, and some
persons were touched, rubbed, and pressed over the whole upper part
of the body. Many people gave no outward evidence of being seriously
affected by the violent handling. In a few cases where young men were
laying-on hands for girls, the rite was performed in such a way that
one could not help thinking that the participants were enjoying sexual
gratification through it.[1]

In one church the 'patients' sometimes collapsed during performance of the rite. A sturdily-built girl once gradually reached a
complete state of collapse when the prayer was a young man, and half-
collapsed on another occasion when the rite was performed by a
woman. At the same service a younger girl of about thirteen also collapsed. She was thin and physically undeveloped and had a bad squint,
but she always appeared lively and took a leading part in the singing,
also preached at times. Her mother told me that she often had visions,
which usually came when she was in such a condition of physical
collapse. One might have thought that in this church collapsing is a
recognized form of behaviour, probably connected with the idea of

[1] For a similar sexual element in Zulu Separatist churches, see Sundkler, *op. cit.*,
p. 247.

RITUAL AND REVELATION IN THE CHURCHES   179

having a particular spiritual experience, and that it provides an opportunity for drawing attention and perhaps even gaining prestige in a manner which is socially approved. However, the local leader could not explain their collapsing and said that it was not the 'custom' in their church.[1] As we have seen (ch. IV, pp. 72 f.), similar experiences, usually of a more serious and prolonged nature, influenced some of the church leaders to join the churches they are in now.

The beating of some of the people who were prayed for and the accompanying shouts (ch. V, p. 134) were afterwards explained to me as follows: 'It is to scold the enemies that are in the person. By beating they feel the pains which are in the person. In Tlhaping it is [called] massaging (*go sedila*).'[2] The 'enemies' he explained to be such 'as the depositing [of medicines of sorcery] by people'.

In the less violent type of Pentecostal churches the laying-on of hands is less violent, although these also sometimes have smaller elaborations in the rite. In one of these churches the members do not wear special robes, but the two Preachers wear wide white tunics gathered with green cords round their waists. When praying for the sick they stand facing each other, their cords hung around their necks. Two or three people come at a time, and kneel between them, facing one of them. The ends of the cords are laid over the heads or shoulders of the two 'patients' on the outside. (Illustration 7.) The Preachers pray loudly, each saying his own prayer, and the laying-on of hands takes place simultaneously. They move their hands around, touching the heads of the 'patients', sometimes also their shoulders, backs or chests. When a baby is prayed for, one Preacher takes it in his arm, gathering his tunic around it and prays with his hand on the baby's head. The other places the one end of his cord around the child and also holds his hands around it.

The laying-on of hands itself was explained as 'fulfilling the command of the Book', with particular reference to the Epistle of St. James. The significance of the cord was explained as follows: 'It is received from the "elders" of the church [such as the minister and Evangelist]. They "pray for" it. They put on the cord for you. This garment [the tunic] is prayed for. When it is placed over someone else, the one who prays is helped by the prayers of those numerous people who prayed for these clothes of the church. . . .'

In the Church of St. Paul Apostolic Faith Morning Star the members of the congregation file past the officiant and each is very lightly

---

[1] For collapsing in American Negro revival meetings, cf. Dollard, John, 1937, pp. 226 ff.

[2] The verb denotes the application of ointment (as medicine) by rubbing.

180   RELIGION IN A TSWANA CHIEFDOM

touched, mostly on the head only. As a person is touched he goes down on his haunches, or inclines forward. Some turn round like a top and some keep on stepping about, waving their arms gracefully, writhing their bodies, and making sounds. On one occasion two of the women kept on acting in this manner for more than twenty minutes, long after everybody had filed past and even after the service had ended. On ordinary Sundays the rite takes place during the latter part of the service in the church building, but on special occasions, as when a baptismal ceremony has been performed, it takes place on the holy place toward the end of the proceedings. In this Church a prayer is not said simultaneously with the laying-on of hands.

What may be termed '*holy water*' plays an important role in connexion with health in several churches. Mostly it is ordinary water which has been 'prayed for'[1] by an office bearer. Such water is often immediately consumed in church, but in at least two churches the members regularly take home bottles of holy water to be consumed regularly, or when they do not feel well. On one occasion a young girl who had just received a bottle of water was told by the leader that there were snakes in her liver. The snakes were said to be of the kind called *seleke* (or *seleka*).[2] Later he explained to me that the snakes were the result of sorcery.

The person praying for the water usually handles the bottle while praying for it or places his hands over it and perhaps also covers it with a part of his robe. One leader removes the cork of the bottle before he starts praying because 'water cannot be prayed for when it is closed'. Another collects water from deep below the surface where a baptismal ceremony of the church has been performed, for use as holy water.

In the St. Paul Apostolic Faith Morning Star a rite of drinking water follows the laying-on of hands in an ordinary Sunday service. The members of the congregation proceed to a table where they kneel and drink water from small 'Vaseline' jars. The minister, in explaining the rite to me, said: 'It is their medicine (*setlhare*). It helps the spirit, the blood, the body, the understanding.' He referred to Rev. 22:17, where there is reference to drinking 'the water of life', and also pointed out that Christ prayed for the water at the wedding in Cana. It is the same Church in which most of the people 'go through the water' after the performance of a ceremony of baptism.

In three of the churches *ashes of cow-dung* are used for purposes of healing. It is sometimes added to the holy water, and one leader

---

[1] The Tswana term is *go rapêlêla metsi* (lit., to pray for the water).

[2] *Seleka*, 'An earthworm, a species of small harmless snake.' (Brown, *Secwana Dictionary*.)

RITUAL AND REVELATION IN THE CHURCHES 181

said that besides the ash he also adds salt. Some of the ash may also be rubbed on the affected part of the body. Once it was sprinkled in the middle of the floor before the rite of praying and laying-on of hands started, and on the same occasion, the leader rubbed some of the ashes on his hands before praying for one of the people. The leader said that it was 'ash from the hearth, only [ashes] of dung of cattle. It is grass, because cattle eat grass.' He further explained that: 'The ash is a horn; it is medicine (*setlhare*). It is a command; it is the law of the church. It is *sewasô*' (see below). I did not hear any particular text mentioned in connexion with the use of ashes, but one church leader, after having described the use of ashes in some detail and having mentioned the custom of prayer with laying-on of hands, said that he used this method because he read about it in the Bible. This remark might have referred to the laying-on of hands only, but I think it also referred to the use of ashes. It might be connected with Numbers 19, where prescripts are given for the slaying of a heifer which had to be burnt with 'her skin, and her flesh, and her blood with her dung'. The ashes had to be preserved 'for a water of separation', and anybody who had touched a corpse had to be purified on the third and seventh days after the incident by being sprinkled with some of the water of separation. These churches would not find it practicable to slaughter and burn a whole animal, skin, flesh, and blood, but they can burn dung and they probably feel that since the dung is particularly mentioned, it might as well be used alone. However, I have no direct evidence for this interpretation.

More than once the term *sewasô* was used in connexion with rites in which ash was used, and it was also used of other rites which are very distinctly purification rites, although no ashes are used in them. Zulu Zionists use the term *isiwasho* 'for the various kinds of *purgatives and enemas* (water mixed with ashes or soap) used in connexion with ritual purification'.[1] *Sewasô* and *isiwasho* do not seem to be indigenous Bantu words but are probably derived from the English word 'wash'. Purification will be discussed in greater detail in the following section, but the connexion of ashes with purification supports the suggestion that its use is connected with Numbers 19.[2]

In three of the churches the *elaborate* kind of *robes* are worn which have been described in the previous chapter (ch. V, pp. 131 f.).[3]

[1] Sundkler, *op. cit.*, pp. 211–212.   [2] See also p. 197.

[3] At a service of a fourth church the leader and two women each wore some or other piece of clothing decorated with a pattern or two. A man also tied a cord round his body. When I asked about the significance, no mention was made of health-giving powers, however. In a fifth church I sometimes saw individuals wearing a coloured cord round the waist.

182   RELIGION IN A TSWANA CHIEFDOM

These are closely connected with health and healing. Sometimes a coloured or white flag, which may also be adorned with patterns, is added to the ensemble. In another church a greater variety of figures than those described above appeared on the garments. Besides star symbols, crescent moons, crosses, and rings, there also appeared letters of the alphabet, while one figure resembled a hand and another the character 3. Several had quaint figures representing angels, strongly reminiscent of children's drawings of human beings. Other unidentifiable figures also occurred.

A church member procures his outfit piece by piece according to revelation. One church leader said that at baptism every new member is given a cord, but the other pieces of the uniform are gradually procured as they are revealed. In another church young children, not of an age to have been baptized yet, also sometimes wear a cassock with a few figures on, or a head cloth. The colours and the forms of the figures on garments are also revealed. The figures on a particular garment are not necessarily revealed at the same time as the garment itself, but it may be revealed that certain figures must be placed on a garment someone already possesses. People do not receive revelations pertaining to their own garments, but are always told by another member of the church what they should wear. In one church it was said that superior church officials do receive revelations about their own garments.

In all three churches these garments are worn as means of improving or at least sustaining health. It may be revealed to one that a fellow-member should wear a cloak or a cord or a band of a particular colour and with particular figures in order to recover from, or to ward off illness.

In one church members of the congregation relate revelations they have received before the service closes. Mostly these take the form of visions (*ditšupô, dipônô*) which are usually said to be received while the person is awake. Some relate to the wearing of garments. A young woman, for instance, related: 'This morning as I was praying I saw a red cloak (*sephika*).[1] I was praying this morning as I was going to church. Further, I saw that my father, the Preacher, had stars on his robe (*pura-pura*). I saw that my mother had put on a cloak of sackcloth with white stars. . . .' This meant that the people she had 'seen' had to procure the garments or figures with which they had been seen.

---

[1] This word was not known to me and does not appear in Brown's *Sechuana Dictionary*, neither in Mabille, A., and Dieterlen, H. (revised R. A. Paroz), *Southern-Sotho English Dictionary*, Morija, 1950. The church people explained that it denotes a cloak such as the ones they wear.

RITUAL AND REVELATION IN THE CHURCHES 183

On a white 'cassock' which a young man was wearing under a red cloak were the characters T J X J in blue. When he was ill, a young girl had 'seen' that he should put it on his clothes to recover. There was also a red band which had been 'seen' by the Evangelist, some blue and red crosses seen by a young woman and a blue star (with about seven protuberances looking more like the petals of a flower than the points of a star) which had also been seen by the girl.

These garments were explicitly compared to medicines by one church leader. They do not go to a doctor, he explained, and whereas a doctor throws his bones and then tells you to take a goat and cut it, they do not cut a goat,[1] but a piece of cloth. He said the cords, which exceed the clothes in power, are his 'horn', and claimed that he fixes cords crosswise in his house when there is lightning, and that they resist every medicine of sorcery that may be used against one. Through someone else the spirit will reveal to one how the cords should be placed.

I have very little information as to whether particular values and associations are attached to particular symbols and colours. When asking about the significance of particular figures I usually received the answer that they 'stand against' or prevent illness. With reference to the stars and crescent moons one leader said that 'they are all the lights which come from heaven; also that you should have the brightness of light'. The sackcloth was once connected with the Ninevites who reacted to Jonah's preaching by repenting in sackcloth and ashes. These examples, and particularly the use of crosses and angels, suggest that these symbols are not taken from the indigenous background. Much more case material would probably be required to discover the symbolism of particular colours and figures.[2]

Particulars about sticks, staffs, and flags are revealed in the same way as for the cords and garments. Of these accessories it is said that 'they give you strength'. (Incidentally the flags are often found very useful as face cloths when sweat flows freely!) One leader spoke of a flag as a broom with which to 'sweep the things that are in front', for instance when he enters the water to go and perform baptism. He also said that it represented 'the ground he has won in his spiritual move-

---

[1] In traditional rites where the slaughtering itself is significant, a sheep or a head of cattle is slaughtered. When a goat is slaughtered in connexion with ritual, some part of it is usually needed as medicine.

[2] Among Zulu Zionists the wearing of white robes is connected with traditional notions of impurity and purification. Impurity is referred to as 'blackness' in traditional Zulu-ritual and has to be removed by the use of 'white' medicines. No such parallel seems to exist among the Tlhaping. (See Sundkler, *op. cit.*, p. 214, and *Krige*, 1950, p. 82, n.)

184   RELIGION IN A TSWANA CHIEFDOM

ment' and that it would give him strength for further progress. The
same man also has a walking stick surmounted by a curved piece of
metal, giving it the appearance of a short crook, and a crucifix is also
attached to it. Of this he said that it revealed where there was danger,
so that if, for instance, he placed the point of the stick somewhere
where a snake was hidden, it would cause the snake to appear.[1] The
same man often wears a beret to which several metal objects such as a
small chain, crucifix, and other metal objects are attached. Of the
chain he said that another person to whom it was revealed that he (the
leader) should wear it put it on for him after 'praying for' it. Its purpose was to help revelations to come to him clearly. Another leader
said of the staffs that they give one power to pray against diseases and
enemies.

Special prayers are said by a Prayer or other church official over
every garment, cord, staff or flag before the owner starts wearing or
using it.

When a cord was given to a girl a woman first rubbed some ashes on her
hands and with the point of her staff poked at the cord which had been
placed on the floor, moved it about a little, then knelt, placed her hand over
it and prayed.

In at least one church the garments must be prayed over anew every
time they have been washed. When once I saw this performed the
Prayer draped his flag over the clothes and later held the clothes in
his hands, wrapped in his flag, as he prayed over them.

On the whole these garments are only worn to church services, but
sometimes one sees people wearing just a cord or a band round a limb
or round the body even in everyday life. One leader always goes about
more elaborately dressed.

A few less common usages and methods of healing must still be
mentioned. One minister is known to prescribe and administer *enemas
of salt water* in some cases. Another who has abandoned this method
after clashing with the law said that using salt was 'according to the
law of God', and referred to the Gospel of St. Mark saying that 'if they
[people] live by salt it is said that they live with (in) peace. [Cf. Mark
9:50.] Just as Elisha put salt into the water in which there was death,
saying: "So speaketh Jehovah the God of Israel." On that day death
came out.' (II Kings 2:19–22.)

In the St. Paul Apostolic Faith Morning Star church members who
are in ill-health *go to the minister's homestead* to spend several days

[1] This man claims to have passed his Junior Certificate and to have been a teacher.
I have every reason to believe that this is true.

RITUAL AND REVELATION IN THE CHURCHES   185

there so that he can pray for them.[1] As far as I could make out this praying usually takes place in the regular devotions in the church building, but people with very particular troubles such as insanity or barrenness are prayed for on the holy place. The minister also prays for the sick when visiting other parts of the reserve.

One leader said that when dealing with difficult cases he *burns seven candles* in candlesticks 'like the seven candles that were there when the Revelation was made' (cf. Rev. 1:12 ff.). He held that when these candles burn he has a certain power, and that the candles may reveal something 'that is in the darkness' for him.

Of the church 'healers' active at present, I know of only one who has come into conflict with the law on account of his healing activities. The reason why he was charged, and none of the other church leaders who also perform healing, is probably that he charged fees for examining patients and administering enemas—one shilling for an examination, ninepence for the first enema, and threepence for each succeeding enema. Before judgement was delivered, the accused made the following statement in court.[2]

'I came to the country[3] as a man of prayers and I told the chief that I use enemas consisting of salt and water. I am in the Apostolic faith and we used no medicines. The chief allowed me. All the people that are here to-day in court[4] is the people I prayed for. What I called a doctor is a man going to the veld digging for roots and dispensing as a chemist. I used no drugs and no roots. All I used is a solution of salt in water. Doctors will demand cattle from their patients. I am only charging only a very small fee from my people in order to buy salt and rubber tubes. The money I am charging is equivalent to the amount collected in other churches to keep the mission work going. Nobody will work for such small amounts unless he is a man of God alone. I am not in position [sic] of a certificate. I am not a doctor but is a man of prayers. I don't want people who are dealing with witchdoctors because I don't believe in roots and other such articles.'

He was found guilty on four counts and his wife on two, and they were charged ten pounds or one month imprisonment on each count. They paid the fine.

After having got to know this man personally, who, ironically

[1] It was hinted by outsiders that in some cases staying at the minister's home is a form of doing penance.

[2] From *Criminal Records* in the Native Commissioner's Office at Taung, Case No. 178 of 1947. I quote the report verbally. I take it that it is a verbal rendering of the interpreter's version. The accused, I am sure, would not have spoken English.

[3] He is a local inhabitant but refers to his return after a long absence during which he had joined the church.

[4] From other sources I heard that a large number of his followers were present in court.

186   RELIGION IN A TSWANA CHIEFDOM

enough, is the one who lays so much stress on submissiveness and on obedience to the authorities (ch. IV, p. 115), I am perfectly convinced of his *bona fides* in the matter, and I am sure that he was not aware of his acting contrary to the law in any way. He still finds it difficult to understand why he was convicted. To him it is a matter of having been punished for doing good, since many people have been healed by his treatment—so he, and at least some of the people he has treated, and many of the general public believe. Nobody gave evidence that his treatment harmed them. He still performs healing by prayer and some of the other means that have been described.

At present I know of no church leader who charges fees for healing. People who recover after treatment sometimes join the church of the person who treated them. In one or two cases it was said that people might make thank-offerings after recovery if they wished.

A particularly interesting case is that of J—— N—— who, during 1951, performed healing and other activities which resulted in his arrest. He is described as a 'Shangaan' (probably a Shangana-Tonga) and a 'minister of religion',[1] originally from Beira, Portuguese East Africa.[2] According to the evidence presented in court, N—— on more than one occasion revealed the presence of objects which were supposed to be the cause of various misfortunes which had befallen the homesteads where these were found. The following is a summary of the evidence of a male teacher, a Nguni, to whom we shall refer as X.

When X consulted N—— for the first time he did not discuss anything about illness with him beforehand, neither was he ill himself. X proceeded as follows: 'I gave accused half-a-crown and he opened his Bible and told me there were many things happening at our home, things disappearing, things dying and misunderstandings among our whole family. He even told me that my wife had no children and the cause of that and of the misunderstandings in our home was something buried in our home. He also said that during this whole period there had been deaths in our home, and we had just recently lost a child, and that one of my horses was dead, which was the truth.' N—— also intimated that he could discover and remove the object, and it was later agreed that he would do so.

At a week-end about two weeks later he went to X's home with his congregation and announced that he charged £7. 10. 0 to remove the spell from X's house, £2. 10. 0 for its future protection, and another £2. 10. 0 to protect his mother's house. X agreed to these payments. 'Accused first held a religious service, during the course of which he said it was time for him to go and dig out that thing.' He produced a stick he used to have with

[1] I could not identify his church, but some of his techniques of healing resemble those of Separatist Pentecostals.

[2] *Criminal Records* in the Native Commissioner's office, Taung, No. 310 of 1951.

RITUAL AND REVELATION IN THE CHURCHES 187

him and a 'girdle' and gave one end of the latter to X's brother to pull it along the ground where N—— directed him. They left the house where they had been. Outside 'there was a wall where we make our fire and there was a pot on the fire. When we came to the fire the girdle sort of coiled itself at the end. Accused made a circle round the spot with his stick'. N—— directed the brother to dig on that spot while he read his Bible silently. On N——'s directions some water was thrown into the hole and N—— himself poked about in the mud with his stick until he 'pushed it down' at a certain spot. With both hands he took some mud from next to the stick and deposited it in a basin which N—— told X's brother to take into the house while the others followed. N—— called everybody to come and see, and on his directions more water was poured over the mud. 'I then noticed,' X said, 'there was an article in the mud and the accused took it out with one hand and put it on the floor and I saw it was something wrapped in a cloth. Accused opened the cloth with a knife and took out something black and sticky and which gave off a very bad smell. He said this was the cause of the bad spell which had been cast over the house. After telling X to burn the object N—— 'went to the benediction and closed his service' and X forthwith paid him twelve pounds ten. N—— also still searched for and produced a wristlet that had been missing. In his search he held his stick in front of him. Under cross-examination X said that this performance took place at night.

At another man's homestead N—— in much the same manner produced from the mud a piece of a beast's horn which was filled with 'something like black grease'. He broke three eggs into the horn and put it into a bottle which he told his client to bury.

A woman gave evidence of how N—— treated her child 'who was suffering from fits'. After N—— had seen the child and had placed his stick on her chest he said she was suffering from '*Mafufinyane*' (said to be a sickness caused by drugs causing people to go mad). N—— produced special 'water' which he mixed with ordinary water for the child to drink afterwards. He prayed and held a service and after touching the girl with his stick again, 'tied a girdle round her body and round her wrists'. He charged thirteen pounds but the witness' husband 'paid him with a head of cattle'.

A fourth witness gave evidence that the accused, in treating her, made her stand over boiling water and covered her with a blanket. He put nothing in the water, however. After this he prayed for her and gave her some water to drink. N—— is also said to have administered enemas, prescribed the wearing of spectacles, and to have given the same patient medicine with which to wash the eyes, and to have undertaken to bring about the return of a child who had been away from home for a long time. There was also a female teacher among his clients.

188   RELIGION IN A TSWANA CHIEFDOM

N—— was charged on five counts of 'wrongfully and unlawfully pretend[ing] to practice witchcraft [sic]', or alternatively of theft by means of false pretences, and on seven counts of practising as a medical practitioner without a licence. He was finally found guilty on nine of the counts and sentenced to ten pounds or one month imprisonment on each count.

As I shall try to illustrate in greater detail later, pagan rites and beliefs or elements of these have been incorporated into the ritual and beliefs of Zulu Zionist churches to a larger degree than in any of the Separatist churches in Taung. In view of this, it is significant that the Shangaan 'minister', a foreigner, accepted and incorporated certain aspects of traditional belief and custom into his activities and teaching more openly and spectacularly than any of the local church leaders. Not only did he accept the reality of sorcery as the others do, but he also acted against it in accordance with tradition by revealing the objects of sorcery, although his methods of discovering it did not follow a traditional Tswana pattern.[1] His discovery of lost objects and the administering of a steam bath have precedents in the activities of Tswana native doctors. Further, the readiness with which local people patronized the Shangaan 'minister' is in keeping with the tendency in former times for foreign native doctors and rainmakers to be readily patronized and to be considered more powerful than the local ones.

Like some other church leaders, he administered enemas, a method also known to native doctors. This may, however, have been borrowed from European techniques of healing. (The native doctor uses a horn for administering enemas, not a rubber tube, etc., like the church leader cited above.) Treatment with holy water, a usage which the Shangaan minister has in common with several others, also has a precedent in traditional practice. Tolonyane, who is held to be 'a real Tswana prophet', made the people drink water for which he had prayed (ch. II, p. 30).

The only other examples of traditional elements entering the ritual of healing in these churches are the laying-on of hands, seen as a parallel to the native doctor's technique of massaging (p. 179), and the fainting of Pentecostals, which might be associated with the fainting of the *ngaka ya sedupi* (p. 205). It is doubtful, however, whether the latter association actually exists, since this type of doctor is little known nowadays.

The outstanding instance of traditional belief being incorporated in

---

[1] His methods do, however, resemble that of a type of Shangana-Tonga diviner who, when in a peculiar psychological state 'could guess anything'. (Junod, Henri A., 1927, Vol. ii, p. 538.)

RITUAL AND REVELATION IN THE CHURCHES 189

the ritual and belief of these Pentecostal Separatists is the belief in sorcery, of which we have already observed several examples. It was most explicit in the Foundation Apostolic Church in Jerusalem, and emerged particularly in connexion with the visions which church members related (cf. p. 182). The Evangelist once related that he had 'seen' someone passing the Preacher's homestead, carrying a bag of medicines. All were agreed that this meant that someone intended performing sorcery against the Preacher. When a girl told of her seeing a woman remonstrating with her and asking why she (the girl) could read, whereas her own child could not, it was interpreted as a sign that the woman wished to perform sorcery against the girl. The same girl also saw a baboon following her, which was immediately interpreted as a sign of sorcery. The association of the baboon with sorcery is not peculiar to this church only but it does not seem to be a typical Tswana belief, and is regarded as of Nguni origin.

On one occasion when the Preacher himself was absent there was a quarrel between his wife and the Evangelist, so that the former 'walked out'. At the end of the service a girl said that while she was praying she saw a *mongana* tree[1] behind the Evangelist. This was interpreted as a sign that someone disliked him and contemplated performing sorcery against him. I never heard a particular person's name mentioned in connexion with such visions about sorcery, but in the latter instance I had the feeling it was being connected with the quarrel which had taken place that morning. I am not aware of a regular association between a *mongana* tree and sorcery outside this church.

Outsiders say that the leader of the church of St. Paul Apostolic Faith Morning Star does not deny the reality of sorcery, but he holds that sorcerers have no power over Christians, and encourages his followers to give up the use of traditional anti-sorcery charms and medicines. It is said that people who had ardently believed in such techniques, surrendered their protective medicine horns to be burnt.

Although the validity of traditional beliefs about sorcery is recognized by these churches, the techniques used to counteract it are innovations. Where it is held to have no power over Christians no measures are taken of course. The same kinds of treatment applied against illness and misfortune in general may also be used where sorcery is supposed to be the cause, and the choice of such treatment usually depends on revelation.

The instances of traditional elements being incorporated into church ritual and belief connected with illness and healing, are not particu-

[1] A species of thorn tree (*Acacia detinens*).

190   RELIGION IN A TSWANA CHIEFDOM

larly numerous, but it is significant that the rites of healing performed in the Pentecostal Separatist churches often bear a distinctly magical character. It is clear that the flowing coloured robes of some of these churches, adorned with their coloured figures, and all their bands and cords, their flags, and staffs are magical charms which have a strengthening, protective or healing influence. The staffs of leaders that have been prayed over are supposed to be imbued with particular potency. The consecrated cords which the two preachers placed over the heads or shoulders of people for whom they were praying, were said to link them with the prayers of the superior officials who had consecrated them. They were not mere symbols of such a spiritual link, but were themselves efficient links, magical links. A prayer said over a bottle of water imparts healing powers to the water and the water itself heals and is no mere symbol representing a healing influence. The belief that such water possesses healing power surely belongs to the domain of magic; so also the idea that water from the places of baptism may be used for healing. The ashes sometimes put into the water might have some real medicinal value, but when it is rubbed on the hands of the person performing the laying-on of hands, or when it is sprinkled on the ground beforehand or on the cord before it is put on for the first time, a magical value is attached to it, although, of course, the Tswana does not make this distinction between magical and non-magical medicine.

The laying-on of hands tends to become not a mere symbolic action representing the blessing or healing influence that is imparted by God Himself, but an action which, if performed in the correct circumstances and by the proper persons, is supposed to have a healing influence in itself. This was clearly illustrated by a remark made by a church leader to the effect that he could not pray for others with laying-on of hands when he was ill himself, because if he were to do it, he would cause his own ailment to 'enter' them. The laying-on of hands literally becomes 'the magic touch'. I suggest that that is why it has with some churches become not just a light touch with the hand on a single place, but a violent pressing and rubbing over various parts of the body. That would also explain why the bottle of water is often handled by the person praying over it, not just touched. The same applies to the consecration of church garments and other accessories before they are put on for the first time or after they have been washed.

Candles are connected with revelation not only because of a certain logical association between light and revelation, but more particularly because of the mention of candles (actually candlesticks) in the book of Revelation. Their use is magical in that they are not merely inter-

RITUAL AND REVELATION IN THE CHURCHES   191

preted as symbolic representations of the process of revelation, but as giving the officiant a certain power, and helping him to 'see' more than ordinary persons in everyday life. The scripture reference here again illustrates the fragmentary and literal use that is made of Scripture, a tendency which will presently be shown to be connected with magic.

When all pray at the same time, as is the custom in Pentecostal Separatist churches, it is impossible to follow even a single prayer, but these prayers gave the impression of consisting of rigmaroles of clichés, and of sounds which in ordinary conversation have no meaning, but which are interpreted as speaking with tongues (see below). The repetition of the same sounds and the same set phrases, and the quick tempo at which they are expressed, give these prayers the character of magical formulae rather than of attempts to formulate and express heart-felt needs as petitions very consciously directed to a personal God. Two cases I recorded seem to suggest that conducting a church service may have the effect of 'charming' a house or homestead against sorcery.

Water rites and purification

A number of rites have already been described or referred to in which water plays an important role. I refer to baptism and passing through the water after baptism, to feet washing, drinking of holy water and salt-water enemas. To these several others can be added, which are either explicitly called rites of purification or in which water is used and which are mostly connected with death. Again it is in the Pentecostal Separatist churches that these rites are important (see Table VII). I witnessed only one of the rites described in the following paragraphs.

In three of the Pentecostal Separatist churches a rite of purification is performed involving immersion in water as at baptism, and prayer. A Preacher of one of these churches described the rite as follows:

'When a person has been bereaved we take him to the water; we wash (*tlhapisa*) him with water.' The rite is referred to as *sewasô*. Before entering the water and while entering the officiant prays that 'the water should be right', because there may be a snake in the water. The one who has to be purified then follows him into the water and the officiant immerses him as many times as he considers suitable. As to the purpose of the rite he said: 'We remove his *sehihi*.'

In this and in another church, those requiring purification after a funeral are the close relatives of a deceased such as parents of a

192   RELIGION IN A TSWANA CHIEFDOM

deceased child or the children or spouse of a deceased adult, but in the third church all the church members who attend a funeral are thus purified after a day or two.

In two of the churches the same rite is also performed for a woman after childbirth, as well as in connexion with illness. One leader said it is performed for a person who has recovered from an illness 'to make him clean' (or pretty—*ntlahatsa*). Another said that if a patient does not recover after the usual prayers, they 'take him to the river and make him stand in the water and pray for him'. In the third church it was said that apart from bereaved persons anybody who 'is not right', such as a church member who still drinks a lot of beer, should also be purified thus.

In the Zion Apostolic Church a rite of sprinkling is performed for a close relative of a deceased person to purify (*itshekisa*) him. The officiant and the person undergoing the rite first wash their hands in the same dish of water. The officiant has his green cord hanging loosely round his neck as in the rite of the laying-on of hands (see above, p. 179) he dips the tassels of the cord in the water and sprinkles the person, and then he and another church official pray. It is said that if the person is not purified in this manner, he cannot live 'nicely' (*sentle*) and cannot forget the deceased person.

In the church of St. Paul Apostolic Faith Morning Star water plays a more prominent role than in any other church. It is in this church that the members pass through the baptismal pool for health purposes. Several other water rites already mentioned are also performed by them (Table VII). After a death they perform ritual similar to the Mosaic ritual of purification which they explicitly connect with Numbers 19:11. In their funeral rites all the people present at the funeral are sprinkled with water when the funeral is over. For seven days subsequent to it church members who have attended any funeral may not take an active part in church activities. They may attend services but may not, e.g., preach and pray in public. On the seventh day they are finally purified. One set of informants said they wash with water that has been 'prayed for' while others held that they wash in the pool at the leader's homestead.[1] The leader himself is also subject to the rule of abstaining from church work until he has been purified.

At one service of this church I observed a rite of sprinkling which was performed in respect of newly bought articles belonging to church members.

[1] For reasons already mentioned I was not able to discuss this rite with the minister or members of the church.

13. The Sexton ringing the 'bell'. In the background the simple church building beside some ruins (Bechuana Methodist Church)

14. Interior of a Separatist church

RITUAL AND REVELATION IN THE CHURCHES   193

After the rite of drinking water the minister announced: 'Let the things to be prayed for, come.' About five people came forward and placed the following new articles on the floor: a jar of 'Vaseline', a pair of child's shoes, one or two coloured shirts, a man's sports jacket, a towel, and a pair of child's shorts. The minister spoke about gratitude and added: 'These things are gifts of God; it is not by the power of man. May God glorify (or sanctify) them.' After he stressed that one may not steal, a prayer was said by the congregation. The owners were asked whether any of the things had been stolen and they denied it. The minister warned them that the 'side-car will come'[1] if anything had been stolen. While the congregation sang, the minister moved around the articles, sprinkled water on them from a mug and touched each in turn. With each step he acted as if his knees gave way, more or less as some people do when he lays hands on them. (See p. 180.)

The leader explained to me that the articles are presented 'to be thanked for before God. If we do not thank, Jehovah will give us a roguish spirit. I sprinkle them with water so that they may become blessed'. It was further explained that he encircles the articles so that everything may be included; if there was only one object he could merely have placed his hand over it.[2]

Water and general cleanliness are also important in this church, apart from ritual. On the occasion of a feast which followed a baptismal ceremony (see p. 166) the guests of honour who were served inside the house, were served with a basin of water. soap, and a towel before sitting down to the meal. A woman made the round, holding the basin for every guest in turn, and fetching clean water for each one. On another occasion, when the minister and I were alone, he ordered the girl to pray before he washed. Furthermore, an outsider reported that he once heard that the leader had come into the church in a state of excitement and after he had calmed down told the congregation that 'a voice' had told him that the people should not spit just in any place but use their handkerchiefs or spit somewhere away from the houses, and they should not drink from the same containers without first washing them. Another said he exhorts his congregation not to worship with dirty clothes or without cleaning their teeth or washing their feet. (It should be realized that injunctions such as these are by no means superfluous in the society with which we are concerned.)

All the rites mentioned so far in this section are rites of Pentecostal

---

[1] In towns a motor-cycle and side-car were formerly used by the police to 'pick up' arrested persons.

[2] One informant maintained that they sometimes slaughter sheep or a head of cattle as a sacrifice in respect of a person who is ill, as a means to procure healing. Of this the informant said: 'It is their purification' (*tlhapisô*). I have no further material to substantiate or explain this. (See further, p. 207.)

R.T.C.—14

194   RELIGION IN A TSWANA CHIEFDOM

Separatist churches. In a Baptist Separatist church of group 'A' the clothes of mourning are ritually removed from persons bereaved of a close relative, two or three months after their bereavement. Laying-on of hands forms part of the rite, which was described to me as the church's rite of purification (*tlhapisô*). The Bishop of the church connected it with Zach. 3:3–5, where mention is made of the high priest Joshua whose 'filthy garments' were removed and who was given other garments to put on.

Before discussing the significance of these rites we should note that the Pentecostal Separatist churches, as well as most other churches, are opposed to the traditional Tswana rites of purification in which a doctor officiates.

With reference to baptism and purification rites Dr. Sundkler laid down the thesis 'that the propensity of the Zulu Zionist to total immersion is intimately linked up with traditional Zulu ritual practices in streams and pools'.[1] He also shows how baptism tends to be repeated, thus distinctly becoming a rite of purification. This does not hold in respect of the Tswana Separatists and traditional Tswana ritual practices. The churches attaching particular value to baptism by immersion have a considerable proportion of the total membership of the Separatists in Taung. They also tend to view baptism as a rite of purification (p. 163) and to repeat a rite similar to baptism by immersion as a rite of purification. Yet in the traditional ritual of the Tlhaping we search in vain for numerous rites connected with rivers and pools. Hardly anything of the kind is performed nowadays, while in the past such rites were only performed in very special circumstances, as when the fabulous water snake (*phikakgolo*) had 'taken' a person. For rain ceremonies driftwood from the river was used and some doctors also claim that they spent some time in a pool of water during their period of initiation. In the literature on Tswana ritual I have come across very little beyond these examples. When this is compared with the numerous occasions on which Zulus wash in a pool or a river as part of a ceremony of purification,[2] the contrast is striking.

Baptism by immersion, then, has no close morphological parallel in traditional Tswana rites. Moreover, some of the churches have rites of purification which are definitely connected with traditional notions of 'impurity', such as *sehihi*, for which the traditional rites of purification were performed, but the church rites performed to remove the impurity often resemble the rite of baptism by immersion, and not the

---

[1] *Op. cit.*, p. 201.

[2] Cf. Sundkler, *op. cit.*, pp. 22, 314; and Krige, 1950, pp. 82 (n.), 90, 158, 165, 228, 319, etc.

RITUAL AND REVELATION IN THE CHURCHES 195

traditional rites. The propensity for baptism by immersion and rites of purification in rivers or pools must therefore have a different explanation in the Taung churches.

As I have hinted above (p. 163), the explanation seems to be found in the nature of the teaching which is usually connected with baptism in the European churches which favour baptism by immersion as opposed to other forms of baptism. It is typical of many 'western' Baptist[1] churches that they tend to make baptism all-important to salvation, so that one cannot be saved, or one can scarcely be saved, without being baptized, whereby a certain efficacy is attached to the rite itself. It is not regarded as a mere representation of a spiritual process or action which makes one acceptable to God, but the rite itself is seen as bringing one in that condition, or at least as contributing a great deal toward the attainment of that goal. This type of doctrine I hold to be distinctly magical (pp. 146 ff.). Its magical nature is also shown in the stress that is laid on the particular form the rite must take. Baptists in general tend not only to consider baptism as very important for salvation, but also hold that it must be just the one particular form of baptism; only that is valid, not the other forms. When a rite is merely a symbolic representation, the minor particulars of form need not be stressed, as long as it arouses the appropriate associations in the minds of those concerned, but in magic even a minor deviation from the proper form of a rite may render it ineffectual.

I suggest that it is the magical value usually attached to baptism by immersion that renders it particularly acceptable to the Tlhaping. The traditional religion of the Tswana bore a strongly magical character and such of its ritual as still exists is predominantly magical. Having this background of magic, new doctrines attaching a magical interpretation to the modes of behaviour with which they are concerned will have a stronger appeal than doctrines which are distinctly non-magical.

I also drew attention earlier to the literal and fragmentary application of portions from Scripture, which not only characterizes teaching about baptism in the Baptist churches in Taung, but is a characteristic of their teaching in general. (See pp. 83, 162.) It also emerges in various scripture references made in connexion with some of the rites described in the present chapter, e.g. the consecration of the parents together with the children, ritual drinking of water, and the use of ashes, candles, and salt.

[1] I use 'Baptist' in its broad sense of churches which stress the necessity of adult baptism by immersion, as opposed to infant baptism by sprinkling or pouring.

196   RELIGION IN A TSWANA CHIEFDOM

This tendency is also typical of many 'Western' churches. Certain passages which favour the particular view of a church receive all the attention and stress, without reference to the context or to the general trend of Scripture as a whole, and this is often combined with a very literal interpretation of Scripture. This mode of interpretation must be contrasted with that which aims at obtaining a comprehensive impression of the content of Scripture as a whole, and which seeks to interpret every particular verse or passage within its immediate and wider context. I suggest that the former method, i.e. a literal and fragmentary application of Scripture, is closely akin to the mode of thought underlying magic. What Evans-Pritchard writes about Zande beliefs seems to me to apply to the combined beliefs of any society in which religion bears a strongly magical character. Commenting on Zande magic, he writes that Zande beliefs 'are not indivisible ideational structures but are loose associations of notions. When a writer brings them together in a book and presents them as a conceptual system their insufficiencies and contradictions are at once apparent. In real life they do not function as a whole but in bits. A man in one situation utilizes what in the beliefs are convenient to him and pays no attention to other elements which he might use in different situations.'[1] In other words, the beliefs are not seen in their totality, and a particular belief is not seen within the context of the whole body of belief. This applies to traditional Tswana belief, and, I think, to all systems of belief which are predominantly magical. In a society whose members are accustomed to this mode of thought, particular receptivity to the type of Christian teaching which uses Scripture in a fragmentary and literal manner could be anticipated.

This explanation of the predilection shown for the particular form of baptism—(immersion)—as opposed to the other forms—(sprinkling and pouring), does not exclude some direct connexion of church rites of purification with traditional beliefs and practices. No doubt the importance of water in church ritual must in a general sense be related to the traditional notions of impurity, particularly malevolent 'heat', and the purifying or 'cooling' ritual in which water was (and still is) so important. There are also some close parallels between particular aspects of church ritual and tradition. Both in tradition and in the churches, death is connected with *sehihi* and calls for purification. In two churches some purification rites take the form of sprinkling as in traditional purification. Further, the drinking of holy water for purposes of health is very similar to the traditional prophet

[1] 1937, p. 540.

RITUAL AND REVELATION IN THE CHURCHES   197

Tolonyane's use of ritual water called *letsididi* (coldness) (see ch. II, p. 34).

Mention must here be made of the fact that there are religious bodies among Europeans which also lay great stress on the use of water in healing. The possibility of influence from that source is not excluded.[1]

In Zulu Zionist churches the use of ashes is closely connected with purification. They are particularly used as an emetic, the vomiting being part of the process (of which confession also forms a part) of cleansing both body and soul.[2] The leaders in Taung did not refer to the use of ashes as *tlhapisô* (a purification) but one spoke of it as *sewasô*, which is the Tswana form for the Zulu *isiwasho*, the name for the purgatives and enemas used by Zulu Zionists in connexion with purification. Another Taung leader, when questioned about *sewasô*, said it was the Nguni term for *tlhapisô*. This shows some connexion of ashes with purification. In Zulu Zionist churches the use of ashes as a purificant finds a precedent in traditional Zulu rites of purification, but I do not know of any traditional Tswana purification in which it is used, so that in Taung it lacks the sanction of tradition which it has in Zulu churches. Probably its use as purificant was first introduced by Zulu Zionists and this example was followed by non-Zulu leaders. It should also be remembered that some of the churches in Taung have Nguni people in their ranks, and it is known that important higher officials of some are Zulus. Whereas the use of ashes as a purificant is not sanctioned by Tswana tradition it seems as if in Taung churches its use is again more closely connected with Mosaic law (see above, p. 181).[3]

One suspects that more or less all the rites of purification bear a magical character. In some cases the evidence is not conclusive, but where a rite is thought of as removing a dangerous condition such as *sehihi*, there is no doubt about it.

Revelation and the Spirit

In this section we shall again be almost entirely concerned with the Pentecostal Separatists. It is not that members of other churches do not also believe that individuals may receive direct revelations, but

[1] Several of the Separatist 'Prayer-healing Churches' in Ibadan which are described by Dr. Geoffrey Parrinder also make use of holy water in healing. The author does not say whether this practice has any connexion with the pagan or Islamic background. (Parrinder, 1953.)

[2] Sundkler, *op. cit.*, pp. 210–212. In the Zulu churches the vomiting is related to the significance of vomiting in traditional ritual. Among the Tlhaping vomiting does not play this important role, neither in the churches nor in traditional ritual.

[3] Though the use of ashes in Zulu churches is related to traditional custom, it is also connected with Mosaic law. (Sundkler, op. cit., pp. 211–212, 232.)

198   RELIGION IN A TSWANA CHIEFDOM

belief and behaviour connected with revelation are not such important and integral parts of church life and doctrine as in some of the Pentecostal Separatist churches. In these other churches many people believe that particular revelations may be received through dreams, and these are partly interpreted on traditional lines. Christians say that dreaming such dreams is 'a gift of God'.

Some dreams are interpreted as directing a particular course of behaviour, usually calling for a change or reform in behaviour. A number of church leaders as well as ordinary members are known to have changed their church affiliation as a result of dreams or visions (ch. V, pp. 72 f). The following is an example of a dream calling for a reform in behaviour (in a Separatist church of type 'A').

In his dream X saw the minister beside a deep hole in the ground calling him to come and look. X came and saw a coffin at the bottom of the hole, but the minister told him that that was not a coffin but a man, and that he would call him and that he would come out. When the minister called out: 'Elijah!' the man came out, taking only one step to reach the top, and walked off toward the east. Then the minister said to X: 'Do you see what happens to those who do the work of God? That man is going now to earn his everlasting life.'

X thought it meant that he had been busy with 'bad works' and that in the dream the minister was trying to bring him back and show him that if he did not do the works of God he would not inherit eternal life.

Several church leaders said that members sometimes come to consult them about dreams and that they try to explain such dreams as they understand them. A leader of a Sabbatarian Separatist church said 'the Bible refuses' dreams, referring to Jer. 23:16–17 which cautions against false prophets.

In two Pentecostal Separatist churches no more attention is paid to dreams and revelations than in the churches referred to above. A leader of one of these said that if people of other churches prophesy to them, they only accept these prophecies if their content agrees with Scripture. The rest of the material in this section pertains almost entirely to the remaining four Pentecostal Separatist churches (cf. Table VII).

The Holy Spirit, mostly just spoken of as 'the Spirit' (*Môya* or *Môwa*) or 'the spirit of God', is particularly thought of as the source of revelation. Revelations sometimes come in the form of dreams, but more often as visions, or as the speaking of a voice. The Spirit also reveals His presence in people by making them perform certain bodily movements and pronounce utterances which do not form part of everyday language (speak with tongues).

RITUAL AND REVELATION IN THE CHURCHES   199

Revelations through visions and through dreams appear to be of the same nature, but people usually distinguish clearly between what they have 'seen' and what they have dreamt. A few instances are known of people receiving visions when they were unconscious, but most visions are received in a waking condition. Sometimes a vision comes when someone is moved by the Spirit to dancing and similar movements (see below), but it may also come when he sits still. One leader said of such visions that he saw them 'like a bioscope'. Visionary and audible revelations are referred to in terms such as 'a gift of the Spirit', being 'shown (*bontshiwa*) by God' or 'revealed (*senolwa*) by God', and 'the Voice says (*lentswe le re*)'. In one church it is spoken of as prophecy.

One leader is said to have been able to predict events before he joined the church. Another one himself speaks of his 'seeing' as a gift of God which he inherited from both his father and mother. He refers to it as 'being born with *maséré*',[1] which was said to be equivalent to 'being born with the caul'. Even in the churches of these two men the gift of prophecy or receiving revelations is not confined to the leader only, but is shared by most, if not all members of the congregation.

In the church in which revelation is referred to as prophecy (which is a predominantly Nguni church), one becomes a prophet by going alone 'to the mountain' to fast for three or four days, and to pray that God should enable one to diagnose illness, to pray for patients and prescribe the manner in which they will be healed. A person seeking this gift will know that he has acquired it if, while praying for a person, he hears with his ears what has to be done.

A leader of another church explained that one starts receiving revelations in the following manner:

After baptism 'Prayers' regularly pray for you that God should help you, that He should forgive you. 'You keep on praying; you have observed prayers. Now one day God will visit you; He will show you visions. It comes to you as if you feel dizzy. . . . God is busy making something manifest (*senosetsa*) to you. Now you will speak with new tongues of angels. Those who are not in the Spirit cannot understand [lit. hear] you; you will be heard only by those who are in the Spirit—what are you saying. . . . It is the Hebrew language.'

He also explained the manner in which the Voice comes to him: first he hears a sound like that of a bee and then he hears the Voice

---

[1] This was said to be a Southern Sotho expression. *Leséré* according to Mabille and Dieterlen's Dictionary is 'light beer'.

200 RELIGION IN A TSWANA CHIEFDOM

speaking to him 'in Hebrew',[1] sometimes also in a language commonly known.

Speaking with tongues is often accompanied by movements of the body, which are explained as 'the entrance of the Spirit into the person'. It is hardly possible to discern a general pattern which the sounds and the movements follow and I can only give some examples at random in addition to the description of the violent type of Pentecostal service given in the previous chapter. The buzzing sound like that of a bee seems to be commonly connected with the working of the Spirit and was heard in different churches. Others make blowing or hissing sounds, or snort. When praying or preaching, whole phrases of apparently meaningless sounds are often interjected. They may phonologically resemble (or partly resemble) Bantu speech: one leader often ended such phrases of speaking with tongues with something like 'ntikala ba kurrrrr'. When I asked him the meaning of it, he said it was a prayer. He also sometimes smacked with his lips when praying, producing a sound like a kiss: this meant 'amen'! Others sometimes utter sounds more reminiscent of the phonology of English words. Sounds like 'great pied' and 'thiripied guide' often recurred in one leader's blessings and prayers. Whether all such sounds and phrases which recur have a recognized meaning, I do not know.

The jerks of the body, stooping postures, twitchings, shivering, waving of arms, and similar bodily movements which have already been described are also interpreted as the work of the Spirit. Further examples of the manner in which the Spirit is thought to work may be observed in the following account of a night service for the 'opening' of a house of the Preacher of a Pentecostal Separatist church.[2]

The Evangelist was also present, but the Preacher conducted most of the service. A young man and a young girl were so restless through the Spirit working in them that the Preacher became quite desperate at times. They were up and down, in and out at the door, interrupted the speaker, and chattered to each other, mostly speaking with tongues and often talking simultaneously. Once when everybody was singing and jumping about as if performing a kind of dance, the girl stood with her arm round the Preacher's waist. Later again, while someone was speaking, she stood beside the Preacher with her hands on his head, as if praying for him. While she was busy he uttered a kind of roar and eventually jumped up, his body vibrating. The girl and the young man remained restless for hours, causing endless interruptions although the Preacher had scolded them several times and at last

[1] An informant from another church also referred to the speaking with tongues as 'Hebrew'. On a different occasion he said there are two kinds of speech of which the one is 'Gabos, dimêg, gasêg' (with aspirated g as in Afrikaans and Tswana).

[2] For a description of the service as a whole, see p. 101.

RITUAL AND REVELATION IN THE CHURCHES 201

burst out in a series of English and Afrikaans words of rather uncouth and blasphemous nature! The young man seemed to be as disturbing as ever after this.

Once when the Preacher was again speaking, he suddenly interrupted himself, and called out: 'Who has got shoes on?' He started hunting around and came to a man (not a member of the church) sitting next to me. Both he and I had our shoes on.[1] Yes, said the Preacher his stick had told him so! Soon after this, my friend and several other people who were also wearing shoes, chose to hurry out of the room.

Later on there was singing and dancing as before, but the Preacher started dancing in the middle of the room, waving his arms, and spinning around like a top, as people often do in this church. Once he came to me and put his hand on my head and the other on the head of my neighbour, praying and speaking with tongues. When he had finished he asked whether I had felt something and seemed rather taken aback that I had not.

This kind of behaviour seems so disconnected and without a fixed pattern that it is impossible to present an adequate description of it in words.

The episode shows how the belief in direct inspiration and revelation by the Spirit can be a source of internal troubles and disputes. From an outsider's point of view the two young people were all the time flouting the authority of a church official. When I discussed the service with the Preacher a few days later, he said that the disturbers held that it was the Spirit (or 'their Spirit') which made them act in such a manner, but he doubted it. He was 'a man of the Spirit' himself, but the Spirit did not move him to act as they did. It was not the custom of the church, but the young man had returned from Johannesburg with this kind of behaviour. He, the Preacher, had now written to the minister (the Leader or a senior church official) in Johannesburg to enquire about this behaviour because the minister did not teach him to act in such a manner.

An expression he used during the service also implied that he doubted their claim to being moved by the Spirit. When scolding them once he said: 'We should leave *badimo* [spirits of the deceased] outside.' Apparently he was hinting that they were not being moved by 'the Spirit' (i.e. God's Spirit), but by the spirits of the dead, thereby implying that their behaviour was not genuine from a church point of view.

The presence of someone wearing shoes was also connected with the disturbance. The Preacher explained that 'if we enter with shoes on,

---

[1] I usually observed these rules myself and had done so on this occasion, too, but with the endless sitting, and with so little space to move, my feet had become cold and I slipped on my shoes again!

202   RELIGION IN A TSWANA CHIEFDOM

we cannot agree', but also added that if this was really what was troubling the two they would have revealed it. His staff had 'told' him about the shoes. These staffs are generally thought of as 'giving strength' when one is praying or preaching but are also particularly connected with divination or prophesying.

Spinning around as the Preacher did during the service is also connected with revelation. This kind of dancing is called 'tress' (pronounced as in English). The same term is also applied in this church to the running around in a circle in the manner described in the previous chapter (illustration 9), the former being a substitute for running around in a circle when space is restricted. The Preacher said he performs the action so that the Spirit should tell him something, '. . . so that understanding will come to me, whatever it may be . . . so that I may know something that will happen'. 'Tress' is often also performed by the whole congregation during a service, particularly around a Prayer and a member for whom he or she is praying. When the service is over they usually file out and run around in a circle for a little while before disbanding. About this it was said: 'If someone has a bad spirit it will throw him out of the circle.' 'A bad spirit' was defined as 'his original spirit (môwa wa tlhôlêgô ya gagwê)'. A good spirit 'is to be loving'.[1]

In connexion with the act of placing his hands on our heads, the Preacher explained that the hand on the other man's head became heavy. He claimed that even as he spoke to me his hand was still feeling heavy and this was more than three days later! This showed that the man had a very serious ailment. In my own case he said he 'felt' a pain going down my neck and back. He himself experienced the pain coming up his arm to his neck and this showed him that I had such a pain. He said that perhaps I did not feel it at the time, but some time or other I would still feel it and remember what he had said. He added that 'this ailment comes from God only'.

The revelations received are mostly concerned with the treatment or prevention of illness: they are about the cause of illness (including sorcery), about what clothes or figures should be worn, whether to use holy water, whether to use ashes, and so on. A vision about the arrival of a stranger clad in white robes, who came in and knelt in the homestead enclosure before greeting members of the congregation was interpreted as pointing to the expected visit of superior church officials from Johannesburg. About the St. Paul Apostolic Faith Morning Star outsiders say that they undertake no work unless the

[1] The term 'Tress' is probably a mispronunciation of 'dress', in its military connotation, and refers to their proper alignment in the circle.

Spirit has revealed to them that they should do it. The leader's itineraries are decided by revelations he receives. He is the only one I know who foretells events of general importance to the community as a whole. He is said to have given warnings beforehand of a recent epidemic of smallpox and a severe hailstorm which occurred in November 1952. During my second field trip he announced at his headman's *kgotla* that there would again be a severe hailstorm, worse than the previous year (1952). The headman reported this warning at the chief's *kgotla* in a general tribal assembly. When foretelling such calamities the minister in question usually exhorts the people to pray and humble themselves before God so that it may pass soon or come with moderation. Such predictions of general importance are only made by the leader and not by other office-bearers or members. He is the one of whom it is said that he used to receive revelations even before he joined the church.

Mention must be made of the mechanical manner in which the Bible is sometimes used for the purpose of divining or obtaining a revelation. This manner of divination was practised by the Shangaan minister as well as by the other leader who appeared in court. Another man who still follows this method explained that he uses it in connexion with illness. He takes the Bible and prays over it and opens it with his eyes still closed. He reads at the place he has opened and the portion he reads reveals the diagnosis and treatment of the disease.

Dr. Sundkler has shown that a remarkably close parallel exists between the Zulu diviner and the Zulu Zionist prophet.[1] The Pentecostal Separatist 'prophet' or 'apostle' in Taung is comparable to the commonly known traditional Tswana doctor-diviner in that both of them combine the activity of divining with that of healing. There are, however, important differences which for the Tlhaping rule out the close parallel Dr. Sundkler has drawn.

(a) *Becoming a diviner/Joining the church.* Among the Zulu the initial development in becoming a diviner is a deterioration of health which is eventually ascribed to possession by an ancestor spirit. Zulu Zionists often join the church in connexion with healing. An important aspect of their development as church members consists in their 'being entered' by 'the Spirit'. Although healing and being entered by the Spirit play a similar role in Tlhaping Pentecostal churches, the Tswana diviner is not a person who has become ill through spirit possession and does not show particular psychic or somatic characteristics. He has learnt the art of divining and doctoring from a close

[1] *Op. cit.*, pp. 313 ff.; cf. also pp. 109, 238 ff., 256 ff.

204   RELIGION IN A TSWANA CHIEFDOM

relative or from an unrelated person to whom he has made a payment for instruction.

(b) *Ritual in rivers or pools*. The Zulu diviner often has to perform ablutions in a stream and Zulu Zionists as well as Separatist Pentecostals in Taung undergo baptism by immersion and perform purification ceremonies in rivers. Some Tswana doctors claim to have spent some time under water in a river or pool during their initiation but do not regularly perform ritual activities in rivers or pools.

(c) *Methods of divining*. A Zulu diviner divines with the help of the spirits by a process of asking leading questions and observing the reactions of his audience. Zulu Zionists also prophesy by a process of questioning. Taung Pentecostal Separatists mostly receive revelations through direct inspiration by the Spirit but sometimes also by opening a Bible. Tswana doctors divine by the use of sets of dice. In this case the general pattern of Tswana Pentecostal Separatists' revelations is different from that of the Tswana diviner. However, a minor parallel may be observed between the belief that the falling of the Tswana diviner's dice is controlled by the ancestor spirits, and the belief in the role the Spirit of God plays in revelations received by Pentecostals.

A closer parallel is that between the use of a Bible for 'divining' and the throwing of dice. (i) Before throwing them the Tswana doctor recites the praises of his dice. These are interpreted as prayers to the spirits of the deceased to make the divining successful. The prophet or apostle also prays before opening the Bible. (ii) The throwing of the diviner's dice and the basing of a verdict on the position of the dice is of a similar nature to opening the Bible with closed eyes and giving a pronouncement based on the passage of Scripture where the Bible has been opened. In both cases the exact outcome of the action is a matter of 'chance'. (iii) The doctor bases his verdict on an examination of the position of the dice and on the rules relating to the particular praises or formulas connected with the different positions of the dice. The Pentecostal prophet or apostle reads the passage where the Bible has been opened and arrives at a verdict by interpreting the passage in terms of the values and doctrines of his church.

(d) *Group patterns*. Zulu diviners often act as a group and their 'group pattern' provides the pattern on which Zionist congregations are organized. There is no 'group pattern' of Tswana diviners to which the organization of Pentecostal Separatist congregations can be compared. Among the Tswana one becomes a doctor by being apprenticed to an established doctor for a time, but teacher and pupil do not maintain a particular relationship after the period of apprenticeship is over.

RITUAL AND REVELATION IN THE CHURCHES 205

At times the chief may summon a number of doctors to perform divination collectively, for instance, in connexion with rain, but doctors do not 'band together in fairly distinct groups' as is the case among the Zulu.[1]

This comparison shows us on the one hand that there is a whole range of similarities between Zulu diviner and Zulu Zionist prophet. These similarities do not merely consist of a number of isolated aspects, but it is a comprehensive similarity involving a complete pattern: Zionist prophet follows the diviner-prophet in all the important aspects. On the other hand, we immediately encounter two major differences between Tswana Pentecostals and the commonly known Tswana doctors, viz. the manner in which they come into their particular role of divining or prophesying, and the absence of regular group activities and a group pattern on the part of Tswana doctors, to which the Pentecostal church group could be parallelled. Parallels between the two do exist on a number of smaller points, however. There is a degree of similarity between the Tswana doctor's initiation and the Pentecostals' baptism and between some forms of church purification and that which the doctor performs. The more common form of receiving revelations among Pentecostals of Taung (inspiration by the Spirit) is dissimilar to the traditional method of throwing the dice, but there is close similarity between the latter and the method of opening the Bible as occasionally used in the churches.

There are some more precedents for various aspects of Pentecostal Separatists' beliefs and activities in Tswana tradition, but most of these are found in the activities of certain less common and lesser known types of specialists in the field of magico-religious beliefs and ritual. I refer in the first place to the nowadays-little-known *ngaka ya sedupi* (see ch. II, p. 32). His inspiration by the ancestor spirits, the strange sounds uttered during his performances, his fainting when tobacco was used, and his revival by singing, praying to the ancestor spirits and clapping of hands are comparable to the prophet's and apostle's being entered by the Spirit, their speaking with tongues, the fainting of some people under treatment, their opposition to tobacco, and their singing and clapping of hands while a healing ceremony is performed.

There are also points of similarity between the prophet, Tolonyane, who is said to have acted on traditional lines (ch. II, pp. 30 f.), and Separatist prophets and apostles. Tolonyane also received revelations through direct inspiration by the ancestor spirits, as Separatists claim

---

[1] *Op. cit.*, p. 315. Cf. Schapera, 1953, p. 62.

206   RELIGION IN A TSWANA CHIEFDOM

to receive it from the Spirit of God. Someone who accompanied Tolonyane into the cave which he used to frequent is reported to have heard a confusion of unusual sounds, believed to be the voices of the ancestor spirits. This is comparable to the Separatists speaking with tongues when they 'are entered' by the Spirit. The prophecies of one leader (St. Paul Apostolic Faith Morning Star) are of a similar nature to the predictions of Tolonyane: both predicted a smallpox epidemic and made predictions about rain and climatic phenomena on various occasions. One of my most trusted informants on traditional matters, himself not a member of any church, connected the above-mentioned church leader with the prophetess Botlhale (who also came from the ranks of the church, p. 48), whom he again connected with Tolonyane. He holds the activities of all three to be of a similar nature.[1]

Attention must be drawn to certain differences between Zulu Zionists and Pentecostal Separatists in Taung which seem to be related to the differences between traditional Zulu diviners and traditional Tswana diviners. For instance, whereas some Zulu Zionist congregations are unstable vagrant groups, in Taung such groups do not exist (see p. 66). This 'spiritual vagabondage' is related by Dr. Sundkler to the vagrancy of traditional Zulu diviners.[2] The absence of vagrancy in Taung Separatist churches may be related to the fact that traditional Tswana diviners do not roam about the country as Zulu diviners do. Perhaps this could be termed a 'negative' aspect of the relation of traditional beliefs and practices to ritual and belief in the churches.

Another instance is provided by the role of women in the churches. Women are particularly prominent in Zulu Zionist churches. According to Dr. Sundkler 'some 80 per cent' of their members are women, and women may rise to important positions of leadership, which he calls 'the real power basis for women leaders'. This particular predominance of women in Zionist churches he relates to the fact that most traditional Zulu diviners are women.[3] In Taung there is a general predominance of women in the churches (ch. IV), but in Pentecostal Separatist churches, which would roughly coincide with Dr. Sundkler's Zionists, women constitute only 53% of the members, and do not become important leaders. This distinct difference between Zulu Zionists and Tswana Pentecostal Separatists may be related to the fact that few women become diviners among the Tswana, unlike the Zulu.

[1] The particularly important role of water in the ritual of this church also brings it in line with Botlhale and Tolonyane, both of whom made the people drink water that had been 'prayed for'.

[2] *Op. cit.*, p. 316; cf. pp. 96–97.

[3] *Op. cit.*, pp. 141 ff., 316.

RITUAL AND REVELATION IN THE CHURCHES 207

I have already referred to the parallel between the role of the ancestor spirits in traditional notions of revelation (both Zulu and Tswana) and the role of the Spirit of God in Pentecostal Separatist or Zionist churches. In this connexion the question may be asked whether the idea of being ill through spirit possession is altogether foreign to the Tlhaping. I would not deny that the Tlhaping believe in spirit possession, but it does not seem to be a very common belief. In Tswana insanity or a state of mental derangement is indicated by a verb which means 'to be entered' (*go tsenwa*). In connexion with this verb, which he translates as 'to be possessed', Dr. Willoughby says that 'all insane people are held in awe, unless they are harmless simpletons of the milder sort; but not all of them claim to be "possessed" by a particular spirit'.[1] From this we may deduce that at least some such people were believed to be possessed by a spirit.[2] In a few cases in which I heard this word (*go tsenwa*) used or when I asked an informant about it, it was not connected with spirit possession, but I was told that it was illness that had entered the person's head. When I suggested the ancestor spirits, it was denied. It was also said to be caused by God or by people performing sorcery.

This adds to the impression that in so far as beliefs about the Spirit in Tswana Pentecostal Separatist churches can be related to traditional beliefs about the ancestor spirits, the relation is of a vague and distant nature. It is certainly not as clear and distinct as among the Zulu where traditional beliefs about possession by an ancestral spirit— which still show great vitality in Zulu society—have been transferred to the idea of being filled with the Holy Spirit as found in some churches.

The belief in the Spirit, however, does not completely displace the belief in ancestors in Zulu Zionist churches, and in spite of substituting it in some instances, it is nevertheless used to uphold and sanction it in others. Dr. Sundkler says that 'Spirit and Angel are concepts which Zionists use rather indiscriminately' and then points out that 'the Angel's main reproach in churches of Zionist type is that the ancestral spirits have been neglected', and Zionists often slaughter animals as sacrifices to their ancestral spirits.[3] We have noted one instance in which a Pentecostal Separatist church in Taung slaughters an animal, and interprets it in terms of the belief in ancestor spirits (see above, p. 161), but this is a unique example.

In one church, the Church of St. Paul Apostolic Faith Morning Star, animal sacrifices are known to be made, but these do not seem to be

[1] 1928, p. 110. [2] Cf. also *op. cit.*, pp. 105 ff.
[3] *Op. cit.*, pp. 249 ff.

208 RELIGION IN A TSWANA CHIEFDOM

connected with the ancestor spirits. According to two informants who are not members but have close contacts with this church, the animals slaughtered are definitely spoken of as sacrifices (*ditlhabêlô*) and reference is made to Old Testament sacrifices to sanction them. Cattle and sheep are sacrificed, as many head at a time as church members bring. They are slaughtered in the stock pen and each animal is prayed over before being slaughtered. All the meat is eaten at a feast in which the congregation as well as visitors take part. Such sacrifices are made at about Easter and September each year. The latter is spoken of as a thanksgiving (*tebogô*). On a Saturday in January I visited the leader of this church and on my making a remark about two carcasses hung outside to dry, he remarked: 'I am making a feast. It is a thanksgiving. I am thanking God.' This seems to have been a New Year thanksgiving.

On the evidence available we may say that Taung Pentecostal churches also differ from Zulu Zionists in that in the latter the belief in ancestor spirits is still strong and sacrifices to them are common, whereas in the Taung churches this is not the case. The immediate explanation is to be found in the fact that among the Tlhaping the cult of the ancestors has obviously disintegrated much further than among the Zulu. I would suggest that even in traditional Tswana society the ancestor cult was less important and sacrifices were less numerous than in traditional Zulu society, a theory which is discussed in greater detail in the following chapter.

Prayers for rain

At the beginning of the rainy season, weekly prayer meetings for rain are held. During the 1953 season the first reference I heard to it was when a headman, speaking in a tribal assembly, asked that the chief should 'open' the prayers for rain. The prayer meetings were started at the chief's *kgotla* on a Monday morning and on subsequent Mondays similar services were also held at the headmen's places. At the chief's place the services were conducted by the L.M.S. African minister by request of the chief's chief councillor. At the headmen's places the local leaders of different churches took turns in officiating. In the services at Taung the chief and his two important councillors sat in the central position, facing the congregation. The officiating minister and the church leaders accompanying him took up positions to one side. (Illustration 6.)

The idea that the chief should 'open' the prayers for rain and that they are organized by councillors acting on his behalf appears to be a remnant of the old tribal structure in which the chief also had religious

15. The entrance to Mmoloki's Cave

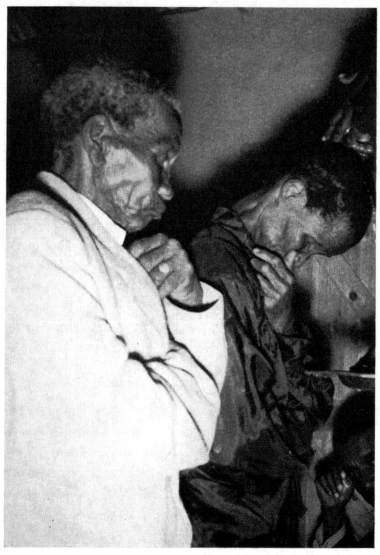
16. Two old people receiving baptism in Lutheran church

RITUAL AND REVELATION IN THE CHURCHES 209

functions and was responsible for having certain important rites performed on behalf of the whole tribe, albeit through specialists appointed or summoned by him. This was particularly the case with rain rites.

I suggest further that the Christian prayer meeting for rain has developed as a substitute for some of the pagan rain rites which have fallen into disuse, although some of the pagan ritual in connexion with rain is still performed (ch. II, p. 27 f.).

Summary

It is a commonplace that Christian missions and churches have profoundly influenced the life of the indigenous peoples of South Africa. The material in this chapter shows in respect of Tlhaping society that the traditional culture and the social structure on which it was based has on the other hand also influenced the forms of belief and worship that are found in the churches.

In some instances *elements of pagan ritual and belief have found their way into church ritual and belief.* In one church the rite of eating the *mogôga*-animal is performed in much the same way and with much the same significance as in pagan ritual. The role of the chief in connexion with prayer meetings for rain is also a remnant of the traditional background. Most funerals contain remnants of pagan ritual, but these seem to have lost their traditional significance. The belief in *phikakgolo* (the water snake) is recognized in the ritual of one church, while several recognize the belief in sorcery. We observed an instance of a Christian woman holding what is apparently the belief that the spirits of people who die in discontent do not rest. The belief that children are sinless may also be a remnant from paganism.

A few Christian rites and usages which are not part of the heritage which Christian churches have brought with them from abroad have developed as *substitutes* for traditional rites or social ceremonies. This is the case with prayer meetings for rain, the service for bringing out a new-born baby, and memorial services some time after the death of important persons. The Roman Catholic priest also sometimes performs a rite of 'blessing' the food for a wedding feast, with the express purpose of encouraging church members not to summon a native doctor to perform traditional ritual. Divining with the use of the Bible might also be regarded as a 'Christian' substitute for the traditional custom of divining with dice.[1]

[1] Some of the usages mentioned here may show a certain resemblance to usages which are found outside Bantu churches, but from their particular form and from the particular situations in which they occur it is clear that among the Tlhaping they have developed as substitutes for indigenous customs.

R.T.C.—15

210   RELIGION IN A TSWANA CHIEFDOM

There are also a number of instances in which *parallels* may be seen between church rites and traditional rites, as between the role of the Holy Spirit and ancestor Spirits in divining or prophesying, the secrecy of communion and of initiation ceremonies, rules of avoidance in the churches and traditional taboos, beliefs about dreams, visions and revelation through 'the voice' in the churches and traditional beliefs about dreams, and between beating during the laying-on of hands and massaging as part of traditional techniques of healing. Such parallels also exist in respect of the occurrence and purpose of rites of purification, the drinking of holy water, and the combination of healing activities with divining (or the receiving of revelations). Similarity in form need not imply that traditional beliefs and rites have influenced beliefs and rites in the churches, particularly when such beliefs and rites do not occur in Bantu churches only. However, as we have shown in some cases, it is possible that the existence of such similarity in form has given particular sanction to the church rites and beliefs in question and has made them particularly acceptable to Bantu converts.

In Zulu Zionist churches ritual and belief display much closer and more striking morphological resemblance to traditional beliefs and practices than is the case in Taung. This, I think, is to be explained by the fact that the pagan system of magico-religious beliefs is still much stronger and much more of it can still be observed among the Zulu than in Taung.[1]

We have seen, however, that much of ritual and belief in Taung churches, particularly with the Pentecostal Separatists, bears a *magical character*. This is particularly evident in connexion with baptism, healing and rites of purification. This, I suggest, is the most important aspect in which Christianity has been influenced by the traditional background. This traditional background of magic not only influences African converts to attach an 'indigenous' magical interpretation to Christian rites and beliefs which they are not generally given in 'western' churches, but it also makes them particularly susceptible to the teachings of the branches of Christianity which tend to attach magical value to their ritual. This has been illustrated with particular reference to baptism.

Finally we should note that some of the rites in the churches are new '*inventions*' with no precedent either in the heritage of Christian churches or in the indigenous traditional background. Several such examples come from the St. Paul Apostolic Faith Morning Star, e.g. the reinstatement of a 'lost sheep' through partial baptism, passing

[1] For a discussion of this point, see ch. VII.

through the baptismal pool after baptism, the coffin as ritual symbol on the holy place, and blessing newly bought articles. Other examples are the coloured robes and patterns worn by some Pentecostal Separatists in connexion with health, and the use of candles to assist in revelation. Other rites again, for which there are precedents in Western churches, are elaborated, particularly by the Pentecostal Separatists, as we have shown in connexion with the rite of the laying-on of hands. In other instances Old Testament ritual which is usually no longer adhered to by Christians, has been revived in these churches, as is the case with the use of ashes as a purificant, the slaughtering of animals as sacrifices, and some rules of avoidance. This tendency toward an increase in ritual is discussed in greater detail in the next chapter.

CHAPTER VII

TRENDS AND INTERCONNEXIONS

I N concluding we may review the main trends in the present religious situation in the Phuduhutswana chiefdom and note how religion and changes in religion are connected with other aspects of the social structure. The trends in paganism and Christianity respectively will be dealt with separately, but we should remember that the society is not divided into two distinct groups, one attached to paganism and the other to the Christian churches. There is considerable overlapping between the two, which in itself is an important trend. Although paganism is receding before Christianity, the break with the traditional pagan background is not easy.

Trends in paganism

Apart from the general waning of paganism as illustrated by the fact that some pagan ritual has already become completely obsolete and some people have abandoned paganism altogether, the most important fact about it is that different aspects of the traditional system of magico-religious beliefs and activities are not receding in equal proportion. The ancestor cult has largely disintegrated but traditional magic tends to *persist* to a considerable degree. Moreover, even where traditional beliefs about the role of the ancestors are still adhered to, the belief in God is much more prominent, more clearly expressed and more consciously held than appears to have been the case in former times. These trends ask for explanation. Why is it that the ancestor cult is disappearing more rapidly than magic? Why is Christian monotheistic teaching being accepted while teaching against pagan magic is not, or at least not to the same degree?

The explanation seems to be found in the connexion between ancestor cult and the social structure. Professor Radcliffe-Brown has already made this point in respect of South African (indigenous) societies in general.[1] He holds that an ancestor cult is a concomitant of a kinship system which stresses unilineal descent, and that its social function is the strengthening of the sentiments which bind together the members of the lineage. Where these sentiments are weakened through the impact of 'European culture', as is the case in South

[1] A. R. Radcliffe-Brown, 1952, p. 164.

TRENDS AND INTERCONNEXIONS 213

Africa, the ancestral cult disintegrates. In Chapter I I drew attention to the weakening of the principle of unilineal descent among the Tlhaping, which is particularly reflected in the scattering of the population and the fact that the rule of patrilocal residence is fast disappearing. As the lineage ceases to be an important group in the social structure, the ancestor cult also becomes unimportant and disintegrates or is easily substituted by a new set of rites and beliefs.

I would suggest, however, that an ancestor cult may have a wider social significance than in respect of the solidarity of the lineage. In a patrilineal society the spirits of the dead other than those belonging to one's own lineage may also be believed to influence one or they may be the objects of the rites performed.

Among the Tlhaping the ancestor cult is not only concerned with deceased patrilineal relatives, but also with others, e.g. those on the mother's side. As we have observed (ch. II), the remnants of the cult hardly reflect the predominance of one's lineage ancestors which apparently used to characterize the cult in former times. Apparently then the social function of the cult among the Tlhaping was not only that of strengthening the sentiments which served to preserve the unity of the lineage, but it also sanctioned the relations that one was expected to maintain with one's kinsmen generally.[1] The disintegration of the ancestor cult is related then, not only to the decreasing importance of the unilineal principle of kinship, but to the neglect of kinship obligations in general.

Remarks made by some of my informants implying that the performing of sacrifices to the ancestor spirits is not important in Tswana ritual, suggest that among the Tswana the cult is less elaborated than among the Nguni and Southern Sotho peoples.

Sacrifices and prayers directed to the ancestors are of course not the only forms of ritual implying the existence of an ancestor cult.

---

[1] To give another instance of an ancestor cult having a wider social significance than in respect of lineage solidarity, I refer to the Mende. Dr. Kenneth Little has shown that the Mende (like the Tlhaping) believe that the ancestral spirits occupy a position in the cosmos nearer to the Supreme Being, serving as a link between the living and 'the final source of supernatural power'. The rites performed by the Mende imply that the spirits expect a share of the prosperity experienced by their living relatives and the latter's households. 'These relatives are surviving sons, grandsons, and great-grandsons, and nephews *on both sides of the family*.' It is obvious, therefore, that among the Mende one is not only concerned with the spirits of one's deceased patrilineal relatives. Dr. Little also makes clear that the ancestor cult sanctions the relationship that should exist between oneself and one's important living kin generally, not only one's lineal kin. 'The ancestral spirits stand, conceptually, in the same relationship to the family as do its senior members on earth to their own sons and daughters and nephews and nieces.' (Little, 1954, pp. 116, 120 ff. The italics are my own.)

214   RELIGION IN A TSWANA CHIEFDOM

Among the Tswana the belief in *dikgaba* and the rite it involves also seem to be part of the cult (see ch. II, p. 29). However, although it may be believed that the misfortune referred to as *dikgaba* is caused by the ancestors, they seem to be in the background in the ritual: the rite is essentially a magical rite of purification (it is called *tlhapisö*, washing). It shows more concern with appeasing the living senior whose displeasure at the misbehaviour of his junior is the initial cause of *dikgaba*, and with washing away the 'impurity', than with the ancestors, although they enter the train of belief. Prayers and sacrifices on the other hand imply more direct dealings, more direct concern, with the ancestors themselves. In spite of the importance of *dikgaba*, I think the unimportance of sacrifices (and the prayers which usually accompany them) is evidence of the lesser elaboration of the ancestor cult.

At present sacrifices to the ancestors certainly seem to be less common among the Tlhaping than among the Nguni and Southern Sotho peoples. We have observed that among the Zulu, sacrifices to the ancestors are common, even as a part of Zionist church ritual. Fairly recent accounts of the Pondo and Swazi show that sacrificial slaughtering and other rites connected with the ancestor cult are still common among these people.[1]

Among the people of Basutoland, particularly the Tlokoa, the ancestor cult also appears to persist with greater vigour than among the Tlhaping, although here too it seems to be rapidly disintegrating.[2] In part this difference between the Tlhaping (and, in fact, the Tswana generally[3]) on the one hand, and the Nguni and Sotho peoples on the other, is probably due to the Tlhaping having been in closer contact with European culture than the others. They inhabit a relatively small reserve which is surrounded by European farms and is within easy reach of large European centres by rail or road and which therefore has nothing of the relative isolation of some parts of Swaziland, Zululand, Pondoland, and Basutoland. Furthermore they are isolated from any large unit of Tswana people. In these circumstances it is to be expected that the traditional culture as a whole, and the ancestor cult as part of it, should have disintegrated further than among the other peoples mentioned.

My Tlhaping informants' remarks, however, seemed to imply that even traditionally sacrifices were not as common among them as among the Nguni and Southern Sotho. This emerged from casual

[1] Hunter, 1936, and Kuper, 1947 and 1952, p. 43.
[2] See Ashton, 1952, pp. 114–116.
[3] See Schapera, 1953, p. 61.

TRENDS AND INTERCONNEXIONS 215

remarks, as well as from answers to my questions. The idea is supported by the fact that even among the Tswana of the Protectorate, who do not seem to have been as heavily exposed to influences of European culture as the Tlhaping of Taung, little of the ancestor cult persists at present. It is also consistent with the Tlhaping attitude to cattle. Cattle still have more than economic value to them, but their ritual and social value is certainly not as great as it used to be, so that they are not prevented from selling large numbers of cattle at the monthly stock fairs. Whereas cattle used to play a very important social role in the form of marriage payment (*bogadi*), such payment is falling into disuse with many people, while some substitute small stock or cash for cattle. The significance of these facts comes out when they are contrasted with the position in the Keiskammahoek Reserve in the Ciskei, which has a Nguni population. There also there is much evidence of social change, but sacrifices are still common, marriage payment almost universal, and few cattle are sold.[1]

Leaving the Southern Sotho out of the argument for a moment, I think this difference in the ancestor cults of the Tswana and Nguni respectively could be related to difference in traditional social structure. Granted that the anger or displeasure of ancestor spirits on the one hand and sorcery (and/or witchcraft) on the other are two alternative possibilities for explaining misfortune (although not necessarily the only two possibilities), and 'that accusations of practising witchcraft or sorcery are an expression of conflict',[2] I suggest that the lesser importance of sacrifices to the ancestor spirits among the Tswana may be related to their traditional pattern of territorial distribution. As we have observed, this pattern was one of concentration in large, relatively densely populated towns. In contrast with this the Nguni pattern is one of decentralization of the population in scattered homesteads or small villages.[3] It seems reasonable to assume that in a large, densely populated town an individual comes into regular contact with a much greater number of people than would be the case in a society of which the members are scattered. Consequently conflicts and suspicions may develop in greater number in the former type of society. If this assumption is correct, it follows that the structure of Tswana society offered more opportunities for interpreting misfortune in

[1] *Keiskammahoek Rural Survey*, Vol. II, Houghton and Walton, and Vol. III, Wilson, Monica, and others. Perhaps this lesser elaboration of the ancestor cult among the Tswana partly explains why Moffat did not recognize the existence of a cult of the dead. Fritsch also maintains that the ancestor cult is less elaborated among the Tswana than among the Xhosa. (Fritsch, 1872, p. 198.)

[2] Wilson, 1951, p. 313.

[3] Kuper, Hilda, 1952, p. 17; Gluckman, 1950, p. 169; Hunter, 1936.

216   RELIGION IN A TSWANA CHIEFDOM

terms of witchcraft and sorcery than Nguni society. I suggest that because of this the Tswana tended to be more concerned with witch-craft and sorcery and less with the displeasure of the ancestor spirits as a cause of misfortune than was the case among the Nguni. For this reason they were also less concerned with propitiating the spirits of the dead and did not have such an elaborate ancestral cult as the Nguni.

I have no information on the incidence of accusations of sorcery among the Tlhaping. The findings of diviners in this connexion are not published and I never heard accusations directed against particular persons. Moreover, if such information should provide a check on the hypothesis put forward above it would have to come from a large Tswana town, and this no longer exists in Taung. The argument put forward is therefore nothing more than a hypothesis which needs further testing.

I left out the Southern Sotho from the argument because there are not the same clear-cut contrasts between them and the Tswana. In their pattern of territorial distribution the Southern Sotho fall between the Nguni and Tswana: villages show great variation in size, some being quite small and some being as large as four or five hundred 'families'.[1] There is some concentration of population but it is not such a consistent pattern as among the Tswana. Probably the Southern Sotho fall in an intermediate position between Tswana and Nguni in respect of the elaboration of the ancestral cult also.

The main argument with which we are here concerned, however, is that the ancestor cult is related to the kinship system and that as the kinship system of the Tlhaping disintegrated, their cult of the dead was bound to fade in importance also. As we have observed that the ancestors were believed to form a link between the living and God, it is understandable that as the ancestors became less important, it became easy to accept the idea taught by the missionaries, that God is directly interested in the affairs of men and can be approached in direct prayer. The fact that there is greater approximation, even among non-Christians, to Christian monotheistic teaching than used to be the case formerly, is therefore not merely a result of missionary teaching, but it is also connected with the waning of the ancestor cult which on its part is related to the disintegration of the kinship system.

Whereas the belief in the ancestors has been undermined unob-trusively by the disintegration of the kinship system, the missions and schools have not been assisted by such an unseen ally in combating

---

[1] Ashton, *op. cit.*, p. 21.

TRENDS AND INTERCONNEXIONS 217

the belief in magic. The conditions calling for the practice of magic persist.

General trends in the churches

In the course of the previous chapters we observed how the organization, ritual, and belief of the churches are in many ways *related to the traditional background.* Examples of this trend have been summarized at the end of chapters IV and VI.

In the latter chapter it was shown that the influence of traditional belief and ritual emerges particularly in the *magical value* often attached to church ritual and belief. Admittedly even some Western churches show a tendency toward magicality, but although such magicality would be rather difficult to measure, we are surely justified in saying that much of the magic in these Taung churches, to the mind accustomed to scientifically based modern technology, appears much cruder and not far removed from the pagan forms of magic.

When considering this in conjunction with the fact that pagan forms of magic also show considerable tenacity among the Tlhaping, and considering further the long-established position of schools in Tlhaping society, and their thorough acquaintance with many forms of modern technology, one may well ask why such forms of magic persist. One should remember, however, that mere knowledge of the existence of scientific techniques is not enough to dispel the magic which so obviously runs counter to our knowledge acquired through science. It is only a real insight into the processes involved, particularly an insight into the causes of disease, death, crop failures, droughts, and other natural phenomena, that will lead to a more complete rejection of magic. It may be relatively easy to educate isolated individuals to an understanding of such processes, but to attain this for a society as a whole seems to be a tedious task. It certainly has not been attained for Tlhaping society. There are highly educated individuals possessing a considerable degree of knowledge (and even some of them sometimes turn to magic) but the larger proportion of the members of this society still lacks this knowledge. In spite of the considerable extent to which schools have become part of the society, most scholars attain only an elementary standard of schooling. As long as only a small margin of the society possesses real insight into the processes referred to, one must expect traditional magical patterns of thought to persist.

In another context I discussed the tendency toward a *literal and fragmentary interpretation of Scripture* which shows affinity with the traditional pattern of thought underlying magical ritual (see ch. VI, pp. 195 f.). In both cases there is a lack of a comprehensive approach which seeks to view each particular rite and belief within the framework of the totality of rites and beliefs.

A distinct *moralistic and legalistic trend* has also been observed in ritual and teaching. The essence of Christianity for many people consists of the adherence to a particular code of behaviour—putting aside traditional practices such as initiation and beer drinking, not having extra-marital sexual relations, going to church, giving church contributions, and doing good 'works'. Some churches stress particular objects and activities which have to be avoided and preach the keeping of 'the law'. 'Baptist' churches stress the necessity of adult baptism by immersion, Sabbatarians make the keeping of Saturday as Sabbath an indispensable part of Christianity. The particular pattern of behaviour is usually connected in a very direct manner with the judgement which will decide the individual's condition in future life.

This trend may in part be related to particular missionary methods. Missionaries in southern Africa have tended to require of converts certain outward observances, such as the wearing of European clothes, abstinence from native beer, and the renouncing of traditional customs such as initiation ceremonies, giving of *bogadi*, polygyny, and the use of magic. Apparently the missionaries enforced these observances long before native converts themselves realized their true significance. Most Protestant missionaries would not have viewed the observance of the rules they were laying down as means to salvation, yet by the Bantu they came to be considered as the essence of becoming a Christian. Moreover, church discipline has been largely concentrated on the rules pertaining to traditional practices and to sexual relations in general, and there has been a tendency to conduct disciplinary action in church on much the same lines as a traditional court session. All this has fostered the idea that the most important aspect of Christianity is that it involves obedience to a certain set of rules of behaviour.

I further suggest that this moralistic trend is also related to the disintegration of society. Through the changes in the old social structure, old values (e.g. respect for the chief and for old age, and filial obedience) are passing away, old rules of behaviour are disappearing and there is the feeling that the society is becoming increasingly lawless. In this situation there is an acute need for a new clear-cut set of rules of behaviour backed by a strong sanction. A form of Christianity stressing adherence to a definite set of laws sanctioned by the notion of future judgement undoubtedly meets this need. This connexion between a Christian moralism and the instability of present-day social relations was clearly expressed by the minister who exhorted the

TRENDS AND INTERCONNEXIONS 219

parents to teach the children 'the law' and enforce filial obedience with chastisement if necessary, 'because to-morrow you will find them playing dice' (see ch. VI, p. 152). In part the values stressed are new values, but in part they are a restatement of old values in a new (Biblical or Christian) idiom or backed by a new sanction as, e.g., the enjoining of filial obedience and strict discipline enforced by corporal punishment.

It also seems, however, that there is a connexion between this moralism and the tendency toward magical ritual and doctrine. We have seen that a close causal connexion exists between the pattern of behaviour in this life and one's fate in future life. It is not that this process is thought of independently of the belief in God: God is the Law-giver and Judge, and His judgement, based on man's behaviour, decides one's fate; but within this pattern of belief, keeping of the law, adherence to the proper pattern of behaviour, is thought of as an effective guarantee for obtaining favourable judgement.

To bring out more clearly the affinity of this moralism to magical belief, it should be contrasted with a different form of Christian belief which, without denying the reality of a divine law or of future judgement, denies the ability of man to ensure a favourable judgement by adhering to a particular pattern of behaviour, i.e. by keeping a set of laws. The only way of salvation is through grace and faith. Man has to recognize his transgression of God's law and in sincere repentance of this, believe that he is granted forgiveness and salvation by virtue of Christ's accomplishment as Mediator. The 'good works' of the believer are then in no way efficacious in attaining salvation but testify to man's gratitude for grace received.

The difference between such teaching and the moralism described above lies in the value attached to adherence to a particular pattern of behaviour. In the moralistic pattern of belief the activities of the individual have a certain degree of direct efficacy in ensuring salvation, in the other these activities have no such efficacy but serve as an expression of gratitude. As I have shown in the previous chapter, I hold that in as far as a ritual object or act is believed to have a certain direct efficacy it bears a magical character. Therefore the moralistic teaching attributing a certain direct efficacy to correct behaviour is akin to magic. This affinity with magic, I suggest, makes this kind of moralistic teaching particularly acceptable in a society in which belief in magic is still strong.[1]

Another trend is the tendency toward *emotionalism*. Emotionalism

[1] Cf. what the Wilsons have termed 'magical morality'. (Wilson, Godfrey, and Monica, 1945, p. 92.)

220 RELIGION IN A TSWANA CHIEFDOM

has not been mentioned very often, but it is evident in the descriptions of Pentecostal services. I also observed it to a lesser extent in the delivery of some preachers of churches of type 'A' and 'B'. The emotionalism is particularly intense in the more violent type of Pentecostal churches where the service takes place in an atmosphere of high tension forming a striking contrast with the casualness of relations immediately after the service.[1]

A tendency which must be mentioned in connexion with emotionalism is the *elaboration of ritual*. This ritualistic trend is particularly evident in Pentecostal Separatist churches where we have observed how new ritual has been added to that of non-Bantu churches, while known ritual has been further elaborated. In churches of type 'A' and 'B' this trend is less obvious, but even here one may notice liturgical additions which are not found in the Western church pattern followed. The processions and formalized greetings at the end of services are also relevant here (see ch. V).

Ritualism and emotionalism may be interpreted as expressions of a desire for a religion which is vividly experienced. Ritualism provides a religion which is seen and sometimes also felt, it provides for sensual experience. The liturgical additions in churches of type 'A' and 'B' perhaps do not give a definite sensual or emotional experience but they provide for active participation of the rank and file. Significant are also the Pentecostals' preference for a 'swing'-type of rhythm in singing, which more or less impels bodily movement, the wide range of movements and utterances ascribed to the working of the Spirit, the laying-on of hands, and the freedom ordinary members have to address the congregation and to interrupt other speakers with the customary exclamations and singing. The avowed reception of direct revelations through dreams or visible or audible revelations also illustrates the desire for a vividly experienced religion. Baptism by immersion is also relevant in that it provides a more vivid sensual experience than baptism by sprinkling or pouring.

The question arises whether ritualism and emotionalism may be related to the traditional background. Traditional magico-religious practices did not include long sermons; they did include prayers, but they included more action. Sacrifices (which meant sacrificial meals), sprinkling or washing with medicines in rites of purification and observing the fall of the dice in divination provided the opportunity for seeing, feeling, and actively participating in the magico-religious

[1] The first marked success that Moffat saw of his missionary labours at Kuruman was a spiritual awakening accompanied by considerable display of emotion. (See Moffat, 1856, pp. 328 ff.)

TRENDS AND INTERCONNEXIONS

sphere. It is difficult to say what role the display of emotion played in traditional society, but with the dullness and lack of excitement which typifies life in the society at present, religious emotionalism may well be a form of compensation for the loss of other forms of excitement.

Dr. Sundkler has shown that among Bantu on the Witwatersrand new class distinctions, based on education and economic success, are emerging, and that the 'upper class' are turning to a church like the A.M.E. Church. The Zionists, similar to our Pentecostals in respect of emotionalism and violent ritual, 'take care of the uneducated'.[1] In Taung there is also some evidence of the emergence of a 'professional' class, but it is still too small to allow of generalizations of this nature. We may say that the bulk of the population is still at a relatively low stage of economic development and that in the society as a whole the standard of empirical knowledge is still low.

In this connexion I think it is significant that the kind of religion which produces vivid emotional or sensual experiences is popular with American Negroes. This is more apparent in the Southern states than in the North and is particularly evident in 'Lower Class' churches.[2] Their patterns of 'getting religion' and 'shouting' are typical examples. On the other hand, denominations whose teaching and ritual are held to appeal to the intellect are said to have had little success among Negroes in the Southern States. However, Negroes of the 'Upper Class' generally prefer these churches.[3]

Furthermore, it is significant that the same type of religion, although perhaps not in such extreme forms, is also found among lower class Whites of the Southern States of the U.S.A.[4] Among Europeans in South Africa the churches in which the more extreme forms of emotionalism and a relatively violent type of ritual are found seldom attract followers from the ranks of those prominent in the field of economy, politics, or 'cultural' activities.

The foregoing facts suggest the hypothesis that a religion of intense emotional or sensual experiences goes with a low standard of

[1] *Op. cit.*, pp. 81, 86.

[2] Cf. Dollard, 1947, p. 225; Frazier, 1940, p. 133; Powdermaker, 1939, p. 252 and ch. 12.

[3] Frazier, *op. cit.*, p. 128; Powdermaker, *op. cit.*, ch. 11; Woodson, C. G., *History of the Negro Church*, p. 97, quoted by Dollard, *op. cit.*, p. 224 n.

Cf. also what Arthur T. Porter (1953, p. 7) relates about religious affiliation in Freetown, Sierra Leone: 'In the earliest period the more respectable and wealthy members of the population belonged to the various Wesleyan denominations.' The rest of the population was divided among other 'less orthodox' churches in which 'were to be found displays of emotionalism—shouting and shaking and what has been described as "an exciting exhibition of finding the Lord"'.

[4] Powdermaker, *op. cit.*, chs. 11, 12; Dollard, *op. cit.*, p. 220.

222 RELIGION IN A TSWANA CHIEFDOM

knowledge and economic conditions offering a relatively small degree of security. When societies are stratified on the basis of the standard of knowledge and economic success this type of religion may also serve as a form of compensation for those in the lower strata of society.

Preferences for certain denominations and types

From the analysis of church statistics given in chapter III, a few trends emerged which call for further elucidation in the light of the material presented in subsequent chapters. I refer to the exceedingly large number of Roman Catholics, the strength of Methodism among Protestant denominations and, perhaps less spectacular, but neverthe-less important, the total strength of Sabbatarian and Pentecostal churches.

(a) *Roman Catholicism.* It is remarkable that in an area where a Protestant Mission has had the advantage of a much earlier start, and in which many Protestant denominations have been working in later years, nearly half of the people who have official connexions with churches are Roman Catholics. I think the main reason for this is the intensive and comprehensive nature of their missionary effort (see ch. III, p. 56).

I suggest, however, that certain aspects of Roman Catholic ritual and doctrine add to its acceptability. I have tried to show above that a type of religion which is vividly experienced seems to have particular attraction in this society and that ritualism does increase religious experience. If this is correct, it goes without saying that the elaborate ritual of Roman Catholicism adds to its acceptability. There is even a certain morphological resemblance between certain Roman Catholic ritual acts and some traditional Tswana rites. The sprinkling of holy water is comparable to the central act in Tswana rites of purification, and the burning of incense (e.g. over a corpse) is reminiscent of the burning of medicines by a Tswana doctor.

Roman Catholic ritual may also produce a certain type of emotional effect. I experienced this myself during a service celebrating the Immaculate Conception of the Virgin. After an evening service in church a congregation of about a hundred and twenty people, mostly young people and children, moved in procession to the artificial grotto containing an image of the Virgin. Each one was carrying a burning candle and the grotto was illuminated with candles and small electric lights. During the short service which followed there was an atmosphere which one could 'feel': the candles threw a soft light on the faces of the audience and the singing was particularly pleasing— to my personal taste the best I heard at any service I attended. I could

TRENDS AND INTERCONNEXIONS

223

not help thinking of the violent Pentecostal services where I also experienced 'atmosphere', but of a very different nature. With its elaborate ritual Roman Catholicism appeals to the senses and can provide distinct emotional experiences.[1] This, I suggest, adds to its acceptability.

I would also suggest that the Roman Catholic doctrine of the sacraments is more acceptable than the teaching of some Protestants in this connexion. Roman Catholics see in the sacraments not merely symbols representing certain divine acts of grace, but they also believe that the sacraments, when administered in the right way, necessarily communicate divine grace to those to whom they are administered. In connexion with baptism, for instance, a Roman Catholic writer writes of 'the Catholic doctrine of *regeneration* of infants *effected infallibly* through baptism'.[2] The bread and wine becomes in the Mass the actual flesh and blood of the Redeemer and the celebration of the sacrament imparts the supernatural grace associated with Christ's death to those who partake of it. To me it seems that this view of the sacraments gives them a magical character. They are not purely magical, of course, but the direct connexion made between the sacraments and the grace received by those who partake of them, gives them a distinctly magical character, in the sense of magic as we are using it.[3] It is this that makes them particularly acceptable to people accustomed to thinking in terms of magic.

Reference must here also be made to the positive efforts made on the

---

[1] The repetitive element in R.C. liturgy, e.g. in the responses of the congregation, reminds one of the repetitive element in other churches where it is a particular 'African' development. (Ch. V, p. 136.)

[2] Magrath, 1943. (Italics my own.)

[3] The following definition is given of the sacraments: 'According to the teaching of the Catholic Church . . . the sacraments of the Christian dispensation are not mere signs; they do not merely signify Divine grace, but in virtue of their Divine institution they cause that grace in the souls of men.' *The Catholic Encyclopedia*, Robert Appleton Company, New York, 1912.

Cf. also the following: ' . . . For the Reformed the grace symbolized (in general, increased union with Christ) is not conveyed by and through the sacrament, but is the fruit of an independent working of the Holy Spirit (and of Christ) in the soul, making it respond to the symbol of the sacrament and the seal it carries of God's promises by an increased faith (in the Reformed sense of faith). Hence for the Reformed the connexion between sign and grace is moral only, and, though normal, is not infallible even if the sacrament is received with due dispositions. Whereas for Catholics the connexion is casual [should be: causal], and the grace is always given if no obstacle is placed by unsuitable dispositions, independently of the actual faith and love of the recipient. They work, as it is said, ex opere operato. . . .' The same writer says of the Catholic view: ' . . . The grace is caused immediately by God, but yet has an *infallible connexion* with the Sacrament, which, when rightly performed, always obtains this effect from God.' (Magrath, *op. cit.* Italics my own.)

224 RELIGION IN A TSWANA CHIEFDOM

part of Roman Catholic missionaries to substitute Christian rites for pagan rites. Sometimes new rites are evolved to suit local customs, as in the case of blessing the food for wedding feasts (see ch. VI, p. 209). Other rites which are also said to be performed with the express purpose of counteracting the activities of native doctors are the blessing of new houses (which includes the sprinkling of holy water), the blessing of fields, of stock and stock pens and cattle byres, and the blessing of women before and after childbirth. Of particular interest also are the medallions bearing the images of saints, which are very commonly worn by adults and children. Roman Catholics may buy these from the church and then wear them, after they have been blessed. The wearing of these medallions is encouraged to counteract the use of pagan amulets. There are then in Roman Catholic ritual many rites or ritual objects performed or used in circumstances closely parallel to the circumstances in which pagan ritual acts and objects are performed or used. I should think that the change of allegiance from paganism to Christianity is made easier by the existence of such parallels.

We have noticed above that there is a general trend in the churches toward a type of moralism which closely connects a person's pattern of behaviour in this life with his fate in future life. I have also tried to illustrate that such a type of moralistic teaching has affinity with the pattern of thought underlying magic. If it is possible to show, as I think it is, that the same type of moralism is typical of Roman Catholicism, it follows that we have in such moralism another factor making for acceptability. Such moralism is apparent in the Roman Catholic doctrine of the meritoriousness of good works according to which 'the just, in return for their good works done in God through the merits of Jesus Christ, should expect an eternal reward'.[1] It is also apparent in the idea that the duration of the period the faithful have to spend in Purgatory is conditioned by the good works performed by them during their earthly sojourn.

(b) *Methodism.* The numerical strength of the Methodist Church also calls for comment. The only Protestant church rivalling it in strength is that of the L.M.S., both having over a thousand members (communicant and non-communicant members—cf. ch. III). Third comes the Anglican Church with less than four hundred. The missionary undertaking of the L.M.S. is by far the oldest and it is the only Protestant mission which has had a permanent European missionary in the reserve. If perhaps the Methodists formerly had an ordained minister in the reserve, they have not had one for a considerable time

[1] *Catholic Encyclopedia,* 'Merit'.

TRENDS AND INTERCONNEXIONS

now. In these circumstances it is remarkable that the Methodist Church, which has only six church buildings compared to the twelve of the L.M.S. and only one school (and a share in another) compared to the eight (and a share in one) of the L.M.S., to-day has a larger official following than the L.M.S.

There are a few factors which may have played a part in furthering Methodism in Taung. First it is important to note that the Methodist Church—unlike the L.M.S.—has branches throughout South Africa, and has among the Bantu population of the Union of South Africa a very marked lead on all other denominations. In the 1946 census 1,008,344 natives were enumerated as Methodists. As already pointed out, this is about 25% of all Bantu professing adherence to churches according to the above-mentioned census. After the Methodists come the Anglicans with 552,633.[1] In view of the numerical predominence of the Methodist Church among the Bantu population of the Union as a whole, it seems probable that in Taung they have benefited from the influx of 'foreigners' more than any of the other churches. This is borne out by the fact that there is a strong 'foreign' element in the Methodist Church in the reserve. (Not all these people, who themselves or whose forbears immigrated to Taung from other areas, are Nguni. There are also many Tswana, e.g. Rolong from Thaba'Nchu.) It is said that the leadership in the Methodist churches of Taung is largely in the hands of this foreign element and none of the leaders I personally knew had been born in Taung.

As I have already shown (p. 67), the small size of the local church group with its intimate in-group relations appears to have particular appeal in the society with which we are dealing. We have also observed the important role of the lay element in leadership in most churches (p. 67). These factors, which seem to appeal not only to the Tlhaping, but to the Bantu of South Africa in general, are inherent in the typical Methodist pattern of church organization with its 'class' system making for the forming of small regularly co-operating groups of church members, and its range of lay preachers (Local Preachers, Preachers on Trial, Exhorters) and Class Leaders offering extensive opportunities for leadership.[2]

---

[1] 758,810 were enumerated as belonging to Native Separatist churches. No single Separatist church could have a following comparable to that of the Anglicans.

[2] As Dr. Sundkler has shown, the Methodists have with this type of organization set a pattern followed by other churches in their missionary activities. 'Other Mission Churches in South Africa . . . have with certain modifications followed the Methodist scheme of lay organization, and now find themselves with a much stronger emphasis on lay work in the Bantu Church than is the case in the mother-Churches in Europe.' (*Op. cit.*, p. 137.)

R.T.C.—16

226   RELIGION IN A TSWANA CHIEFDOM

The acceptability of the 'class' system, and the extensive mobilization of the lay element in spreading the gospel,[1] combined with Methodist ardour for 'winning souls' have probably contributed to the remarkable strength of Methodism in Taung and among the Bantu of South Africa in general.[2]

A final remark about Methodism refers to emotionalism. I attended only one service of the Methodist Church in Taung[3] and that was an ordinary Sunday morning service which was not characterized by a particular degree of emotionalism. Revivals which are marked by the display of a considerable degree of emotion (e.g. strong feelings of fear of the coming judgement, feelings of remorse, and tearfulness) are, however, usually taken to be typical of Methodism.[4] In view of what I have said above about the significance of religious emotionalism as providing a vivid experience in religion, the tendency to emotionalism which is typical of Methodism has probably also added to its acceptability.

(c) *Pentecostalism and Sabbatarianism.* Out of a total of 10,203 church members in the Phuduhutswana chiefdom 1,130, or just over 11%, belong to Sabbatarian and Pentecostal denominations. It might be said that these figures do not give reason for speaking of a trend toward Pentecostalism and Sabbatarianism. It should be appreciated,

[1] From the numbers of preachers given in Table IV, it might appear as if lay preachers are comparatively speaking more numerous in some of the other churches. It should be born in mind, however, that I could only enumerate full Preachers, and that there are a large number of Preachers on Trial, Exhorters and Class Leaders of the Methodist Church who are not included in the statistics. All these, nevertheless, take part in spreading the gospel.

[2] (a) Cf. the movement known as *Unzondelelo*, which arose subsequently to a revival in 1866, in which Bantu Christians (Methodists) 'banded themselves together to carry the Gospel to the heathen kraals and reserves which abound in Natal'. Du Plessis, 1911, pp. 301–302.

(b) In view of the fact that Methodism has spread rapidly in other parts of the world as well (e.g. in Britain and the U.S.A.) the factors mentioned are probably not relevant to its spread among the Bantu only, although the degree of their importance could be expected to vary in different societies.

[3] Had I realized the strength of the Methodists while I was in the field, I would probably have made an effort to attend more of their activities. I did not get the impression that they had a particularly large membership until I obtained their statistics, and this was only shortly before the termination of my field-work.

[4] Methodism is mentioned as one of the 'schools' in which religious feeling or experience (Dutch: 'gevoel als affect') takes 'an important place, if not the most important place'. (Article on 'Gevoelstheologie' in *Christelijk Encyclopedie voor het Nederlandsche Volk*, J. H. Kok, Kampen (1st Edition).) Cf. also what Prof. Latourette writes of John Wesley's sermons: '. . . As with those of Whitefield and as in the Great Awakening in the Thirteen Colonies and some of the later revivals in the United States, they often released striking emotions. Men and women screamed, were physically convulsed, or fell insensible.' (Latourette, 1953 p. 1026.)

TRENDS AND INTERCONNEXIONS

however, that most of these denominations started their activities in Taung quite recently (see Table II). Moreover, the missionary activities of churches and missionary bodies conforming to these types are very limited compared to the activities of those conforming to type 'A'. I think this is true not only of Taung but of the Union of South Africa as a whole. Bearing this in mind, the numerical strength of the Pentecostals and Sabbatarians in Taung does seem to be remarkable. They definitely have a larger proportion of the Bantu church members in Taung than amongst the European population of the Union professing adherence to churches.[1] But it is when we take only the Separatist churches, where the Bantu are on their own, that the appeal of Sabbatarianism and Pentecostalism is unmistakable: they form 37% (i.e. 765 out of 2,070) of the total membership of all Separatist churches in Taung. This appeal is also reflected in the drift to these churches as illustrated by the life histories of church leaders (see p. 74).

In the previous chapter I tried to show that in a society with a traditional background in which magic was important there should be particular receptivity for a type of Christian teaching which uses Scripture in a fragmentary and literal manner. I think there is reason for saying that Sabbatarians and Pentecostals in general tend to use Scripture in this manner.[2] If this is agreed, it follows that it constitutes a factor making for the acceptability of Pentecostals and Sabbatarians in this society.

I also tried to show that the typical Pentecostal and Sabbatarian doctrine imparts to baptism a certain degree of magical value, and this, I argued, makes for acceptability among people like the Tlhaping, whose extant traditional (pagan) ritual is predominantly magical. Baptism by immersion may also be viewed from the angle of the tendency toward a type of religion which is sensually or emotionally vividly experienced, since it provides a more vivid sensual experience

---

[1] According to the 1951 census, 2,503,591 Europeans professed adherence to Christian churches or religious bodies. Of these, 2,327,789 or 93% were enumerated under the following churches, all of which are very definitely not Sabbatarian or Pentecostal: the three Afrikaans-speaking Reformed churches, Anglicans, Presbyterians, Congregationalists, Methodists, Lutherans, Roman Catholics and the 'Greek Church' (probably the Greek Orthodox Church). Besides denominations which are distinctly Sabbatarian or Pentecostal the remaining 7% include the Baptist Church, Christian Scientists, Salvation Army, and Plymouth Brethren.—Extracted from Union of South Africa, *Population Census, 8th May, 1951: Vol. iii.*

[2] Cf. the concentration on passages dealing with adult baptism, particularly the baptism performed by St. John the Baptist in Jordan; on Old Testament passages about the Sabbath and on Old Testament ritual prescripts; or on certain outward characteristics of the Primitive Church such as the performance of miraculous healing and speaking with tongues.

228 RELIGION IN A TSWANA CHIEFDOM

than baptism by sprinkling or pouring, and therefore adds to the acceptability of a denomination or type. People already baptized in infancy are not excluded from this experience because they are usually baptized again, since the earlier baptism in childhood is not recognized.

Pentecostalism particularly 'caters' for this desire for a vividly experienced religion. As we have seen, the greatest elaboration of ritual and the most violent forms of it are found in these churches, and all this makes for vivid, often distinctly sensual experience. The particular stress on the role of the Spirit as agent of revelation has the result that these churches are less strictly bound to forms handed down from the past, and if they wish to, can easily give a very individualistic interpretation of Scripture which is supposed to be sanctioned by their own revelation. All this makes for greater freedom of expression generally, and particularly clears the way for greater elaboration of ritual or the development of altogether new ritual.

The church of the L.M.S.

The question why the L.M.S. has fallen behind other churches in numbers, in spite of its advantage of an earlier start and the prestige of being to a certain extent considered as a tribal church, is also important. Church life at present does not create an impression of vigour and vitality. Think of the lack of opportunities for the younger generation and educated men, the very small number of male members and the large undefined body of adherents who nominally claim adherence to the church but nevertheless do not come to an open acceptance and confession of Christianity. The services conducted by untrained workers are often uninspiring and contain little ritual, while the singing often lacks the enthusiasm and vigour which is typical of the singing in some other churches.

The statistics of membership for the whole L.M.S. district (in which Taung is one of four sub-districts)[1] suggest a condition of stagnation after the earlier rapid growth. The figures which follow give the numbers of *communicant* members for different years. The only pre-1900 figure available is the one for 1879.

1879— 207	1916—1,183	1936—1,468
1901— 710	1921—1,173	1941—1,575
1906— 807	1926—1,200	1946—1,595
1911—1,200	1931—1,355	

[1] Figures for the Taung sub-district, which more or less coincides with the Phuduhutswana chiefdom, are not available for a stretch of time long enough for comparative purposes. The district figures presented here have been extracted from Haile, 1951.

TRENDS AND INTERCONNEXIONS 229

In the earlier stages the progress was relatively rapid: during twenty-two years (1879–1901) there was an increase of 503 (or 243%). In 1910 part of the Barkly West Mission of the L.M.S. was transferred to other missions, while the part which was retained by the L.M.S. was incorporated into the Taung district. That explains why the figure for 1911 is so much higher than the one for 1906. Then for fifteen years, from 1911 to 1926, there was no increase in membership at all, while after 1926 there was only very slow progress, making for an increase of 395 (or 32·9%) during the twenty years up till 1946.[1]

I can only suggest a few factors that may have contributed to this loss of vitality. No doubt the entrance of other denominations into the field had a discouraging effect on the L.M.S. churches and their leaders. A missionary writes in his report for 1929: 'The Church work seems to progress slowly. The opposition of the Roman Catholic, the Seventh Day Adventists, the Church of England, the Wesleyans, and the Independents, not to speak of the Ethiopians, seems to have taken much of the vigour out of the remaining workers in the L.M.S. Church.'[2]

The scattering of the population also seems to have affected the L.M.S. churches in the reserve adversely. In times of drought the people not only scattered to outlying parts of the reserve, but some left to settle elsewhere, e.g. in the Transvaal. Clearly such a process affected an old established church like the L.M.S. more seriously than others of more recent origin.[3] The 1928 report particularly refers to the 'withdrawal of young life' from the church as a result of the large number of young people 'disappearing' to the towns or diamond diggings in search of work. Probably this contributed to the present condition in which the older generation seems to monopolize church organization and leadership.

The high standards required for acceptance into church membership, and the strict church discipline of the L.M.S. seem to have been responsible for such a large number of people remaining adherents, without officially joining the church. No doubt many who had already been influenced by the preaching of the L.M.S. eventually joined other

---

[1] It may be that some Taung outposts were transferred to other districts during later stages. I know of one such instance: in 1904 the Madibogo church with 145 members was transferred to the Vryburg district. This example, however, does not affect the argument based on the statistics. On my knowledge of the area it seems unlikely that any other churches were transferred in this manner.

[2] *Annual Report* for Taung Mission, 1929 (L.M.S. Archives). All further references to L.M.S. reports in this section are to reports in the L.M.S. Archives.

[3] Many of those who went to the Transvaal, nevertheless still remained within the Mission district to which the statistics given above apply.

230 RELIGION IN A TSWANA CHIEFDOM

churches which set lower requirements and imposed less discipline. The L.M.S. report for 1923 states that new members had on an average spent four years in the enquirers' class. Nowadays, the general term is three years. In many churches the period is considerably shorter. Generally speaking, the L.M.S. discipline is strict, but it is of particular importance that non-payment of church contributions has also led to disciplining, except in the case of members who lack the means. At times this has caused many lapses. The report for 1923, after stating that there were 1,059 members and 391 catechumens, adds that 'it should be remembered that the real membership stands at about 2,000. Owing to the hard times there are many lapses and the names of these do not show for the current year until they have secured their new membership card [on payment of their contributions, I presume]. The same applies to the enquirers who really number about 700.' The present figures show that many of these lapsed members never rehabilitated themselves and either remained adherents of the L.M.S. or joined other churches.

It is also possible that the size of the L.M.S. personnel and the means at their disposal did not allow rapid progress in numbers beyond a certain point and that once this 'saturation point' was reached the Mission was kept so busy tending the flock that had been gathered that it was not possible to proceed with intensive evangelistic work among that portion of the population which had not yet fully accepted Christianity. Instead, other churches stepped in and reaped the harvest. A member of the Society writes that 'it has often been said that the L.M.S. holds too long a line and holds it too thinly: other Missions ought to be called in to take a share in the work'.[1] In Taung, where there also seems to have been a lack of sustained concentration and intensive missionary labour, the other missions and churches were not 'called in to take a share of the work' but stepped in to gather their own flocks.[2]

Some aspects of Bantu Separatism

We have seen that there are no profound differences in church organization between Separatist and non-Separatist churches, and the trends discussed earlier in this chapter are present in both kinds of churches. One should remember, however, that as far as church activities within the chiefdom are concerned, even the churches connected with Europeans are to a high degree organized and conducted

[1] Haile, op. cit., p. 29.

[2] After the completion of my manuscript the Rev. Joseph Wing of Taung informed me that the total membership of the L.M.S. in the Taung mission district was 2,449 in 1953, which shows that in recent years there has again been more rapid progress.

TRENDS AND INTERCONNEXIONS

by Bantu Christians themselves, and on this level the fact that they are connected with Europeans is not very conspicuous.

With reference to Dr. Sundkler's findings in connexion with Zulu Separatist churches there are two important aspects in which the Taung Separatist churches differ. The first is that those in Taung are less consciously concerned with the inter-racial situation than the Zulu churches, and secondly the Pentecostal Separatists of Taung are not as distinctly nativistic as the Zulu Zionists.

Dr. Sundkler has indicated the cleavage in South African society on lines of colour as one of the main reasons for Bantu Separatism, and he has shown how Zulu Separatists express their resentment of their subordinate position as Africans in the stress that is laid on the Old Testament, on the exodus of Israel from Egypt and the role of Moses as liberator, in the idea of a Black Messiah, and particularly in the idea of a hereafter in which they will no longer have an inferior position. The Separatist Church movement, according to Dr. Sundkler, is often nationalistic and he admits of 'much outspoken anti-white propaganda in *most* Independent Churches'.[1]

In Taung churches also there is evidence of reaction to the inter-racial situation, but I have no evidence of Separatist churches being used as channels for voicing protest against the subordinate position of the African, neither am I aware of any anti-European propaganda forming part of the programme of Separatist churches.[2] I did not receive the impression that such an aspect of the church programme was purposely suppressed in my presence. On the contrary, I am quite sure that in at least two churches submission to the government of the country and to one's European employers is enjoined.

This aspect of Separatism is consistent with the attitude encountered in the society as a whole. Even outside the churches one seldom encounters expressions of acute anti-European feeling, neither does there seem to be particular enthusiasm for a broad Bantu nationalism. In this connexion the absence of any modern political association in the chiefdom is also significant. On the other hand, recent reports

[1] *Op. cit.*, p. 295. (The italics are my own.)

[2] (*a*) Some of the earlier Separatist 'prophets' in Taung do seem to have had an anti-European and anti-government note in their teaching. (See ch. III.) Cf. the following remark made by G. Shepperson: 'After 1916 it might be said that the African independent churches of Nyasaland ceased to act in a genuine revolutionary capacity. Their function had become, perhaps, that of a safety-valve.' (Shepperson, 1954, pp. 233–245.) This seems to apply to Taung also.

(*b*) The Watch Tower Movement, which has the reputation for anti-European tendencies in other parts of Africa, is still very weak in Taung and has so far not displayed such tendencies there. (For anti-European tendencies of the Watch Tower Movement, see Quick, 1940, pp. 216 ff.; and Cunnison, 1951, pp. 456 ff.)

232 RELIGION IN A TSWANA CHIEFDOM

from Zulu reserves indicate a growing sense of solidarity on a broad African front and increasing interest in African nationalism. 'There is much talk of "African liberation", both in the reserves and in the towns.'[1] The contrast is therefore not merely one between Zulu Separatism and Tlhaping Separatism but between Zulu society and Tlhaping society.

There are a few factors which may help to explain this different attitude of the Tlhaping. In the first place, it seems important that they have not been involved in major clashes with Europeans comparable to those in which the Zulu and other Nguni were involved. The two or three clashes that occurred were of minor significance compared to that between the Vootrekkers and the Zulu king, Dingane, and the Zulu war of 1879, not to mention the whole series of wars between the colonists and the Cape Nguni tribes on the eastern frontier of the Cape Colony.

Moreover, the Tlhaping, although they also had their armies and regimental system, do not possess the great military tradition of the Zulu. The Zulu reached the height of their glory, a nation of considerable size having been formed as a result of military conquests, at a time when the Tlhaping lived in a state of unrest and tribulation and when the tribe was on the point of splitting into four or five sections.[2] At this low ebb the Tlhaping began experiencing their more intensive contacts with Europeans, so that their ultimate subordination was perhaps not as keenly resented as that of the Zulu.[3] Further, if ever the warrior was the Tlhaping ideal of manhood, there is nothing left of that attitude at present.

Another factor is the advanced stage which the disintegration of the old social structure and the way of life connected with it has reached among the Tlhaping. The old values have been undermined and have disappeared, and in terms of European values they are economically poor and politically insignificant. Consequently, there is little to bolster up their self-esteem and they give the impression of an uninspired people. Ruins and dilapidated homesteads, inhabited but not kept in repair, are typical of the area around the chief's place. The chieftainship is of little significance and tribal assemblies are small and inefficiently conducted, not seldom ending in confusion. Perhaps the absence of strong anti-European feeling and of interest in Bantu nationalism is part of a general disinterestedness resulting from the breakdown of tribal life.

[1] Koornhof, P. G. J., 1953, p. 482.
[2] Cf. pp. 1, 2. This is, in fact, typical of the Tswana tribes generally. (See Schapera, 1953, p. 15.)
[3] Cf. Agar-Hamilton, 1937, p. 12.

TRENDS AND INTERCONNEXIONS

Although the Taung Separatists do not reveal strong nationalist tendencies, the phenomenon of Separatism, as observed in Taung, is certainly affected by the inter-racial situation and conditions resulting from contact with European society and culture. I hold Separatism to express the African's desire to act independently, free from the control of Europeans and free from the embarrassing comparison with the technically more efficient European leaders. In the field of religion, unlike that of politics or economy, there are no barriers which prevent such independent action. However, the desire for independence, owing to factors mentioned above, is apparently not so strong as to create open and acute hostility to the barriers preventing independent action in other fields.

The large membership of the Roman Catholic Church also seems to imply that the urge for independence must not be overrated as far as Taung is concerned. We have seen that the efficient and comprehensive nature of the R.C. Mission effort is an important reason for their success. Bearing in mind that Bantu Roman Catholics participate much less in church leadership and the conduct of their own church activities than do their Protestant brethren, it could be argued that the preponderance of Roman Catholicism shows that the superiority of European techniques (cf. imposing buildings of R.C. Mission, electric plant, educational qualifications of workers, medical work) carries more weight with a considerable section of the society than the urge for independent leadership in church affairs.

Particular mention may here be made of the St. Paul Apostolic Faith Morning Star. I have already mentioned cleanliness as a particular value in this church. Another is diligence, also in economic undertakings. In sermons the minister enjoins his members to exploit the opportunities offered by the Irrigation Scheme. He himself, with the help of the congregation, has shown a degree of economic initiative which is rare in his society. With a great amount of labour he has planted a number of fruit trees on the stony slope around his homestead, besides a small plantation for timber nearby. Part of his garden can be irrigated from the small reservoir, fed by hand-pump from his own well, but water must be carried to most of the fruit and other trees. In this he is assisted by the members of the church, of whom there always appears to be a number at the homestead. Economic progress, therefore, seems to be included in the church programme. Perhaps the rite of blessing newly bought articles is in part also a form of display of economic progress which serves to enhance it. The stress on hygiene and economic progress expresses a desire to lift the society out of its 'backwardness' which is stressed and aggravated by

234   RELIGION IN A TSWANA CHIEFDOM

the conditions resulting from contact between Bantu and Europeans.

With reference to the inter-racial situation I may point out a certain contradiction in the attitude of some of the churches, particularly the Pentecostal Separatists, to ritual. These are the churches which particularly attach magical value to rites, thus being very definitely influenced by traditional patterns. But the same churches tend to denounce traditional pagan ritual as performed by native doctors even more emphatically than other churches and lay great stress on the Biblical foundation of their beliefs and usages. We observe here two opposing tendencies: on the one hand, the conscious rejection of tradition and acceptance of what is new, but on the other hand, that which is new is re-interpreted—probably unconsciously—according to traditional (magical) patterns of thought and is often given a peculiar elaboration. One could expect that the Bantu, aware of their inferior position in the total South African society, would tend to simulate European patterns of living wherever possible, in order to deny any suggestion of inferiority, because difference from Europeans with their technically superior culture is only too often interpreted as inferiority. Perhaps the very emphatic rejection of pagan ritual and acceptance of ritual which is believed to have a Biblical foundation (thus being in line with Christianity, the dominant European religion) is one way of simulating European patterns and of expressing the desire to be accepted as the equals of the superior European class.

Nevertheless, the break with tradition is not easy and it still asserts itself. The ritual reveals acceptance of the general patterns brought by European missionaries, but as they are, these patterns are too 'foreign' to give full satisfaction. By their greater elaboration and the magical value attached to them they are to some extent brought in line with familiar patterns.

This brings us to the second important difference between Separatism in Taung and among the Zulu, viz. the absence of such a distinct nativistic trend as that found among Zulu Zionists, i.e. if the term 'nativistic' implies the incorporation of traditional pagan *forms* into church organization, belief, and ritual. There are morphological similarities between certain aspects of Pentecostal Separatist ritual and some traditional Tswana practices, but these are vague compared to the parallels found in the Zulu churches. The absence of such distinct nativistic trends in Taung must probably be related to the advanced stage of disintegration of the traditional culture. A traditionally less elaborate ancestor cult among the Tswana (see above, pp. 214 ff.) may also be responsible for this difference. Furthermore, baptism by immersion and beliefs about being filled with the Holy Spirit which

TRENDS AND INTERCONNEXIONS 235

result in certain utterances and bodily movements characteristic also of Pentecostalism among Europeans, have striking precedents in Zulu purification ceremonies and beliefs about possession by ancestral spirits. It does not seem improbable that these similarities caught the imagination of Zulu converts and either served to suggest further elaboration of church ritual on traditional (pagan) lines or at least stimulated the nativistic trend. Tswana traditional culture did not present the same precedents to Pentecostal belief and ritual and therefore there was not the same suggestive or stimulating force to foster nativistic tendencies.

Although I would not apply the term 'nativistic' to Separatist churches in Taung, we do find expressed in Separatism a desire for a religion and a church which is less 'alien', which has greater affinity with the traditional background. In this connexion I may point out that on the whole little has been done by missions to foster the development of indigenous liturgical and other forms. Missionaries seem to have taken for granted that Bantu churches and congregations must necessarily follow the same patterns of devotion, organization, and church life as the 'mother' churches.[1] Whereas the urge for an indigenous interpretation of Christianity finds little scope in mission churches, it can be given free play in Bantu Separatist churches. This urge for more familiar forms I see expressed in a simpler and less formal church organization and in the preference for a hierarchical arrangement of church offices and councils. As we have observed, there are some minor similarities in form between church ritual and aspects of the traditional background, but it is particularly the magical value attached to Christian ritual which illustrates how an 'indigenous' interpretation of Christianity emerges in the Separatist churches. It also emerges in the greater leniency toward polygynists (although all condemn polygyny), the favouring of marriage payment (*bogadi*), and the recognition of beliefs in sorcery and the water snake. The trend toward a religion that is vividly experienced through ritualism or emotionalism is probably also part of the indigenous interpretation of Christianity.[2] I have also tried to show that the kind of moralism which

---

[1] For the absence of indigenous forms in South African missions and churches among the Bantu, see International Missionary Council, *The Life of the Church*, Tambaram Series, Vol. II, Oxford University Press, London, 1939, p. 15.

A well-known instance of the development of indigenous forms of Christianity under missionary guidance is found on the island of Bali. (See Swellengrebel, 1948.)

[2] (i) Dr. Sundkler has described the emphasis on ritual as 'an important intimation of the true *interpretatio Africana* of the Christian message.' (*Op. cit.*, p. 296.)

(ii) I may here draw particular attention to the significance of the coffin as a symbol in the St. Paul Apostolic Faith Morning Star. The holy place with the symbolic coffin

236 RELIGION IN A TSWANA CHIEFDOM

is common in the churches shows a pattern of thought akin to that which underlies magic.

The desire for an indigenous form of Christianity does not find expression in Separatist churches only, but also in churches connected with Europeans. Church organization, for instance, tends to be informal and to be interpreted in terms of the traditional pattern of political organization even in some churches connected with Europeans. Magical value sometimes seems to be attached to ritual in these churches as well. The church papers placed in the coffin as the 'certificates' with which to arrive in heaven, are an example of indigenous interpretation in non-Separatist churches. In the Separatist churches, however, where the clergy generally receive little theological training and where the control of theologically trained missionaries is absent, the tendency toward such an indigenous interpretation enjoys freer play and is more completely expressed.

The progressive multiplication within Separatism has already been related to the fact that Christianity, particularly Protestantism, has not presented a united front to the African.[1] Pentecostalism, which is particularly prone to secessions, even among Europeans, has no doubt given considerable impetus to the tendency toward fragmentation within Separatism, the more so since some aspects of Pentecostalism make it particularly acceptable in a society such as the one we are dealing with (see above, pp. 226 ff.). However, even where a missionizing church or society has brought with it the heritage of a strong sense of church unity or a strong ecumenical sense, there are factors inherent in the traditional background which may well make it difficult to realize the same degree of church unity and ecumenism in the Bantu church.

I illustrate this with a few characteristics of traditional Tswana society and religion. The largest corporate group in that society was the tribe, the bulk of which was often concentrated in a relatively small geographical area. Occasionally the tribe as a whole co-operated in

in the middle is the central feature in the complex of buildings and objects at the church centre. Note that the central symbol is not a cross as one might expect in a Christian church, but a coffin, which is taken to symbolize the universality of death (it must serve as a reminder that all people must die) but like the cross, it also symbolizes the death of Christ. The cross, which is a foreign symbol, is substituted by a more familiar symbol to which a similar significance is attached as that usually attached to the cross. Although the coffin is not an object belonging to the traditional background, it has already become a very familiar object and one of immediate significance in the life of the society, so that it is not something foreign any more. The cross has remained foreign because it lacks a similar association with everyday life from which it may derive its symbolism.

[1] Sundkler, *op. cit.*, pp. 295 ff.

TRENDS AND INTERCONNEXIONS 237

ritual or ritual was performed on behalf of the whole tribe, but solidarity in the magico-religious sphere did not extend beyond it. Furthermore, tribal unity was not inviolable and the splitting of tribes is not an uncommon feature in the history of the Tswana.[1] Moreover, the ancestor cult really centred in the family or family group. This was the regular cult group—a very small unit which did not retain its unity indefinitely but tended in time to split.[2]

The transition from the traditional small-scale society to a large-scale society is of course in progress, but the pattern of thought of many members of the society is still conditioned by the traditional background. To this background the idea of a church as a corporate body of people which far transcends the geographical area known to the individual and which remains united indefinitely is clearly foreign. I suggest that under these circumstances, unless the unity of the Church is very strongly accentuated, malcontents easily secede, and that this is an important factor in the progressive fragmentation within Separatism.

Protestant missions in South Africa have probably failed to draw enough attention to the doctrine of the Church amongst peoples to whose traditional background ideas such as church unity and ecumenism are completely foreign. In the Roman Catholic Church, on the other hand, the unity of the Church has a very strong sanction in the doctrine that there is no salvation outside the Church (*extra ecclesiam nulla salus*) and in the notion that secession from the Church endangers the eternal salvation of the soul. This sanction has no doubt acted as a strong deterrent to Separatist secessions from the R.C. Church.[3]

Interconnexions

If one were to characterize the Phuduhutswana chiefdom from a religious point of view in a single sentence, it could be called a society in an advanced stage of transition from paganism to Christianity. To a large extent this transition is the result of conscious efforts on the part of missions and churches, and in the main it may be seen as a process in which the Christian religion is taking the place of the traditional pagan religion and magic. However, the transition involves

[1] Cf. Schapera, 1952, pp. 8 ff., and 1953, p. 15.

[2] This is typical of a society made up of corporate lineages. (Cf. Fortes, Meyer, 1953.)

[3] Katesa Schlosser points out that the movement connected with the prophet Kimbangu in the Congo affected the Roman Catholic Missions less than the Protestants because of 'der autoritären Doktrin des Katholizismus'. (Schlosser, 1949, p. 303.)

238   RELIGION IN A TSWANA CHIEFDOM

much more; it is a much more complex process than the mere supplanting of one religion by another. In the first place, this complexity results from the fact that the old and the new mutually influence each other in the contact situation. Moreover, because of the complex nature of society, an attempt to change one aspect of its life must necessarily have repercussions on other aspects. Further, other agents besides missions and churches, such as foreign governments and traders, at an early stage exerted their influence to effect certain changes in the life of the people, and in time a range of interacting forces and processes developed, so that the whole society is now involved in a process of transition affecting almost every aspect of its life and involving a comprehensive change of its whole social structure. The changes in the sphere of religion form part of this wider process of change, are linked to it in numerous ways, and therefore cannot be isolated from it. In this final section I shall try to summarize the different types of interconnexions between the old and the new and between religion and the social structure as a whole involved in the present religious situation, which is a stage in the process of religious change.

The simplest type of interconnexion is that between the two religions or magico-religious systems which are in conflict or in contact. Apart from the fact that *Christianity* has largely supplanted *paganism*, the two have also *mutually influenced* each other. E.g. pagan thought has been influenced by Christian monotheistic notions. On the other hand, the religion of the churches has been modified through its contact with paganism in various manners: traits of pagan ritual and belief have found their way into the churches; new rites have developed as substitutes for pagan ritual; there is in the churches a trend toward magical belief and ritual and toward vivid religious experience. There are also parallels in form between rites introduced by European missionaries and traditional pagan rites, which, where they existed, made for the acceptability of such rites. Although the latter cannot actually be described as paganism influencing Christianity, it does constitute a connexion between the two.[1]

Another type of interconnexion which, like the former, also refers to *reciprocating influences or 'relatedness'* between the old and the new, is that *between the religion of the churches and other aspects of the traditional background* (i.e. outside the magico-religious sphere). Missions and churches have directly attacked or tried to modify some

[1] For actual examples of these different types of connexions between paganism and the churches, see pp. 120 f., 209 f., and 217 ff. where these connexions have been formulated.

TRENDS AND INTERCONNEXIONS

traditional institutions such as the initiation ceremonies, polygyny, and the giving of *bogadi*, and, sometimes with the help of other forces, have had some degree of success. Moreover, the attack on the magico-religious sphere of the traditional background, or innovations of a religious nature, sometimes had indirect results or repercussions in the general social structure. It contributed, for instance, to the disappearance of some of the chief's magico-religious functions (as a link with the tribal ancestors and as an initiator of important rites) thereby weakening the religious sanctions of his authority. Further, the fact that missions set up a new type of authority beside that of the chief also lowered his prestige. Or to mention another example: in as far as the churches prevented or discouraged converts from taking part in pagan ritual, they detached them from their cult groups which were kin groups as far as the ancestor cult was concerned, thus contributing to the weakening of kinship ties.

On the other hand, we have observed numerous instances in which the structure and organization of the churches are related to aspects of traditional social organization and structure. There is some connexion between the local church group and traditional groupings such as the family group or ward, and between church organization and the pattern of traditional political organization. The secrecy attached to Holy Communion in some churches has been shown to be related to the secrecy in connexion with initiation ceremonies. The position of women in the structure of the churches is connected with the relation of the sexes in traditional society, as well as with institutions such as polygyny, tribal initiation, and warfare, and with traditional economy (herding). The concentration of the population and concomitant factors fostered the tendency for the L.M.S. to become a tribal church in the earlier stages while the traditional pattern still existed. The importance of leadership in the churches has some connexion with traditional patterns of leadership. Further, the traditional structure was one of a small-scale society which impedes acceptance of ideas of a broad church unity and ecumenism, while the tendency for Tswana tribes, and also smaller units such as wards and family groups, to split into two or more sections, may be related to the fissiparous tendency in Bantu Separatist churches.

The third type of interconnexion is that between *present conditions in the magico-religious sphere or changes in this sphere on the one hand, and other processes of change which do not strictly belong to that sphere.* For instance, *pagan religion* has been affected by other factors besides missions and churches. I refer to the waning of the ancestor cult which is related to the weakening of kinship ties, par-

240 RELIGION IN A TSWANA CHIEFDOM

ticularly the weakening of the principle of unilineal descent. Further, certain characteristics or trends in the *religion of the churches* which form part of the process of religious change are related to processes of change which are not of a magico-religious nature. To this aspect we must pay particular attention.

Reference has been made to the traditional pattern of concentration of population and its relation to the tendency at an earlier stage for one church to become a tribal church. I have also shown, however, that the changing of this pattern which took the form of a scattering of the population, concomitant with the weakening of tribal solidarity and the chief's authority, is related to the multiplication of denominations in the chiefdom and the waning of the prestige of the tribal church. Further, we have seen how the importance of the local church group as a social group is related to the disintegration of the wards and family groups which were localized kin groups and were the important social groups in traditional society. The importance of leadership in the churches, besides being connected with traditional patterns of leadership, is also connected with processes of change. This is shown in the suggestion that the example of European society has fostered the urge for a leadership not tied to inheritance in the male line, and that outside the churches there is not much opportunity for satisfying this urge. Further, we have seen that it is probably also connected with the weakening of the principle of unilineal descent. These examples show how changes in the religion of the churches are related to changes in the pattern of territorial distribution and in the political and kinship structure.

Characteristics of, and trends in the churches are also related to changes which are primarily economic. Migrant labour, which is itself a product of change, is responsible for the relative absence of young males in the churches. I have also shown that migrant labour has contributed to the multiplication of denominations.

It has been suggested that some trends in church religion are related to insecure economic conditions. To a certain extent the relative poverty of the people of the Phuduhutswana chiefdom is a heritage from their past, since their traditional economy did not give them much security. However, their present poverty is also closely connected with processes of change, particularly with the restriction of land through European settlement and with the fact that under these changed conditions they continued to apply traditional methods of production. Therefore, if the trends toward a religion that is sensually or emotionally experienced is related to economic conditions providing only a low degree of security (and to a low degree of

TRENDS AND INTERCONNEXIONS 241

knowledge), as I have suggested, it follows that this trend in religion is related to the processes of economic change mentioned above.

There are also changes of a more general nature which have a bearing on trends in the churches. The social importance of the local church group and its activities may be connected with the disappearance of traditional amusements and excitements, which is a concomitant of the general decay of the old social structure. Another concomitant of this general disintegration is the disappearance of old values, and we have seen that the trend toward moralism in the churches may be related to this.

There are, then, these three types of interconnexions: the mutual influence of paganism and Christianity, the reciprocating influence between the missions and churches on the one hand, and such aspects of the traditional background as do not belong to the magico-religious sphere on the other hand, and thirdly the interconnexions between religion and magic on the one hand, and processes of change which do not strictly belong to the magico-religious sphere on the other. Here I must point out that different interconnexions and even different types of interconnexions may be involved in a particular phenomenon or in a particular trend. The fact that in paganism as it persists to-day monotheistic notions are more explicit than they seem to have been in the past, has been connected with the influence of missionary teaching, but it is also connected with the waning of the ancestor cult, which is largely the result of the weakening of kinship ties. We should also remember that different influences sometimes conflict, so that the one has a neutralizing or minimizing effect on the other. We have seen, for instance, that the activities of missions and churches have contributed to the weakening of the chief's authority. On the other hand, in as far as the chief is given prominence in church ritual and activities, his prestige may be enhanced by this. In this case the enhancement is or was probably not very considerable and has only had a minimizing effect on those influences of the church making for the weakening of the chieftainship. Nevertheless, the presence of such a factor adds to the complexity of the total situation.

To appreciate fully the complex nature of the process of religious change this discussion should be considered against the background of the structural changes summarized in chapter I. This will show that a particular change in religion may link up with a whole series of interconnexions. I give only a single example: we have seen that the waning of the ancestor cult is related to the weakening of kinship ties, particularly the decline in importance of unilineal descent. But these changes in kinship structure are again related to other factors such as

R.T.C.—17

242   RELIGION IN A TSWANA CHIEFDOM

the scattering of the population and the growth of individualism, and the latter is related particularly to economic changes. The scattering of the population is again related to the weakening of the chieftainship. The latter change in turn is related to the process by which Tlhaping territory was hemmed in as a result of European settlement, and to the loss of political independence. In this manner the change observed in the religion of the people links up with a whole network of change.

APPENDIX I

PARTICULARS OF SAMPLE SURVEY

FOR the sample survey which formed part of my field-work, two areas were selected, one including the chief's *kgotla* at Taung and another around the headman's *kgotla* at Mokgareng in the valley area along which the greater part of the population is now scattered. These two areas were selected with the purpose of discerning what remnants of the old pattern of territorial grouping still persist on the site of the old capital and whether any patterns would emerge in an area more recently populated. Neither of these areas constitutes a separate territorial unit. The existing territorial units are headmen's areas, all of which are too large to be submitted to a one-man survey.

At every homestead a detailed genealogy of the head and his or her spouse was taken, with particulars about the marriages of head and married children. Further information was collected on the composition of the homesteads and the whereabouts of each member, and on the educational qualifications and religious affiliation of each, as well as some particulars on economics.

The Taung area included 49 homesteads, and complete information was obtained in respect of 42. The inhabitants of the other seven were all absent at the time of the survey (i.e. absent for several weeks or longer, visiting or working) and these homesteads were not taken into consideration for statistical purposes. At Mokgareng the sample area included 25 homesteads. For 21 full particulars were obtained, at 2 the heads (a father and his son) were unwilling to give information, and at 2 others the inhabitants were absent at the time of the survey. Complete information was therefore obtained from altogether 63 homesteads. (For most of the others some genealogical information could be obtained from kinsmen and neighbours.)

Only the statistical results dealing with religion have been included in this book, but most of the generalizations in chapter I are based on, or were corroborated by, the results of the survey.

R.T.C.—17*

APPENDIX II

ST. PAUL APOSTOLIC FAITH
MORNING STAR

THE most interesting church I came across in Taung is the one called St. Paul Apostolic Faith Morning Star. Many of its characteristics have been described or mentioned, but as these references are scattered throughout the text it may be useful to list them here, in addition to others that have not been mentioned.

The leader's homestead forms an interesting complex not parallelled in the case of any other church. Beside his dwelling is a small church and a separate small building nearby serves as his special office, while there is also a small hut for the convenience of church members staying at the church centre for a while. In front of the house is the holy place, an open area with a cement surface and a coffin-shaped concrete block in the centre. Nearby is also the small reservoir used for irrigation and for ritual purposes (pp. 164 ff.). Around the homestead are gardens and a considerable number of fruit trees, all enclosed by hedges, fences, and stone walls. There is a small plantation of bluegum and other trees, planted to produce timber for building, for their own use, and for sale. Besides some rites which they share with other churches, they have a whole series of rites particular to them, such as the placing of the coffin on the holy place before burial, a set of purification rites different from that of other churches, reinstatement of a lapsed member by a kind of partial baptism, passing through the baptismal pool for health purposes, the performance of certain sacrifices, and the blessing of newly-bought articles. Their rite of laying-on of hands is different from that of other churches, and although others also use holy water for healing, none of them perform a ceremonial drinking of water like this church. Then there is the custom of staying at the church centre for a time and the wearing of long dresses by the women. (All these rites and customs are described or mentioned in chapter VI.)

When church members greet each other on arriving at the church centre they kneel and utter a prayer or a blessing, and when passing graves they stop and say a prayer. The leader is a man generally held in high esteem and has a reputation for kindness and humility. Besides baptism and good works in general, he stresses certain topics such as submissiveness to one's superiors, and diligence.

A particular terminology is used in respect of church organization. This is not evident in the local church where commonly known Tswana terminology is used, but it emerged in correspondence which I conducted with superior church officials in an attempt to obtain more information. The local leader was referred to as the Field Gospel Servant, and there was reference to a Gospel Troop Sectional Overseer. I was first informed that information

APPENDIX II

could only be obtained from 'Quarters of the Divine Government Offices', and after sending a questionnaire I was told that it was receiving 'the attention of the Responsible Division for the Universal Mass Christianity under which this Gospel Troop of "ST. PAUL APOSTOLIC FAITH MORNING STAR" is guided'. Unfortunately, this was the last I heard from them in spite of my repeated enquiries.

Church members render a great deal of assistance in cultivating the gardens, orchards, and plantations at the church centre, but it is not known how the proceeds from this undertaking are used.

APPENDIX III

RELIGIOUS AFFILIATION OF THE
BANTU POPULATION – 1951 CENSUS

No official report has yet been published relating to the religious affiliation of the Bantu population of the Union of South Africa as reflected by the 1951 census, but some figures, based on this census, have been published in the *Official Year Book of the Union of South Africa, No. 29—1956-57*. The following statistics have been extracted from this source, and may be compared with the 1946 figures used in the book in the passages referred to.

Total number of natives enumerated as
members of Christian churches (cf. p. 11) .   .   5,076,861
(i.e. 59 per cent of
total native population)

Total membership of Native Separatist
Churches (cf. p. 57)   1,590,295
(i.e. 31 per cent of all
churches, or 34 per
cent of all Protestants)

Other groups mentioned in note on p. 57:
S.D.A.   .   .   .   .   .   .   Included with
'Diverse Christian
Sects' in 1951
Apostolic Faith   149,790
Diverse Christian Sects   127,198

Methodists (cf. p. 225)   1,039,573
(i.e. 20 per cent of
all native members of
Christian churches)

Anglican Churches (cf. p. 225) .   .   .   599,229

I am further particularly indebted to the Rev. Carl W. Kies of Warrenton, C.P., for putting at my disposal the following statistics which he personally extracted from the 1951 census files with the permission of the Director of Census.

APPENDIX III

247

Religious Affiliation of the Native Population of the
Taung District—1951

Methodists	3,540
'Congregational and L.M.S.'.	9,204
Anglicans	1,887
Lutherans	702
'Baptists'	37
D.R.C. (Nederduits Gereformeerd)	29
Reformed Church (Hervormd)	21
French Protestants	15
Presbyterians	14
S.D.A.	444
'Apostolics'	255
'Pentecostals'	19
'Sabbatarians'	19
Other churches and 'sects'	25
Roman Catholics	3,119
Separatists	7,395
'No church', 'Other faiths', 'Heathens' and 'Unknown'	3,337
Total.	30,062

These figures cannot be compared directly with my two sets of figures collected respectively from the churches and in the sample survey, since the census figures are for the whole district, which includes the Maidi chiefdom, as well as a small number of farms. Nevertheless a few points call for some comment.

(a) Except in the case of the Roman Catholic Church these figures convey the same impression as to the relative strength of the more important churches. The L.M.S. obviously has a large 'appendix' of nominal members or adherents (cf. p. 116).

(b) That only 3,119 persons (including children) were enumerated as Roman Catholics in the whole district, is difficult to understand in the light of the figure, supplied to me by a responsible official of the Church, of 4,745 communicant members and catechumens in the Phuduhutswana chiefdom alone, even when allowing for a certain degree of incompleteness of census figures. It is difficult to avoid the conclusion that the material on which I worked in the book gave an exaggerated impression of the influence of the Roman Catholic Church. Nevertheless there is no doubt that Roman Catholicism constitutes an important factor in the present religious set-up.

(c) It might seem that the proportion without any church connexions is smaller than I have suggested (pp. 10–11), but knowing the reaction of the people to questions about their church connexions, I am convinced that many would have been enumerated as church members or adherents in an official census, who would not have been counted as such in my own investigations, which were particularly carefully conducted on this point.

LIST OF REFERENCES

Agar-Hamilton, J. A. I., 1937. *The Road to the North.* London: Longmans, Green & Co.

Ashton, E. H., 1952. *The Basuto.* London: Oxford University Press for International African Institute.

Breutz, P. L., 1953a. *The Tribes of Rustenburg and Pilansberg Districts*, Dept. of Native Affairs, Ethnological Publications No. 28. Pretoria: Government Printer.

—, 1953b. *The Tribes of Marico District*, Dept. of Native Affairs, Ethnological Publications No. 30. Pretoria: Government Printer.

Brown, J. Tom, 1926. *Among the Bantu Nomads.* London: Seeley Service.

—, 1946. *Secwana Dictionary.* Tigerkloof: London Missionary Society.

The Catholic Encyclopedia, 1912. New York: Robert Appleton Company.

Christelijk Encyclopedie voor het Nederlandsche Volk, J. H. Kok, Kampen. (first edition.)

Cunnison, Ian, 1951. 'A Watchtower Assembly in Central Africa', *International Review of Missions*, vol. 40, no. 160, Oct.

Dieterlen, see Mabille.

Dollard, John, 1937. *Caste and Class in a Southern Town.* New Haven: Yale University Press.

Du Plessis, J., 1911. *A History of Christian Missions in South Africa.* London: Longmans, Green & Co.

Evans-Pritchard, E. E., 1937. *Witchcraft, Oracles and Magic among the Azande.* London: Oxford University Press.

Fortes, Meyer, 1953. 'The Structure of Unilineal Descent Groups', *American Anthropologist*, vol. 55, no. 1 (Jan.–March).

Frazier, E. Franklin, 1940. *Negro Youth at the Crossways.* Washington: American Council of Education.

Fritsch, Gustav, 1872. *Die Eingeborenen Süd-Afrikas.* Breslau: F. Hirt.

Gluckman, Max, 1950. 'Kinship and Marriage among the Lozi of Northern Rhodesia and the Zulu of Natal', in A. R. Radcliffe-Brown and Daryll Forde, *African Systems of Kinship and Marriage.* London: Oxford University Press for International African Institute.

Haile, A. J., 1951. *A Brief Historical Survey of the London Missionary Society in Southern Africa.* Bulawayo.

Houghton, D. Hobart, and Walton, Edith, M., 1952. *The Economy of a Native Reserve*, Keiskammahoek Rural Survey, vol. ii. Pietermaritzburg: Shuter & Shooter.

Hunter (-Wilson), Monica, 1933. 'The Effects of Contact with Europeans on the Status of Pondo Women', *Africa*, vol. vi, no. 3.

—, 1936. *Reaction to Conquest.* London: Oxford University Press for International African Institute.

—, 1951. 'Witch Beliefs and Social Structure', *The American Journal of Sociology*, vol. lvi, no. 4, Jan.

250 LIST OF REFERENCES

Jennings, A. E., 1933. *Bogadi*. Tigerkloof: London Missionary Society.

Junod, Henri A., 1927. *The Life of a South African Tribe*, vol. ii (Second Edition). London.

Krige, Eileen Jensen, 1950. *The Social System of the Zulus*. Pietermaritzburg: Shuter & Shooter. Second Edition.

Krige, E. J. and J. D., 1954. 'The Lovedu of the Transvaal', in Daryll Forde (ed.), *African Worlds*. London: Oxford University Press for International African Institute.

Koornhof, P. G. J., 1953. *The Drift from the Reserves among the South African Bantu*. Unpublished D. Phil. thesis, Oxford University.

Kuper, Hilda, 1946. 'The Swazi Reaction to Missions', *African Studies*, vol. 5, no. 3.

—, 1947a. *An African Aristocracy*. London: Oxford University Press for International African Institute.

—, 1947b. *The Uniform of Colour*, Johannesburg: Witwatersrand University Press.

—, 1952. *The Swazi* (Ethnographic Survey of Africa, Southern Africa, part i). London: International African Institute.

Language, F. J., 1941. *Kapteinskap onder die Tlhaping*, D. Phil. thesis, University of Stellenbosch. (Parts of this work have been published under the titles given below.)

—, 1942. 'Herkoms en Geskiedenis van die Tlhaping, *African Studies*, vol.1, no. 2, June.

—, 1943a. *Stamregering by die Tlhaping*. Stellenbosch: Pro-Ecclesia Drukkery.

—, 1943b. 'Die Bogwera van die Tlhaping', *Tydskrif vir Wetenskap en Kuns*, 4, Tweede Aflewering (1943).

Latourette, Kenneth Scott. *A History of Christianity*. London: Eyre & Spottiswood Limited. (1953?.)

Lichtenstein, H., 1930. *Travels in Southern Africa* (1803–1806), vol. ii. The Van Riebeeck Society.

Little, K., 1954. 'The Mende of Sierra Leone', in Forde, Daryll, *African Worlds*. London: Oxford University Press for International African Institute.

Mabille, A., and Dieterlen, H. (Revised by Paroz, R. A.), 1950. *Southern Sotho-English Dictionary*. Morija.

Magrath, Oswin, P., O.P., S.L.T., 1943. 'Catholic and Reformed Doctrine Compared—VIII: The Sacraments', *Catholic Times*, November.

Mkele, see Mqotsi.

Moffat, Robert, 1856. *Missionary Labours and Scenes in Southern Africa*. Cincinatti. (Twelfth Edition.)

Mqotsi, L., and Mkele, N., 1946. 'A Separatist Church: Iɓandla lika-Krestu', *African Studies*, vol. 5, no. 2, June.

Parrinder, Geoffrey, 1953. *Religion in an African City*. London: Oxford University Press.

Porter, Arthur T., 1953. 'Religious Affiliation in Freetown, Sierra Leone', *Africa*, vol. xxiii, no. 1, Jan.

Powdermaker, Hortense, 1939. *After Freedom*. New York.

LIST OF REFERENCES

Quick, G., 1940. 'Some Aspects of the African Watch Tower Movement in Northern Rhodesia', *International Review of Missions*, vol. 29, no. 114, April.

Radcliffe-Brown, A. R., 1952. *Structure and Function in Primitive Society.* London: Cohen & West.

Royal Anthropological Institute of Great Britain and Ireland, 1951. *Notes and Queries on Anthropology.* London: Routledge and Kegan Paul.

Schapera, I., 1930. 'The "Little Rain" (*Pulanyane*) Ceremony of the Bechuanaland Bakxatla', *Bantu Studies*, vol. 4, pp. 211 ff.

—, 1934. 'Oral Sorcery among the Natives of Bechuanaland', in Evans-Pritchard, E. E. (ed.), *Essays Presented to C. G. Seligman.* London: Routledge.

—, 1936. 'The Contributions of Western Civilization to Modern Kgatla Culture', *Transactions of the Royal Society of South Africa*, vol. xxiv, part iii.

Schapera, I., 1938. *A Handbook of Tswana Law and Custom.* London: Oxford University Press for International African Institute.

—, 1939. *Mekgwa le Melao ya Batswana.* Lovedale.

—, 1940. *Married Life in an African Tribe.* London: Faber & Faber.

—, 1943. *Native Land Tenure in the Bechuanaland Protectorate.* Lovedale Press.

—, 1947. *Migrant Labour and Tribal Life.* London: Oxford University Press.

—, (Ed.), 1951. *Apprenticeship at Kuruman*, Oppenheimer Series Number Five. London: Chatto and Windus.

—, 1952. *The Ethnic Composition of Tswana Tribes*, London School of Economics and Political Science, Monographs on Social Anthropology, no. 11.

—, 1953. *The Tswana*, Ethnographic Survey of Africa, Southern Africa, part iii. London: International African Institute.

—, and others, 1934. *Western Civilization and the Natives of South Africa: Studies in Social Contact.* London: Routledge.

Schlosser, Katesa, 1949. *Propheten in Afrika.* Braunschweig: Albert Limbach Verlag.

Shepperson, G., 1954. 'The Politics of African Church Separatist Movements in British Central Africa, 1829–1916', *Africa*, vol. xxiv, no. 3, July.

Sundkler, Bengt G. M., 1948. *Bantu Prophets in South Africa.* London: Lutterworth Press.

Swellengrebel, J. L., 1948. *Kerk en Tempel op Bali.* N.V. Uitgeverij W. van Hoeve, 's Gravenhage.

Union of South Africa, *Population Census, 8th May, 1951: Vol. iii—Religions of the White Population of the Union of South Africa together with 1946 Census Figures for All Races of the Population.* U.G. No. 62/1954. (Published 1956).

Van Antwerp, C. M., 1938. *Die Separatistiese Kerklike Beweging onder die Bantu van Suid-Afrika.* Unpublished Ph.D. thesis, University of Cape Town.

252   LIST OF REFERENCES

Walton, see Houghton.
Watt, J. M., and Breyer-Brandwijk, Maria G., 1932. *The Medicinal and Poisonous Plants of Southern Africa*. Edinburgh: Livingstone Press.
Willoughby, W. C., 1923. *Race Problems in the New Africa*. Oxford.
—, 1928. *The Soul of the Bantu*. Doubleday Doran & Co.
—, 1932. *Nature-Worship and Taboo*. Connecticut: Hartford Seminary Press.
Wilson, Godfrey, and Monica, 1945. *The Analysis of Social Change*. Cambridge University Press.
Wilson, Monica, and others, 1952. *Social Structure*, Keiskammahoek Rural Survey, vol. iii. Pietermaritzburg: Shuter & Shooter.
(See also Hunter-Wilson.)

REPORTS

International Missionary Council, 1939. *The Life of the Church*. Tambaram Series, vol. ii. London: Oxford University Press.
Irrigation Scheme, Taung, 1950–1951. *Annual Report of the Superintendent*, Taung Irrigation Scheme for 1950–1951.
London Missionary Society. *Annual Station Reports for the Taung Mission*. (Several Reports for the years between 1900 and 1930 are referred to.)
Native Commissioner, Taung. *Criminal Records* in the Taung Native Commissioner's Office, no. 178 of 1947, and no. 310 of 1951.
Pentecostal Holiness Church. *Minutes if the Twenty-ninth Session of the South African Conference of the Pentecostal Holiness Church.*
Union of South Africa, 1925. *Report of the Native Churches Commission*, U.G. 39/25. Cape Town: Cape Times Ltd.

CONSTITUTIONS OF CHURCHES

African Methodist Episcopal Church, 1936. *The Doctrine and Discipline of the A.M.E. Church*. Published by Order of the General Conference held in New York City, N.Y., May.
African United Church, 1917. *Constitutions and Canons of the African United Church*. Johannesburg.
Bechuana Methodist Church. *Constitution*. Johannesburg: Bantu Printing Press.
Ethiopian Catholic Church in Zion, 1919. *Constitutions and Canons of the Ethiopian Catholic Church in Zion*. Bloemfontein.
Ethiopian Church of Africa. *Constitution*.
Holy Church of Christ. *Constitution*.

INDEX

Adherents, 9, 10, 11, 39, 63, 230. *See also Barati*

African Catholic Bantu Church, 54

African Catholic Church, 43, 95, Tables II–VII

African Lutheran Church, 63, Tables II–VII

African Methodist Episcopal Church, 42, 43–44, 50, 52, 65, 160, Tables II–VII

African United Church, 43, 49, 54, Tables II–VII

Age-grades (Age-sets), 8, 19, 156

Alcoholic drinks, attitude of churches to, 43, Table VII. *See also* Beer, *Khadi*

American Negro Churches, 221

American Negro control of Bantu churches, 52, 55

Ancestor cult, 5, 12, 29, 38, 148–149, 161, 208, 212–217, 237, 239. *See also* Ancestor spirits; Prayers; Revelation; Sacrifices

Ancestor spirits, 13, 14, 26, 29–32, 38, 203, 205, 207, 208; as intercessors, between man and God, 29, 31, 216. *See also* Ancestor cult; Prayers; Revelation; Sacrifices

Anglican Church (Mission), 2, 46, 65, 82, Tables II–VII

Anglican church pattern, 43

Apostolic, designation of churches as, 44. *See also* names of individual churches

Ashes, used for healing, 45, 180, 197, Table VII

Avoidance, in churches, 44, 45, 141, 169–171, Table VII; in pagan ritual, 14, 16. *See also* Taboos in pagan ritual

Badimo, see Ancestor spirits

Bantu Baptist Church, 82, Tables II–VII

Bantu Separatist churches, 41–42, 43, 44, 45, 47–50, 57, 61, 64, 70, 74, 80, 95, 98, 100, 104, 107, 108, 114–116, 118–119, 120, 121–122, 129, 135, 141, 142–144, 152, 178, 191, 197, 203–208, 230–237, 246, 247. *See also* Ethiopians; Zionists; and names of individual churches

Baptism, 18, 81, 124, 140, 141, 144, 147, 162, 191; (adult), by immersion, 43, 44, 162–167, 194–197, 220, 227, Table VII

Baptist churches, 43, 44, 108, 162

Barati, 8, 9, 10, 63

Bechuana Methodist Church, 44, 50, 52, 126, Tables II–VII

Beer, attitude of churches to drinking, 67, 84, 117, 139, Table VII; drinks, 67, 150

Bevan, Canon, 46

Bible, place of, in churches, 52, 91, 138, 139, 141, 143, 145, 152, 227. *See also* Divining; New Testament; Old Testament; Scripture

Bogadi (marriage payment), 21; falling into disuse, 7; attitude of churches to, 83–84; connected with rite of eating the animal of the cradle-skins (*dithari*), 17

Bogwêra, see Initiation ceremonies

Botlhale, 34, 48–49, 206

Brander, Rev. James, 52

Brown, Rev. John, 16

Brown, Rev. J. Tom, 50

Burial rites and customs, 21–24, 29, 80, 154, 156–160, 192, Table VII

Candles, used for revelation, 185; giving power, 185, 190

Cape Nguni, 5, 232. *See also* Nguni

Cattle, 7, 15, 215; connected with ancestor spirits, 21, 24–25, 154, 215

Charm(s), 14, 18, 174

Chief(s), Chieftainship, 6–7, 8, 25, 26, 27, 49, 50, 53, 55, 76, 93–94, 208, 241; among Protectorate Tswana, 17. *See also* Churches; Political organization

Childbirth, 34, 36; ritual of, 14–16, 27, 192, Table VII. *See also* Confinement

Children, 15, 17, 66; blessing of, 151–152; of deceased woman, 24, 160

Christianity, impact of, on Phuduhutswana Tlhaping, 5, 9, 11, 39, 209, 237–239; a non-magical religion, 149. *See also* Church; Churches; Indigenous interpretation of Christianity; Pagan religion and magic

Christmas celebrations, 124, 127

Church, nature of the, 62, 236

Church associations, 41, 92, 101–104, 113, 124. *See also* Women's associations.

Church buildings, 95–98, 126

Church of Christ (I6andla lika-Krestu); 64, 66, 98

254   INDEX

Church contributions (dues), 81, 99–100, 230; attitude to, 81
Church discipline, 81, 84–85, 229–230
Church dress, 45, 48, 72, 131, 136, 137; and health, 45, 136, 181–184, 190, Table VII; prescribed by revelation, 182, 183–184
Church finance, 56, 99–104, 124. *See also* Office bearers, salaries of
Church group, *see* Local church group
Church of the First-born, 55, Tables II–VII
Church organization, 43, 62–122
Church origins, 46, 50–56, 58–60, 61
Church property, *see* Church buildings
Church services, 45, 123, 125–137
Church sites, 98–99
Church union, 54
Church or mission schools, 7, 66, 113–114
Churches, history of, 1, 46–50; and political authorities, 48, 49, 50, 55, 71–72, 77, 94, 104, 114–118, 185–186, 208; and race relations, 46, 47, 48, 55, 77, 114, 118–119, 142, 143, 144, 231–235; recognition of, by government, 98, 114; and youth, 111–114, 152. *See also* Ethnic composition; Interdenominational relations; Leadership; Membership; Office bearers; Rural church; Urban church; Zulu churches, etc.
Clan(s), 4, 6. *See also* Totemic groups(s).
Class distinctions and religion, 221–222
Class system (Methodist), 43, 63, 225–226
Collections, 100, 101
Communion, *see* Holy Communion
Concerts, 101
Confinement, ritual terminating, 149–151
Confirmation, 81, 152
Conversion, 92
'Coolness' as ritual concept, 30, 34–35, 37, 149, 196
Cradle-skins, rite of eating the animal of the, 17–18, 29–30, 83 n.2
Culture, of Phuduhutswana-Tlhaping, x, 234–235. *See also* Traditional background
Culture contact, 136, 145. *See also* Social change

Death, causes of, 26; notions connected with, 144–145, 153–156
Dibela, 28, 35, 148
Dice, (used for divining), 13, 19, 20, 25, 29, 31, 72, 204; (used for gambling), 152.
Dikgaba, 25–26, 29, 214
Dithari, see Cradle-skins

Diviners, Divining, 13, 19, 20, 25, 26, 27, 29, 31, 32–33, 203–207; performed by churches, 202–207; traditional (pagan) methods of, 32; with Bible, 72, 186–187, 203, 204, 205
Doctors (native), 13, 32–33, 172, 204; attitude of churches to, 39, 84,174–175; *ngaka ya sedupe* ('hornless doctor'), 32, 188, 205; payment of, 21; training, 32–33, 203–204; treatment by, 13, 19–21, 25, 26, 176. *See also* Diviners; Healing; Medicines.
Dreams, of ancestor spirits, 26, 29, 31, 155; revelation through, 37–38, 198, Table VII
Drought, causes of, 26, 27–28. *See also* Rain
Dutch Reformed Church, 65, Tables II–VII

Easter celebrations, 124
Economic activities, 67, 138, 233, 243
Economy of Phuduhutswana chiefdom, ix, 5, 7, 173, 240–241. *See also* Irrigation Scheme; Labour migration.
Education, 217. *See also* Schools
Emotionalism, 219–222; in Methodism, 226; in Pentecostal and Sabbatarian churches, 44, 130 131, 134, 228; in Roman Catholicism, 222; related to social structure, 221–222; related to traditional background, 220–221
Enemas, applied by ministers, 184, 187, 188, 197, Table VII
Ethiopians, Ethiopianism, 42, 45, 47, 50, 52, 87, 142. *See also* Zulu churches
Ethiopian Catholic Church in Zion, 43, 52, 91, 116, 151, Tables II–VII
Ethiopian Church of Africa, 43, 52, Tables II–VII
Ethiopian Church of Christ by Religion, 43, 55, Tables II–VII
Ethnic composition, of chiefdom, 4–5, 8; of churches, 64–66
Evangelistic work, 88, 89, 94, 123, 124–125, 226, 230
Evans-Pritchard, Professor E. E., 196

Family, 67; role of, in religion, 31, 67, 125, 237; teaching about, in churches, 91, 115–116, 152; weakening of family ties, 173. *See also* Children; Marriage
First-fruits, ceremony of the, 38
Foundation Apostolic Church in Jerusalem, 45, 89, Tables II–VII
Free Baptist Church, 71
Full Gospel Church, Tables II–VII

INDEX

255

Ghosts, *see* Spirits of the dead.
God, belief in, 12, 13, 25, 29, 30, 31–32, 39, 213, 216
Groupings, religious, 8–11, 41–45, 62–67

Headmen, 6, 8, 25, 49, 76, 93–94, 160
Healing, attitude of churches to 'European' techniques, 174, 175–177, Table VII; attitude of churches to traditional techniques, 164, 174, 175, Table VII; ritual of, 43, 44, 45, 130, 133–134, 166, 177–188, 202, Table VII. *See also* Doctors, Medicines
Health of population, 171–174
'Heat' as ritual concept, 34–37, 39, 148, 149, 196. *See also* 'Hot blood'
Heaven, 25, 142, 143, 145, 153–154, 155, 158
Holy Christian Apostolic Church, 45, 65, Tables II–VII
Holy Church of Christ 55, 98, 101, 123, Tables II–VII
Holy Communion, 44, 64, 81, 85, 124, 167–169, 178, Table VII
Holy Gospel Church in Zion, 55, Tables II–VII
Holy Spirit, and ancestor spirits, 207; being entered by, 44, 48, 200; being moved by, 201, Table VII; revelation by, 43, 44, 198–203, 227, Table VII. *See also* Speaking with tongues
Holy water, 180, 187, Table VII
'Hot blood' as ritual concept. 26–27, 34
Hymns, 44, 128, 129, 135

Illness, aggravated by 'hot blood', 26–27; causes of, 25–26, 175–177; prevention of, 27, 202; purification after, 192, Table VII; and religious experience, 48, 72–73. *See also* Healing
Impurity, *see* Ritual impurity
Independence of mission churches, 41, 68–69
Independent churches, 42. *See also* Bantu Separatist churches
Indigenous interpretation of Christianity, 235–236
Individualism, 7, 242
Initiation ceremonies, 8, 16–19; the church and, 16, 81–83, 93–94, 110, 152
Interdenominational relations, 41, 106–110, 229
Irrigation Scheme, Taung, 4, 7, 144, 173; Vaal-Hartz, *see* Vaal-Hartz Settlement

Johane, 48
John the Baptist, prominence accorded to, 139, 141, 144
Judgement, future, 142, 143, 154 156

Kgokong, 49
Khadi, 139
Kinship, 5, 6–7, 8, 26, 66, 67, 80, 149–151, 156, 239, 240; role of, in churches, 66–67; role of, in pagan religion, 31, 212–213
Krige, D. and E. J., and Lovedu concepts relating to rain, 34
Kuper, Dr. Hilda, 93
Kuruman, ix, 1, 46

Labour migration, 5, 7, 93; influence of, on religion, 51, 92, 111, 113, 121, 240
Language, Dr. F. J., 13 n. 1, 16
Laying-on of hands, 130, 134, 178–180, 190, Table VII
Leaders, Leadership, in churches, 46, 55, 67–68, 71–74, 77; in European society, 77; opportunities for women in churches, 85–86, 86–90, 206; in traditional Tswana society, 76–77; *See also* Office bearers
Legalism, *see* Moralism
Lightning, cause of, 36; prevention of, 27, 183
Liturgy, 43, 128. *See also* Church services
Local church group, 62–67; small size of, 62–63; socially important, 66, 67, 104, 120, 125, 136–137. *See also* Ethnic composition; Territorial distribution
London Missionary Society, 1, 46, 47, 53, 62, 63, 64, 68–69, 80, 81, 83, 87–90, 95, 98, 104, 105, 116–118, 123, 124, 137–138, 158, 160–161, 228–230, 247, Tables II–VII
Lutheran Church, 101, Tables II–VII

Magic, 12, 39, 146–149, 176; persistence of, under modern conditions, 212, 217. *See also* Doctors, Medicines, Sorcery
Magical nature of belief and ritual, in churches, 167, 190–191, 195–196, 197, 210, 217, 219, 223, 227, 234; in paganism, 148–149, 195
Magico-religious system, traditional, 12–13. *See also* Pagan religion and magic
Maidi, *see* Tlhaping
Mankurwane, 1, 2, 30, 149
Marriage, ceremonial, 19; civil rites, 7, 152–153; changes in marriage customs, 7; Christian (church) rites, 7, 152–153; ritual treatment before and during wedding, 19–21. *See also* *Bogadi* (marriage payment); Wedding
Mass, *see* Holy Communion
Matolo, Rev. Solomon M., 53

256 INDEX

Medical services, 172; attitude of Tlhaping to, 172

Medicines, connected with childbirth, 15–16; of European origin, 172; traditional, 13–14, 19, 27, 28, 32, 33, 174–176; protective, 20–21, 27. *See also* Healing

Membership (of churches), admission to, 80–81, 229; conduct expected of members, 81, 84; degrees of, 10, 63, 80–81; duties associated with, 81; privileges associated with, 79–80, 81; statistics, 9, 56–59, 246, 247. *See also* Adherents; Religious affiliation

Menstruation, 27, 34, 36

Methodism, 225–226

Methodist Church, 57, 63, 65, 68, 82, 105, 224–225, 246, 247, Tables II–VII

Migrant labour, *see* Labour migration

Ministry, training for, 70, 74–75. *See also* Office bearers

Misfortune, 25–26; causes of, 25–27, 33–37; ritual for prevention of, 27. *See also* Death; Illness

Missionaries (European), 5, 41, 56, 114, 234, 236; position of, in churches, 41, 42, 67–69, 104

Missionary enterprise (activity), 46, 51, 54, 60

Missionary methods, viii, 42, 100, 218, 223–224, 235

Missions, 7; development in rural and urban areas, 105; history of, 46–47. *See also* Missionaries; and cf. names of individual churches connected with Europeans

Mmoloki, *see* Kgokong

Moffat, Robert, ix, 1, 46

Mogôga, see Mourning

Mohapanela, Rev., 54 n., 1

Molotsi, Rev. Marks, 52

Monyakoane, Rev., 54

Moralism, Moralistic trend in churches, 81, 100, 141–142, 144, 152, 171, 218–219, 224

Moses, less prominent in Taung churches than in Zulu churches, 143

Mošwang (stomach contents of animal), use of, in ritual, 24, 26, 28, 149

Mourning, rites and customs connected with, 23, 24–25, 34, 160–162, 194, Table VII; slaughtering of *mogôga*, 23, 24–25, 29, 161

Music in churches, 135. *See also* Hymns

Native Commissioner(s), xi, 19, 55, 114, 116, 153

Native Congress Catholic Church, 54

Native Independent Congregational Church, 43, 47, 52–54, 61, 92, 101, Tables II–VII; Manthe faction of, 53, 54; Schmidtsdrift faction of, 53, 54

Nativistic trend in churches, 234–235. *See also* Indigenous interpretation of Christianity

New Apostolic Church in Zion, 45, Tables II–VII

New Testament, 83, 141, 171

Ngaka (doctor), *see* Doctors

Nguni, 25, 44, 65, 66, 82, 161, 213–216. *See also* Cape Nguni, Pondo, Swazi, Xhosa, Zulu

Night watch, 108, 127, 157, 158

Office bearers of churches, 63, 68–71, 87–88, 178; salaries and other support, 75, 99, 104. *See also* Ministry

Old Testament, 83, 141, 142–143, 161, 171; in Bantu Separatist churches, 141, 231

Pagan religion and magic, 12–40, 214–217; adherence to, 8, 10, 38–39; influenced by Christianity, 28, 39, 209, 212, 238; influence of, on Christianity and churches, 153, 188–189, 195, 196, 209, 210, 224, 238; influenced by general social change, 28, 212–213, 216, 239–240. *See also,* Ancestor spirits; Ancestor cult; Doctors; Magic; Medicines; Ritual, etc.

Pentecostalism, Pentecostal churches, 44–46, 50, 61, 70, 74, 81, 94, 105, 108, 129–134, 137, 138–141, 162, 164, 175, 178, 191, 197, 203–207, 226–228, 236. *See also* names of individual Pentecostal churches

Pentecostal Holiness Church, 45, 129–130, Tables II–VII

Phikakgolo, see Water snake

Phuduhutswana, *see* Tlhaping

Political authorities, 5, 6. *See also* Chief(s); Headmen; Native Commissioner(s)

Political organization, 5, 7. *See also* Chief(s); Headmen; Ward(s)

Polygyny, 93; attitude of churches to, 84

Pondo, 214

Population of chiefdom, 4–5. *See also* Scattering of population

Porte, Father, 47

Prayers, to the ancestor spirits, 23, 29, 31, 149, 213; to God, 29, 39; for healing, 130, 133–134, 177–178; for rain, 23, 28, 30, 208–209

Preachers, 137–138

Pregnancy, 14, 15, 34. *See also* Childbirth

INDEX

Primitive Church, 44, 83

Prohibitions encumbent on members, 81–84. *See also* Avoidance

Prophecy, Prophets, 30–31, 34–35, 46, 47–49, 50, 72–73, 133, 199, 203–206

Protestantism, 41

Protestant churches and missions, 41, 61, 76, 95, 126, 237

Purification, attitude of churches to pagan rites, 194; church rites of, 44, 45, 159, 191–194, 197, Table VII; pagan rites of, 14, 15, 17, 22, 23–24, 25, 26, 27, 28, 37

Race relations, 231–232. *See also* Churches

Radcliffe-Brown, Professor A. R., 212

Rain, associated with well-being, 34; prayers for, 23, 28, 49, 208–209; prevented from falling, 15, 25, 28, 35; prophetess Botlhale and, 34–35, 49; rites (pagan), 27–28, 30–31, 93–94, 149. *See also* 'Coolness' as ritual concept; Drought

Rainfall, 2

Religion, relation of, to magic, 12, 147–149

Religious affiliation of Bantu; in Phuduhutswana chiefdom, 8–11, 39, 56–61; in Taung district, 246–247; in Union of SouthAfrica, 11 n. 1, 57, 246

Research methods, x

Revelation, 72, 197–206, Table VII; and ancestor spirits, 30–31, 32, 48, 204, 205–206, 207. *See also* Church dress; Divining; Dreams; Holy Spirit

Rinderpest epidemic, 2, 16

Ritual, in churches, 125–134, 149–211; pagan, 14–28, 38–39. *See also* Avoidance; Baptism; Burial rites and customs; Childbirth; Church; Healing; Holy Communion; Initiation ceremonies; Marriage; Prayers; Purification; Rain; Sacrifices; Water, etc.

Ritual impurity, notions of, in churches, 191–192, 196; pagan notions of, 34–37

Ritualism, Ritualistic trend in churches, 45, 211, 220–221, 222

Roman Catholicism, 41, 222–224

Roman Catholic Church (Mission), 1, 20, 39, 41, 47, 56, 62, 64, 80, 95, 124, 126 158, 233, 237, 246, 247, Tables II–VII

Rural church, 105

Sabbatarianism, Sabbatarian churches, 44, 50, 61, 74, 81, 94, 105, 108, 109–110, 129, 138, 141, 162, 164, 175

Sabbath, observance of Saturday as, 43, 44, 138, 141

Sacraments, 64; Roman Catholic doctrine of, 223; withheld, 85. *See also* Baptism; Holy Communion

Sacrifices, to ancestors, 24–25, 29, 30–31, 161, 213–215; performed by churches, 161, 207–208

St. Paul Apostolic Faith Morning Star (Church), 45, 56, 63, 64, 71, 74, 115, 151–152, 158–159, 164–166, 179–180, 184, 189, 192, 202, 206, 207, 233, 244–245, Tables II–VII

Sample Survey, x, 9, 243

Scattering of population, 6, 229

Schapera, Professor I., 29

Schools, 7, 93. *See also* Church or mission schools

Scripture, 141; fragmentary and literal use of, 83, 162–163, 195–196, 217–218

Secessions from churches, 47, 50, 51, 53, 55–56, 60, 236

Secularization, 92, 113

Sehapano, 48

Sehihi, 14, 24, 26, 35, 36, 147, 149, 191, 194

Separatism, vii, 42, 47, 61, 230–237. *See also* Bantu Separatist churches; Ethiopianism; Secessions from churches; Zionism

Separatist churches, *see* Bantu Separatist churches

Sermons, 43, 44, 45, 127, 129, 130, 132, 137–145

Seventh Day Adventists, 175, Tables II–VII

Sexual relations, abstention from, 18; connected with 'hot blood' or 'heat', 26, 34, 149; extra-marital, 84, 85, 165; resumption after childbirth, 14, 15; resumption after death of spouse, 25; resumption after long separation, 27

'Shadow' as ritual concept, 14, 17, 26, 29, 34, 35, 36, 148

Social anthropology and missions, viii

Social change, 5–8, 232, 237–242; and religion, 121, 218, 237–240

Social structure, ix; of Bantu, 212, 215; of Phuduhutswana chiefdom, ix, x, 4–5, 6, 7, 8, 120, 209; of Tswana, 5–6, 67, 76, 117, 236–237. *See also* Clan; Kinship; Groupings; Social change; Status; Ward(s); etc.

Sorcery, Sorcerers, 13–14, 18, 20, 21, 22, 26, 28, 172, 174, 176, 215–216; belief in, in churches, 178, 189, Table VII; methods of performing, 21, 33; prevention of, 21, 27, 183; punishment of, 26

South African Native Baptist Church Mission, 44, 71, Tables II–VII

Southern Sotho, 5, 25, 65, 161, 213–216

258 INDEX

Speaking with tongues, 44, 191, 198, 200, Table VII
Spirits of the dead, 154, 161, 201. *See also* Ancestor spirits
State church, *see* Tribal church
Status, 8, 18, 26
Summer, observances in connexion with rain, during, 36
Sunday schools, 10, 63, 113
Sundkler, Dr. Bengt G. M., vii, ix, 42, 45–46, 63, 71, 92, 108, 142, 194, 203, 231
Suping, 49
Supreme Being, 12, 13, 31–32. *See also* God
Survey, *see* Sample Survey
Swazi, 93, 214
Symbolism, of baptism, 147; of coffin, 235 n.2(ii); of colours of women's uniform, 91; of figures and colours in church robes, 183; in magic, 147, 195; of rain rites, 149
Syncretism, 46. *See also* Magical nature of belief and ritual; Pagan religion and magic

Taboos, in churches, 46, *See also* Avoidance; in pagan ritual, 14, 22, 24, 27, 36, 39
Territorial distribution, of population, 215. *See also* Scattering of population; of church groups, 64–65
Thanksgiving, 208
Time, Bantu attitude to, 136
Tlhaping, history, ix, 1–4, 46; Maidi, ix, 2, 4, 47, 52–53; as nucleus of chiefdom, 4, 8; of Phokwane, 2, 46; Phuduhut-swana, ix, 2, 46, 52–53; present distribution of, 2
Tlhapišô, see Purification
Tobacco, attitude of churches to consumption of, 43, 139, 140, 164, Table VII
Tolonyane, 30–31, 34, 38, 188, 197, 205
Totem(s), 4, 8
Totemic group(s), 18. *See also* Clan(s)
Traditionalism in churches, 110
Traditional background, social and cultural, 94, 120–121, 208, 209–210, 217, 220, 234–235, 236–237, 238–239. *See also* Pagan religion and magic; Political organization; Social structure; Tswana

Tribal church, the L.M.S. as, 116–118, 228; Native Independent Congregational Church in Maidi chiefdom, 53–54
Tswana, chiefs, 17; as ethnic group in population, 4–5; initiation, 17, 18; kinship marriages, 7; ward system, 5–6, 67, 76. *See also* Social structure

Unction, 177, Table VII
Uniforms, of women's associations, 89–90, 91–92. *See also* Church dress
Urban church, 105–106, 201, 202

Vaal-Hartz Settlement (Irrigation Scheme), 4, 51
Visions, 73, 199

Ward(s), Ward system, 6, 8. *See also* Tswana
Watch Tower Bible and Tract Society, 45, 126, Tables II–VII
Water, use of, in church ritual, 49, 71, 134, 180, 191–194, 196–197, Table VII. *See also* Holy water; use of, in pagan ritual, 30, 37, 149, 196–197
Water snake, 38, 167, 191, 194
Wedding, feast, 19; outfits, 153
Western civilization, influence of on Bantu, 5. *See also* Social change
Willoughby, Rev. W. C., 13 n.2, 29, 215
Witchcraft, 13 n. 2, 29, 215
Witch-doctors, *see* Doctors
Witness of Christ (Sabbath), 115, Tables II–VII
Women, position of, in social structure, 76; role of, in churches, 85–95, III, 206
Women's associations, 63, 85–92, 158, 160

Xhosa, 66, 82. *See also* Cape Nguni

Youth, *see* Churches

Zion Apostolic Church, 54
Zion Apostolic Church of South Africa, 45, 54, 65, 192, Tables II–VII
Zionists, 45, 46, 66, 71, 72–73, 87, 106, 142–143, 194, 197, 203–205. *See also* Zulu Churches
Zulu, 232
Zulu churches, 45, 71, 142. *See also* Ethiopians; Zionists